Antisemitism

Recent Titles in
Religion in Politics and Society Today

Islam in America: Exploring the Issues
Craig Considine

Religion and Environmentalism: Exploring the Issues
Lora Stone

Antisemitism

Exploring the Issues

Steven Leonard Jacobs

Religion in Politics and Society Today

BLOOMSBURY ACADEMIC
NEW YORK · LONDON · OXFORD · NEW DELHI · SYDNEY

BLOOMSBURY ACADEMIC
Bloomsbury Publishing Inc
1385 Broadway, New York, NY 10018, USA
50 Bedford Square, London, WC1B 3DP, UK
29 Earlsfort Terrace, Dublin 2, Ireland

BLOOMSBURY, BLOOMSBURY ACADEMIC and the Diana logo
are trademarks of Bloomsbury Publishing Plc

First published in the United States of America by ABC-CLIO 2020
Paperback edition published by Bloomsbury Academic 2024

Copyright © Bloomsbury Publishing Inc, 2024

Cover photo: Jewish cemetery Quatzenheim near Strasbourg. (ifeelstock/Alamy Stock Photo)

All rights reserved. No part of this publication may be reproduced or
transmitted in any form or by any means, electronic or mechanical,
including photocopying, recording, or any information storage or retrieval
system, without prior permission in writing from the publishers.

Bloomsbury Publishing Inc does not have any control over, or responsibility for,
any third-party websites referred to or in this book. All internet addresses given
in this book were correct at the time of going to press. The author and publisher
regret any inconvenience caused if addresses have changed or sites have
ceased to exist, but can accept no responsibility for any such changes.

Library of Congress Cataloging-in-Publication Data
Names: Jacobs, Steven L., 1947- author.
Title: Antisemitism : exploring the issues / Steven Leonard Jacobs.
Description: Santa Barbara : ABC-CLIO, [2020] |
Series: Religion in politics and society today | Includes bibliographical references and index.
Identifiers: LCCN 2020005141 (print) | LCCN 2020005142 (ebook) |
ISBN 9781440868733 (hardcover) | ISBN 9781440868740 (ebook)
Subjects: LCSH: Antisemitism—History. | Antisemitism—Historiography.
Classification: LCC DS145 .J27 2020 (print) | LCC DS145 (ebook) | DDC 305.892/4009-dc23
LC record available at https://lccn.loc.gov/2020005241
LC ebook record available at https://lccn.loc.gov/2020005142

ISBN: HB: 978-1-4408-6873-3
PB: 979-8-7651-2509-0
ePDF: 978-1-4408-6874-0
eBook: 979-8-2160-4857-2

Series: Religion in Politics and Society Today

To find out more about our authors and books visit www.bloomsbury.com
and sign up for our newsletters.

For
my grandparents,
Leo Jacob and Ella Israel Jacob,
murdered in Treblinka July 1942,
victims of antisemitic hatred.
precious lives lost

And
my late father,
Ralph Albert Jacobs (1921–1981),
who survived

Contents

Alphabetical List of Entries, ix

Topical List of Entries, xi

Series Foreword, xiii

Preface, xv

Overview, xvii

Chronology, xxxvii

A to Z, 1

Annotated Bibliography, 149

Index, 181

Alphabetical List of Entries

Adversus Judaeos
al-Banna, Hassan
al-Husseini, Amin
Alt-Right
Barnes, Harry Elmer
BDS (Boycott, Divestment, Sanctions) Movement
Beilis Affair
Blood Libel
Carto, Willis
Christian Identity
Coughlin, Charles E.
Crusades
Deicide
Dreyfus Affair
Duke, David
Farhud
Farrakhan, Louis
Fascism
Faurisson, Robert
Frank Trial and Lynching
Goldstein, Baruch
Holocaust
Holocaust, Denial of
Icke, David
Intersectionality

Irving, David
Kristallnacht
Ku Klux Klan
Luther, Martin
Marr, Wilhelm
Martyrdom, Sanctifying the Name of God
National Socialism/Nazism
Nationalism
Oberammergau Passion Play
Pierce, William Luther
Pius XII, Pope
Protocols of the Learned Elders of Zion
Proud Boys
Qutb, Sayyid
Rassinier, Paul
Rockwell, George Lincoln
Social Darwinism
Spanish Inquisition
Usury
Wagner, Richard
White Supremacy
World Church of the Creator
Yockey, Francis Parker

Topical List of Entries

Events
Beilis Affair
Crusades
Dreyfus Affair
Farhud
Frank Trial and Lynching
Holocaust
Kristallnacht
Oberammergau Passion Play
Spanish Inquisition

Ideas
Adversus Judaeos
Blood Libel
Deicide
Holocaust, Denial of
Martyrdom, Sanctifying the Name
    of God
*Protocols of the Learned Elders
    of Zion*
Usury

Individuals
al-Banna, Hassan
al-Husseini, Amin
Barnes, Harry Elmer
Carto, Willis
Coughlin, Charles E.
Duke, David
Farrakhan, Louis

Faurisson, Robert
Goldstein, Baruch
Icke, David
Irving, David
Luther, Martin
Marr, Wilhelm
Pierce, William Luther
Pius XII, Pope
Qutb, Sayyid
Rassinier, Paul
Rockwell, George Lincoln
Wagner, Richard
Yockey, Francis Parker

Movements
Alt-Right
BDS (Boycott, Divestment,
    Sanctions) Movement
Christian Identity
Fascism
Intersectionality
National Socialism/Nazism
Nationalism
Social Darwinism
White Supremacy

Organizations
Ku Klux Klan
Proud Boys
World Church of the Creator

Series Foreword

Religion is a pervasive and powerful force in modern society, and its influence on political structures and social institutions is inescapable, whether in the United States or around the world. Wars have been fought in the name of faith; national boundaries have been shaped as a result; and social policies, legislation, and daily life have all been shaped by religious beliefs. Written with the reference needs of high school students and undergraduates in mind, the books in this series examine the role of religion in contemporary politics and society. While the focus of the series is on the United States, it also explores social and political issues of global significance.

Each book in the series is devoted to a particular issue, such as anti-semitism, atheism and agnosticism, and women in Islam. An overview essay surveys the development of the religious dimensions of the subject and discusses how religion informs contemporary discourse related to that issue. A chronology then highlights the chief events related to the topic. This is followed by a section of alphabetically arranged reference entries providing objective information about people, legislation, ideas, movements, events, places, and other specific subjects. Each entry cites works for further reading and in many cases provides cross-references. At the end of each volume is an annotated bibliography of the most important print and electronic resources suitable for student research.

Authoritative and objective, the books in this series give readers a concise introduction to the dynamic interplay of religion and politics in modern society and provide a starting point for further research on social issues.

Preface

Antisemitism has been labeled by scholars and others as "the world's longest hatred," having its origins socially and culturally within early Egypt, when the ancient Israelites found themselves outsiders in a nation-state empire that initially welcomed them more than three thousand years ago. It then morphed into a religious-theological antisemitism that was able to maintain itself well into the middle Dark Ages of illiberalism, intolerance, and illiteracy. It returned to its social and cultural manifestations in the Enlightenment period, only to culminate in the racial-biological antisemitism of the Nazis and their allies in the most violent desecration of Jews and Judaism known as the Holocaust (in Hebrew, *Shoah*). Today, early in this twenty-first century, a further element has been added: anti-Zionism—now defined as hatred of the State of Israel, its Jewish citizenry, and its philosophy of the longing of an ancient people to return to the land of its origins, which it did with its proclamation of the Third Jewish Commonwealth on May 14, 1948. Each of these appearances of antisemitism—social-cultural, religious-theological, racial-biological, and anti-Zionist—rises and falls with the current political, social, and economic climate.

This text follows the same general outline and format of the series of which it is a part: a general overview of this sad and tragic phenomenon of hatred; a chronology of major historic events that make real what has been described; forty to fifty reference entries with attached bibliographies of people, places, events, and movements, all of which have been part of the antisemitic landscape; and an annotated list of texts, journals, organizations, and websites for further reading and deepening one's knowledge of this ever-present reality.

Even a cursory examination of either the alphabetical list of entries or the topical list of entries reveals two obvious omissions: Adolf Hitler (1889–1945) and Joseph Stalin (1878–1953). The literature surrounding these two tyrants is vast, and their hatred of and violence toward Jews and Judaism is well known. What remains unanswered, however, is the daunting question of why: What prompted their pathological hatred? What persons, events, or cultural moments caused them to regard the Jews as the true enemies of all humankind, kindled by their Jewish religious tradition, and in total opposition to everything they were attempting to achieve? Their "final solutions" were remarkably similar: the total elimination of Jews everywhere and the total eradication of their Jewish religious and cultural traditions.

All of which brings us to this twenty-first century, which continues to experience a resurgence of antisemitism not only on the European continent but also in the United States. Naively, perhaps, many have thought and hoped that, with the revelations of the wanton murders of more than six million Jewish children, women, and men between 1939 and 1945, knowledge of the Holocaust would have eliminated this scourge. And briefly, this was indeed the case—but no more.

Today, Jews and their agencies, institutions, and organizations continue to wrestle with how best to confront antisemitism. Governments, too, have seemingly not shirked their own responsibilities to address it. Yet, like an open sore that refuses to heal or a cancer that continues to grow despite the best efforts of medical sciences, antisemitism refuses to die. Thus, the first step in combating it is to have knowledge of what it was, what it is, and who today are its principal advocates as well as those organizations that continue to attract these haters and engage in such violence. To the degree to which this text aids in the fight against antisemitism, it is reward enough.

Steven Leonard Jacobs
Tuscaloosa, AL
January 1, 2020

Overview

Antisemitism (or *anti-Semitism*), simply put, is the ongoing hatred of the Jewish people, the religion of Judaism, and the culture of the Jews, which all-too-often results in violence against Jews, those falsely perceived as Jews, and those who are supportive of Jews. Further expanding upon this briefest of definitions, this writer also suggests the following:

Antisemitism may thus be further defined, collectively, as the active hatred of the Jews and Judaism from its mildest expressions in group segregation and discriminatory legislation to its most extreme forms in exterminatory and annihilatory activities resulting in the murders of numbers of Jews. Acts of desecration, such as synagogue burnings and graffiti defacements, and the wanton destruction of Jewish ritual objects associated with the religion of Judaism (prayer books, prayer shawls, ritual objects, Torah scrolls, etc.) also constitute active antisemitism. Culturally, shutting down printing presses, forbidding the publication of books and newspapers addressing Jewish issues and concerns, stopping productions of Jewish-themed plays, concerts, movies, teaching and lecture/presentations on these same topics are all further examples of active antisemitism. In this current climate—the early twenty-first century—political and verbal denunciations of the State of Israel and its governmental policies, its military policies, and its Jewish citizenry, including the Boycott, Divestment, Sanctions (BDS) movement and condemnatory resolutions by political and religious groups (e.g., the United Nations Human Rights Council and the Presbyterian Church (USA)) continues to morph into an anti-Zionism that should be more accurately understood as antisemitism.

Definitionally, however, even this expanded attempt is not without problems and difficulties, as the late scholar Gavin Langmuir (1924–2005) wrote in *Towards a Definition of Antisemitism*, "As presently used it impedes rather than aids understanding of hostility toward Jews" (Langmuir, 311). Scholars and journalists have long been aware of not

xviii | Overview

only the controversies surrounding whether the word should be hyphenated (thus giving questionable credence to the word "Semitism" and its inappropriate adaptation from the field of language studies) but also numerous attempts to further sharpen our understanding of antisemitism. German-born publisher, editor of *Die Zeit* ("The Time"), and American academic Josef Joffe (b. 1944), in a 2004 lecture entitled "Nations We Love to Hate: Israel, America and the New Antisemitism," posited what he called "The Five Ways of 'Anti-Ism'":

> "Anti-ism" consists—at all times and in all places—of five elements: One is *stereotypization*, a set of general statements attributing certain negative qualities to the target group. Closely related is *denigration*, the ascription of moral inferiority all the way to an irreducibly evil nature. *Demonization* is the third step, moving from what the target group *is* to what it *does* or intends to do. . . . A fourth feature is *obsession*—the *idée fixe* that Jews (or x) are omnipresent and omnicausal, hence the invisible force that explains all misery. . . . The final step is *elimination*, be it by exclusion, assimilation, or annihilation.

For example, in his 2000 book *Confronting Anti-Semitism: A Practical Guide*, the late Leonard P. Zakim (1953–1999), a Jewish-American religious and civil rights leader, presented his readers with ten different definitions of *antisemitism* by such notables as the leading scholar of the history of antisemitism Robert S. Wistrich (1945–2015) of the Hebrew University of Jerusalem, Israel; British American historian and orientalist Bernard Lewis (1916–2018); author, historian, and animal rights advocate Charles Patterson; American sociologist John Milton Yinger (1916–2011); French philosopher, novelist, political activist, biographer, literary critic, and winner of the 1964 Nobel Prize in Literature Jean-Paul Sartre (1905–1980); scholar of American Jewish history and Reform rabbi Jacob Rader Marcus (1896–1985); and German American attorney and the founder and first president of the Anti-Defamation League Sigmund Livingston (1872–1946). More than thirty years before, American sociologists of religion Charles Y. Glock (b. 1919) and Rodney Stark (b. 1934) defined antisemitism in *Christian Beliefs and Antisemitism* as "the hatred and persecution of Jews as a group; not the hatred of persons who happen to be Jews, but rather the hatred of persons *because* they are Jews" (Glock and Stark, 102; emphasis in original).

More contemporarily, in 2015, the International Holocaust Remembrance Alliance, building upon the Declaration of the Stockholm

International Forum on the Holocaust of 2000, adopted the following *non–legally binding* working definition of antisemitism:

> Antisemitism is a certain perception of Jews, which may be expressed as hatred toward Jews. Rhetorical and physical manifestations of antisemitism are directed toward Jewish or non-Jewish individuals and/or their property, toward Jewish community institutions and religious facilities. (www.ihra.org)

And although it lists as illustrations eleven examples of antisemitism and has been adopted by the European Union and European Parliament, the U.K. College of Policing, and the U.S. State Department, it continues to carry no means whatsoever for prosecution against those who advocate against Jews and Judaism, up to and including violence and murder.

An interesting proposal, however, put forth by Israel's former ambassador to Canada Alan Baker and published by the Jerusalem Center for Public Affairs (www.jcpa.org) in 2015 is his "Draft International Convention on the Prevention and Punishment of the Crime of Anti-Semitism," modeled on the 1948 United Nations Convention on the Prevention and Punishment of the Crime of Genocide. Thus, the "Contracting Parties" (i.e., member nation-states of the United Nations) would agree to twenty-one different articles and move it forward from adoption to ratification to international law. Those found guilty of any "act or manifestation of anti-Semitism" (as defined) would be brought to the bar of justice, both internationally, if appropriate, and nationally, if appropriate. Nation-states would equally commit themselves to monitoring and collecting incidents of antisemitism through its International Anti-Semitic Monitoring Forum, sharing such data across boundaries and educating their citizenry to recognize and combat antisemitism and other forms of hatred and prejudice. To date, to this author's knowledge, Baker's Draft has not been presented to any recognized UN body for initial discussion.

The latest entry into this discussion of antisemitism is that of American attorney, academic, and government official Kenneth L. Marcus in his 2015 book *The Definition of Antisemitism*, in which he writes,

> Anti-Semitism is a set of negative attitudes, ideologies, and practices directed at Jews as Jews, individually or collectively, based upon and

sustained by a repetitive and potentially self-fulfilling latent structure of hostile erroneous beliefs and assumptions that flow from the application of double-standards towards Jews as a collectivity, manifest culturally in myth, ideology, folklore, and imagery, and urging various forms of restriction, exclusion, and suppression. (193–194)

All these attempts at definition are certainly worthy of closer examination and discussion than can be permitted here.

To make things a bit more complicated, Argentine Israeli author and educator Gustavo Perednik—uncomfortable with the term *antisemitism*—in his online course "Judeophobia—Anti-Semitism, Jew-Hate and Anti-Zionism," based on his Spanish-language book *Judeophobia* (2000), argues that "there are at least seven characteristics that make Judeophobia (anti-Semitism) very different from racism, xenophobia, or any other hatred against a group":

1. Judeophobia is the oldest hatred.
2. Judeophobia is strikingly universal.
3. Judeophobia is permanent.
4. Judeophobia is deeper.
5. Judeophobia is obsessive.
6. Judeophobia is more dangerous.
7. Judeophobia is chimerical (based on fantasy). (www.zionism-israel.com)

Even more recently, in 2018, Judea Pearl, a professor of computer science and statistics at UCLA, has suggested replacing *anti-Zionism* and *anti-Israelism* with *Zionophobia*, which he defines as "the irrational fear of Zionism coupled with an obsessive commitment to undermine the right of Israel to exist" (www.haarmorg).

It may very well be, then, that *antisemitism*—or *Judeophobia* or even *Zionophobia*—however defined, remains the world's oldest and longest hatred of others, already manifesting itself even before the Hebrew Bible/Old Testament and making its initial appearance prior to the enslavement of the Israelites in Egypt between three thousand and four thousand years ago. During its long and corrosive journey, antisemitism has presented itself in a variety of iterations, morphing from one to another but never completely ending its previous expressions.

Finally, by defining these different manifestations of antisemitism, albeit however briefly, one sees that common thread of xenophobia,

Overview | xxi

othering, *and* distancing—*fear* of the Jews and attempts to *do* something about it:

- *Social-Cultural:* "We don't like Jews because they are different from us and they do things differently than we do."
- *Political-Economic:* "We don't like Jews because they are a threat to the stability of both our political and economic ways of life."
- *Religious-Theological:* "We don't like Jews because they worship differently than we do and practice a religion different from ours."
- *Racial-Biological:* "We don't like Jews because they are different than we are physically and genetically."
- *Anti-Zionist/Anti-Israel:* "We don't like Jews because their allegiance, no matter where they reside, is to a nation-state that is not us."

Historical Overview

The term *antisemitism* is derived from the German *Antisemitismus* and is largely attributed to the disgruntled journalist Wilhelm Marr (1819–1904) and taken from his 1879 publication *The Way to Victory of Germanism over Judaism* (*Der Weg zum Siege des Germanenthums über das Judenthum*). Marr's concern was a more "academic" or "scientific" term than that of the German word *Judenhass* (Jew-hatred). However, this animus against the Jews and their expressions of Judaism is of much longer standing, though the term itself, despite the concerns noted above, has become almost universally understood for this ongoing hatred and contempt for Jews and Judaism.

Already in the Hebrew Bible/Old Testament, in Exodus 1:8–11, we find the pharaoh of Egypt verbalizing his antipathy to the Jews:

Then a new Pharaoh, to whom Joseph meant nothing, came to power in Egypt. "Look," he said to his people, "the Israelites have become far too numerous for us. Come, we must deal shrewdly with them or they will become even more numerous, and, if war breaks out, will join our enemies, fight against us, and leave the country." So, they put slave masters over them to oppress them with forced labor, and they built Pithom and Ramses as store cities for Pharaoh.

Thus, social-cultural and political-economic forms of antisemitism are in evidence both here and following.

xxii | Overview

In the Scroll of Esther 3:8–11, we find an uncanny parallel to the pharaoh in the words of the Prime Minister Haman to the Persian king Achashverosh, and it is taken to its logical conclusion, genocide:

> Then Haman said to King Achashverosh, "There is a certain people dispersed among the peoples in all the provinces of your kingdom who keep themselves separate. Their customs are different from those of all other people, and they do not obey the king's laws; it is not in the king's best interest to tolerate them. If it pleases the king, let a decree be issued to destroy them, and I will give ten thousand talents of silver to the king's administration for the royal treasury." . . . "Keep the money," the king said to Haman, "and do with the people as you please."

Whether or not either or both are historically accurate or apocryphal and written after they events they describe, they reflect the non-Jews' perception of the Jews; their inclusion in the Hebrew Bible/Old Testament is equally indicative of the Jews' understanding of their enemies' perceptions of them. Further, they both outline criticisms of Jews that have withstood the tests of time and are amazingly parallel and repetitive: there are too many Jews, they cannot be trusted to be loyal citizens, their ways are different from the majority, and, therefore, they must be either enslaved or annihilated.

From these two initial examples, prior to the birth of Christianity, we turn first to Egypt and then on to Greece and Rome.

Rightly argued, the Egyptian priest Manetho, who lived during the early third century BCE, may be regarded as the *first* antisemite. Said to be the author of the *Aegyptiaca* or *History of Egypt* in several volumes, he also included the most venal charges against the Jews—for example, that the peoples of the Exodus were afflicted with leprosy, that their Sabbath was the physical result of having to stop every seven days because of their physical difficulties, that their worship of their invisible God was "cultic" rather than a true religion, and that their practices associated with the cult, specifically circumcision and dietary restrictions, rendered them a "people apart" and unworthy of integration into the larger Egyptian society. Much of what we know of his antipathy toward Jews, however, is found in the writings of the Jewish historian Josephus (37–100 CE)—rather than his own original texts—who also includes the anti-Jewish Greek writer Apion (ca. 20 BCE–ca. 45 CE), who included Manetho's vilifications in his own work. It is, thus, important to note that (a) these foundational antisemitic charges would remain part and parcel of such calumnies throughout Jewish history, and (b) here we see a mix of the social-cultural and religious-theological dimensions of antisemitic hatred.

Historically, it is also important to acknowledge that the *first* outburst of hostility against Jews occurred in Egypt on the military island and colony of Elephantine in 410 BCE, when the local Egyptians, led by their priests and in collusion with their Persian overlords, destroyed the Jewish Temple, though earlier both had welcomed the Jews as allies into their ranks. Although they were later punished by the central Persian authorities, again, we see a mix of the religious-theological and the highly political-economic charges against the Jews, further echoing that presented in both Exodus 1:8–11 and Esther 3:8–11.

The *second* recorded violent outburst against Jews also occurred in Egypt, this time under Roman control in 38 CE, when the governor, Flaccus, who would later be recalled to Rome and executed a year later, allowed the citizenry of Alexandria—Egyptians, Greeks, and Romans—to revolt against the Jewish residents of the city with whom they had a previously relatively positive relationship. The leader of the Jewish community and philosopher Philo (20 BCE–50 CE) remains our source for much of what transpired. False accusations against Jews in the Roman Empire are also found in the writings of Tacitus (56–120 CE), perhaps the most well-known of the ancients, and many others, for example, Chaeremon of Alexandria (fourth century BCE); Lysimachus of Macedonia (360–281 BCE); Posidonius of Rhodes (135–51 BCE); and Appollonius Molon (first century BCE), also of Rhodes.

The irony of the "Roman situation" was its initial tolerance of the diverse religions and peoples found within its conquered empire, coupled with its harsh oppression and put downs of all attempts at political independence, and always perceived as acts of rebellion and revolution.

Enter nascent Christianity and the New Testament two thousand years ago prior to its allying itself with the various Western power structures and one finds the Jews primarily culpable for the death of the Christ—the pernicious and false charge of *deicide* (the killing of the God/Christ)—resulting in religious-theological antisemitism coupled with social-cultural and economic-political forms of discriminatory legislation, ghettoization, and restrictive economic opportunities. The New Testament, most particularly the four Gospel accounts of Jesus's life, crucifixion, and death (written by four unknown authors who were, by and large, ignorant of the

xxiv | Overview

Judaism of the day) place the blame upon the Jews, falsely exonerate the procurator Pontius Pilate (who would later be drummed out of the Roman civil service), and mediate Roman participation and complicity as largely the result of Jewish perfidy. Any number of New Testament texts can be cited in support of these conclusions; sadly, and tragically, the following are but representative examples:

- Matthew 27:24–25: When Pilate saw that he was getting nowhere, but that instead an uproar was starting, he took water and washed his hands in front of the crowd. "I am innocent of this man's blood," he said. "It is your responsibility!" All the people answered, *"His blood be on us and on our children!"*
- Revelation 2:9: "I know your afflictions and your poverty—yet you are rich! I know about the slander of those who say they are Jews and are not but are *a synagogue of Satan.*"
- Acts 2:36: "Therefore let all Israel be assured of this: God has made this Jesus, *whom you crucified,* both Lord and Messiah."
- Acts 7:51–52: *"You stiff-necked people! Your hearts and ears are still uncircumcised. You are just like your ancestors: You always resist the Holy Spirit! Was there ever a prophet your ancestors did not persecute? They even killed those who predicted the coming of the Righteous One. And now you have betrayed and murdered him."*
- John 8:44: *"You belong to your father, the devil,* and you want to carry out your father's desires. He was a murderer from the beginning, not holding to the truth, for there is no truth in him. When he lies, he speaks his native language, for he is a liar and the father of lies."
- Luke 11:50–51: "Therefore *this generation will be held responsible for the blood of all the prophets that has been shed since the beginning of the world,* from the blood of Abel to the blood of Zechariah, who was killed between the altar and the sanctuary. Yes, I tell you, *this generation will be held responsible for it all.*"
- Matthew 23:13, 15, 16, 23, 25, 27, 29, 30: "Woe to you, teachers of the law and Pharisees, *you hypocrites!*" . . . *"You snakes! You brood of vipers!"*

  (All the translations are from the New International Version (NIV); emphases added.)

Uncomfortable though these verses are to all who read them today—or hear them shared from the pulpits of Christianity—and our willingness to accept the scholarly understanding that they reflect not only an inter-communal rancorous debate but the desire of a newly emerging faith to separate itself from its parent, what must always be kept it mind are two things: (1) that they were *literally* understood by the faithful for close to two thousand years and (2) that they were read as such by the leaders of the church, who saw them as their inspiration and sources of their preaching to the largely unlettered masses. Thus, several of the most important and illustrious church fathers demonstrated, both orally and in their writing, their contempt for Judaism and the Jewish people, including Ignatius of Antioch (ca. 35–ca. 98 CE), Justin Martyr (100–165 CE), Melito of Sardis (?–180 CE), Irenaeus of Lyons (130–202 CE), Origin of Alexandria (182–254 CE), St. Ambrose (340–397 CE), St. John Chrysostom (347–407 CE), St. Jerome (347–420 CE), and St. Augustine (354–430 CE).

This was the normative way of the West for approximately twenty centuries, from the Roman destruction of Jerusalem and the Second Temple in the year 90 CE until the rise of Nazism in the twentieth century. Toward the end of the Middle Ages, in Germany, professor, priest, and monk Martin Luther (1483–1546), after first reaching out the hand of love to the Jews in his desire to convert them (They rejected his offer!) wrote and published the most hate-filled tract to appear in Europe, *On the Jews and Their Lies* (*Von den Juden und Ihren Lügen*, 1543), offering the following "suggestions":

First, their synagogues should be set on fire, and whatever does not burn should be covered or spread over with dirt so that no one may ever be able to see a cinder or stone of it.

Secondly, their homes should likewise be broken down and destroyed.

Thirdly, they should be deprived of their prayer-books and Talmuds in which such idolatry lies, cursing, and blasphemy are taught.

Fourthly, their rabbis must be forbidden under threat of death to teach any more.

Fifthly, passport and traveling privileges should be absolutely forbidden to the Jews.

Prior to Luther, however, four events must be mentioned during the period of what most Westerners label the Middle Ages but, from a Judaic perspective, are better understood as the "Dark Ages" of ignorance, hostility, superstition, and violence against the Jewish communities on the European continent.

First of these is a series of Crusades from the eleventh through the thirteenth centuries (ten in all), religiously motivated military expeditions

xxvi | Overview

from the European continent to "reclaim" the holy city of Jerusalem and its environs from the "infidels" (i.e., Muslims). On the way east, Jewish communities were sacked and their people tortured and murdered as their "just deserts" for being enemies of Christ and responsible for his death (the crime of deicide).

Second is the Inquisition of Spain, beginning in the twelfth century, which saw the Roman Catholic Church under its inquisitors put to death, usually by fire, after various tortures designed to extract confessions of religious infidelity—including the rack—of "insincere Christians," primarily converts, many of whom were originally Jews who had converted to preserve their social and economic way of life in a previously well-integrated society. Ultimately, the Jews of Spain were expelled from Spain in 1492 under an edict of King Ferdinand II of Aragon (1452–1516) and Queen Isabella of Castile (1451–1504) and later from Portugal as well, where they had initially fled.

Third is the Black Death, or bubonic plague, of the fourteenth century, which saw an illiterate and ignorant peasantry observe fewer deaths within Jewish ghettos while they experienced the agonizing horrors of this rat- and flea-infested death. Not that Jews did not also die within their ghettos, but their ritual requirement of symbolic handwashing prior to eating and full ritual immersion for both males and females during any given month (e.g., postmenstruation, prior to marriage) tended to act as its own kind of prophylaxis and safeguard against the spread of the disease within their own closely confined living conditions.

The last is the Khmelnytsky Uprising of 1648—which Jews remember as the Khmelnytsky Massacres—inspired by the attempted overthrow of the Polish nobility and government by the Ukrainian *hetman* (leader) Bohdan Khmelnytsky (1595–1657). In a place where Jews had previously been welcomed with open arms and developed their own autonomous governance and successful ways of life, they saw the murders of up to one hundred thousand Jews or possibly even more. Those murders would only be rivaled by those of the Nazis and their European—including Polish and other—collaborators during World War II.

In the eighteenth century, the European Enlightenment somewhat diminished, but not completely, the religious-theological expressions of antisemitism, but it offered different forms of political-economic antisemitism, even after France granted its Jews citizenship in 1791, epitomized in the phrase, "To the Jew as an individual everything; to the Jews as a people nothing." That goal was translated into the strong desire of those in power as well as the intellectual elite agreeing with them—the most well-known of whom was Voltaire (François-Marie Arouet, 1694–1778)—that the Jews should surrender their particularity as the price of full civic equality. Further, the emperor of France, Napoleon Bonaparte (1769–1821), as a show of civic unity, convened first an Assembly of (Jewish) Notables in April 1806 and a Sanhedrin in February 1807, twice forcing Jewish leadership to affirm its commitment to the French nation and their membership as citizens by answering a series of questions, all designed to test their loyalty.

By the beginning of the nineteenth century, the Jews' situation had begun to dramatically improve, especially in the United States, but dark clouds were starting to form over the European continent, apart from the always precarious and vulnerable position of the Jews in Russia, where the Russian secret police turned a French political satire into one of the most notorious and enduring documents of modern antisemitism, the *Protocols of the Learned Elders of Zion.*

The situation of the Jews of Russia, both before and after the Russian Communist Revolution of 1914–1917 mirrored the plight of Jews in the long history of the European continent and its antisemitism: restricted places of residence (the so-called Pale of Settlement); economic deprivation, including restrictions against Jews in certain occupations; and bouts of violent antisemitism fueled by a manipulated and largely illiterate peasantry on the part of the political leadership and further exacerbated by the Russian Orthodox Church.

In 1864, French lawyer and publicist Maurice Joly (1829–1878) anonymously published a satiric attack against the government of Napoleon III (1808–1873) entitled *The Dialogue in Hell between Machiavelli and Montesquieu (Dialogue aux enfers entre Machiavel et Montesquieu ou la politique de Machiavel au XIXe siècle)*. Originally published in Brussels and smuggled into France, the book was seized almost immediately and banned. Its author was soon discovered and arrested. He was convicted and served eighteen months in prison, after which he committed suicide.

An unknown member of the Okhrana, the Russian secret police, saw its potential in a totally other context and brought a copy back to Russia where it would later be rewritten and published as an addendum by the Russian writer, mystic, and disgraced priest Sergei Nilus (1862–1929) in his 1905 book *The Great within the Small and Antichrist, an Imminent Political Possibility* as the twenty-four "Protocols of the Learned Elders of Zion." The text was supposedly a midnight speech in an unknown

xxviii | **Overview**

cemetery by a supposed leading rabbi as a blueprint for world takeover. Thoroughly refuted already as a forgery in 1921 by Philip Graves of the *Times of London* and brought to trial in Berne, Switzerland, in 1934–1935, and even refuted in Russia itself in 1993, it continued to be published in a variety of languages and took on a life of its own, most notoriously in a four-volume extended commentary published by Henry Ford (1863–1947) entitled *The International Jew: The World's Foremost Problem,* a collation of the ninety-one articles published in his newspaper, the *Dearborn Independent.* Today, it remains a foundational text of antisemites the world over and can be found in a variety of languages, including English and Arabic, and easily downloaded off the Internet. Attempts to combat its dissemination and refute its scurrilous falsities have, apparently, met with precious little success.

Mention must also be made of the notorious trial of Mendel Beilis (1874–1934), who was prosecuted for the murder of a thirteen-year-old boy, Andrei Yushcinsky, in Kiev, Ukraine. Beilis was accused of ritual murder (the pernicious *blood libel*), murdering the boy to drain his blood in preparation for the making of the *matzot* (flat unleavened cakes) for the Passover. Although the trial lasted from September 25 to October 28, 1913, and ended with his acquittal, it was too reminiscent and too familiar: accusations of ritual murder/blood libel are part of the negative past histories of England, France, Germany, Hungary, and elsewhere throughout Europe and even later. In 1928, in Massena, New York, a child wandered off and then the rabbi and other Jewish communal leaders were brought in for questioning by the local police. (The child was later found, having fallen asleep after becoming lost and disoriented and later wandering back to town.) The charge later became the subject of Syrian defense minister Mustafa Tlass's (1932–2017) 1983 *The Matzah of Zion,* a retelling of the "Damascus Affair" of 1840, when members of that Jewish community were interrogated, tortured, and some murdered after being accused of the ritual murder of a Christian monk and his assistant.

Prior to the Nazi takeover of Germany and Adolf Hitler (1889–1945) becoming its chancellor on January 30, 1933, a twelve-year event in France (1894–1906)—what has come to be called the "Dreyfus Affair"— showed all of Europe the *power* of political antisemitism to too easily gather support and rally the masses. A French Jewish army captain, Alfred Dreyfus (1859–1935), was initially found falsely guilty of selling secrets to Germany, stripped of rank in a publicly humiliating ceremony to the delight of the crowd, and exiled for life to the prisonlike Devil's Island off the coast of South America. Brought back for a second trial, he was again found guilty and returned to Devil's Island. A third trial, after a public outcry led by France's leading journalist, Emile Zola (1840–1902)—who would himself be forced to flee as a result of his open front-page letter "J'Accuse" in the newspaper *L'Aurore*—resulted in Dreyfus's vindication, pardon, and restoration of rank. An unexpected consequence of Dreyfus's acquittal was, ultimately, the breaking of the stranglehold relationship between the Roman Catholic Church and those who wanted the return of the monarchy.

The Nazi "contribution" to antisemitism in the twentieth century was the injection of a racial-biological component, that is, that the Jew was a lesser, albeit savvy, form of human being, responsible for the totality of *all* of the ills of Western civilization, and thus the *only* solution to this menace was their total extermination/annihilation, not only in Germany itself but throughout all the territories, present and future, under German-Nazi hegemony. The murder of more than six million Jewish men, women, and children was an event we now know as the Holocaust (English) or *Shoah* (Hebrew). It took antisemitism to a logical, if not inevitable, conclusion— extermination/annihilation of the Jews no matter their age (1.5 million children eighteen years old or younger); gender (both females and males); secular and religious; and assimilated or connected to the various Jewish communities of Europe. Thus, in this instance, building upon such "scientific" late nineteenth-century and early twentieth-century concepts as *eugenics* (the improvement of the human "race," a concept itself of dubious factuality) and *Social Darwinism* (only the strong survive in a biologically competitive and adaptive environment), Jews (whom the Nazis defined as *full* (four grandparents), *half* (two grandparents), or *quarter* (one grandparent) in the Nuremberg Race Laws of 1935, where the German term *mischlinge* is better understood negatively as "half-breed" rather than the more neutral translation of mixed biological parentage/grandparentage) could not escape their biological destiny of destruction. Conversion or assimilation were not options for themselves or their children. This false understanding of the "biological Jew" remains strong throughout the antisemitic world and is found today on numerous hate websites and in their printed publications.

Before concluding this historical overview with a look-see at the situation of the Jews in the United States, we turn, logically, to the Middle East. Here, we must distinguish three periods: (1) that of Muhammad and the Qur'an; (2) the post-Muhammad period until the nineteenth century;

xxx | Overview

and (3) the modern period, including the ongoing Arab/Palestinian-Israeli conflict.

Even before the refounding of the Third Jewish Commonwealth, the State of Israel, on May 14, 1948, almost three years to the day after the end of World War II, Arab/Muslim hatred of Jews and Judaism was already in evidence, primarily as an unwelcome presence in *Dar al-Islam* (the world of Muslim/Islamic hegemony). With Israel's successive victories in its wars in 1948, 1956, 1967, 1973, 1981, and beyond, and its military, technological, medical, economic, educational, and political successes, there has come a further importation of a European antisemitism—for example, the employment of former Nazis in Egypt and Syria in the aftermath of World War II as anti-Jewish propagandists, fueling an already negative environment, and the republication of that most notorious antisemitic forgery the *Protocols of the Learned Elders of Zion* into Arabic and its availability in bookstores throughout the Middle East already beginning in the 1950s. (King Faisal of Saudi Arabia (1906–1975), for example, presented leather-bound copies of the *Protocols* as gifts to visiting dignitaries.)

Moving into the middle of the twentieth century, this relatively modern antisemitism had morphed to now include hatred of Zionists (both Jews and non-Jews, including the United States continuously viewed as Israel's most powerful supporter) and Zionism (the national liberation movement of the Jewish people), Israel, and Jewish Israelis. Historically, antipathy toward Jews had already surfaced during Muhammad's (570–632 CE) drive to unify the Arabs of the Arabian Peninsula when the Jewish tribe of the Banu Qurayza and the Battle of Khaybar (627 and 628 CE) rejected his Qur'anic and religious overtures, as did other Jewish tribes in the area, and were subjected to expulsion and death. Furthermore, once Jews found themselves under Muslim/Arab hegemony throughout the Middle East, they were regarded as "second class" or lesser (in Arabic, *dhimmis*), though Muhammad originally respected them as "peoples of the (Sacred) Book" along with Christians, who, on many occasions, fared worse.

It is important to keep in mind, however, that, early on, Muhammad's enmity toward the various Jewish tribes was more political-economic rather than religious-theological. As stated, he regarded both Jews and Christians as "peoples of the (Sacred) Book," even if they had "rewritten" those scriptures to displace the "correct" understanding as the true people of Allah/God and failed to embrace his vision and understanding of the divine-human encounter. Seeing himself as the Seal (Final) of the ancient prophets and the Qur'an as setting forth the direct oral revelations and transmissions from God, one also finds within those holy texts both positive and negative comments about the Jews. Examples of both are found in the *suras* (chapters) 2–7, 9, 10, 17, 20, 22, 26, 27, 32, 40, 43–46, 59, 61, and 62.

In the aftermath of Muhammad's death, and throughout the next several centuries as both Arab unification and conquest coupled with the spread of Islam came to dominate the region, the relationship of the conquerors to the conquered became both positive and negative. Jews achieved economic and political successes under Arab leadership despite such disabilities as having to wear distinctive clothing, residence restrictions, and the like. Into this turbulent world—always facing the danger of an encroaching Christian presence and a different religious-theological affirmation—Jews were able to somewhat successfully negotiate their own situation, posed no real political or religious threat, and largely went about the business of communal safety, security, and survival.

World War II, however, brought about a dramatic change to the situation of the Jews in the aftermath of the disintegrating Ottoman Empire, already in disarray after World War I, in the person of the Palestinian Arab nationalist Mohammed Amin al-Husseini (1897–1974), who was appointed grand mufti of Jerusalem by the British. Virulently antisemitic, he allied himself with Hitler and the Nazis, spent part of World War II in Berlin, lived off a German stipend, and broadcast on Nazi radio his continuing hatred of Jews and Zionists. His goal was for German military success in the Middle East and the implementation of the Final Solution (*die Endlösung*) throughout the region.

Two other important figures of note in the days following World War II were Hassan al-Banna (1906–1949), an Egyptian schoolteacher and founder of the Muslim Brotherhood (later assassinated by the secret police), and Sayyid Qutb (1906–1966), an author, educator, and theorist against the regime of Egyptian president Gamal Abdel Nasser (1918–1970), who would have him hanged while in prison. Qutb's 1950 book *Our Struggle against the Jews*, along with the writings of al-Banna and the work of al-Husseini, remain cornerstones today in the antisemitism and anti-Zionism that remain pervasive throughout much of the Middle East.

As noted, Israel, having successfully fought wars with its neighbors, remains an anathema within the larger geographic region encompassed by the term *Dar al-Islam* ("the world of Islamic hegemony") as a foreign

xxxii | Overview

element and worse. Violence directed toward Israel and Israelis in the form of suicide bombings inside the state against civilian targets, including women and children, became a regular occurrence at the end of the twentieth century and beginning of the twenty-first century. Antisemitic publications, including the notorious forgery the *Protocols of the Learned Elders of Zion* and former Syrian minister of defense Mustafa Tlass's (1932–2017) *The Matzah of Zion* (addressing "blood libel"), are staples within the Arab world, as was the serialization of the TV series *Horseman without a Horse* in Egypt in 2002 and again in 2012.

In 2006, then Iranian president Mahmoud Ahmadinejad (b. 1956, president 2005–2013), already a well-publicized foe of Israel, Zionism, and the Jewish people in general—including calls to "wipe Israel off the map" of the Middle East in 2005 (and following)—hosted a conference in 2006 entitled the "International Conference to Review the Global Vision of the Holocaust and Surrounding Controversies" in Tehran, which was in line with his consistent Holocaust denialism. The year before, in 2005, he had hosted a conference called "The World without Zionism." (Ahmadinejad, it should also be remembered, was among the students who took over the U.S. Embassy in Tehran and held fifty-two U.S. citizens hostage for 444 days in 1979.)

What must also be brought to public attention is the expulsion of Jewish communities throughout the Middle East in the wake of Israel's statehood in 1948 and prior to it as well. Whatever remains of those once-vibrant communities, they are now small, struggling, without political or economic influence, and religiously diminished. By far, however, the most egregious example of that displacement was an event known as the *Farhud* (violent dispossession) in Baghdad, Iraq, in 1941, when almost two hundred Jews were murdered, one thousand injured, and nine hundred Jewish homes destroyed. Ten years later, in 1951–1952, a mass exodus of Jews to both Israel and the United States was almost a fait accompli; those who remain are a quasi-protected minority subject to discrimination, and the fate of their communities depend on Israel's relations with its neighbors, for good or bad.

As more Arabs, both those committed to Islam, especially radical youth, and heavily politicized secularists, have immigrated to Western Europe—especially France and Germany—and Great Britain, bringing with them increasing vulnerability and violence to formerly safe and stable Jewish communities, European Jews have experienced an increase in antisemitic incidents. For example, in February 2006, in Paris, twenty-four-year-old Ilan Halimi (1982–2006) was murdered by a Muslim group calling itself the "Gang of Barbarians" after having been kidnapped the month before. In May 2014, in Brussels, Belgium, the Jewish Museum was attacked, and four persons were murdered. In January 2015, the Hypercacher Kosher Supermarket was attacked; four people were murdered, and nine were wounded. In November 2015, the Bataclan concert venue was attacked in Paris, and nearly one hundred persons were murdered. (Its owners are Jews, but it is questionable whether that fact was already known to the perpetrators of this massacre.) Lastly, in the United States, the Anti-Defamation League (ADL), in its annual audit, reported 1,986 acts of antisemitism in 2017, more than double that of 2015, and a 57 percent increase from 2016.

Conversations among those residents in France and elsewhere continue to raise the tragic question of whether it is not the full and total end of Jewish life in Europe, whether it is time to leave—for Israel, the United States, or elsewhere—and whether the United States itself is no longer the haven for Jews it once was. The jury is still out, but the evidence is clear. *This longest hatred has not died but only reenergizes itself in different iterations and different locations.* Ways that can successfully combat it—through stricter laws and punishments; innovative educational programs directed to young people, primarily economically disadvantaged youth; tightened security for Jewish institutions; building interreligious networks; and the like—are continuing sources of discussion.

Finally, there is the situation of the Jews in the United States. As noted above, according to the Annual Audit of Antisemitic Incidents reported by the Anti-Defamation League (ADL), 2017 saw an increase of *more than* 50 percent of such reporting, revealing a political climate where such assaults are apparently perceived as "righteous acts" of indignation by those who see themselves as under attack by deviant Jewish forces within the country and forced to pay the military and economic prices for U.S. support of Israel and the war on terrorism in Iraq and Afghanistan.

Taking the longer historical view, however, other than at certain periods of unrest—for example, the economic dislocations of the 1920s and 1930s that saw the rebirth of the Ku Klux Klan (KKK) and its public opposition to Jews, African Americans, and Roman Catholics and the civil rights movement in the 1960s, particularly in the South—for much of its history, the United States has proven to truly be a safe haven whereby Jews have both successfully integrated and assimilated themselves into the fabric of American life on every level: social, cultural, educational, military,

xxxiv | Overview

political, and, yes, economic. And while discriminations have been experienced at every level, what has significantly changed Jewish reality from that of Europe has been the high wall of separation of church and state, whereby neither have exercised jurisdictional control over Jews and other members of minority faiths. Thus, despite the various manifestations of antisemitism that continue to present themselves to, for, and against Jews and Judaism, Israel, and Zionism in the United States, Jews remain safer, more secure, and more optimistic about their future here than anywhere else on the planet. The inaccuracy of crystal balls and other predictors of the future aside, whether such will continue remains an open question, as the Jewish population shows little numerical increase in relation to the larger population, and Jewish voices and concerns, especially political concerns about Israel and its survival in hostile surroundings, continue to diminish.

Antisemitism—*Why* It Is

As stated early on, one possible source of antisemitism may very well be what we have labeled *xenophobia*, othering or distancing. This psychological malady whereby we human beings are uncomfortable—or worse—with those who are not like us remains part of what we are as biological entities. That discomfort, coupled with the various iterations of power—social, cultural, educational, religious, political, and economic—by the dominant majority, or those who aspire to dominance, against a decided minority, Jews, always remains a powder keg waiting for the right spark of ignition and resulting in various forms of deprivation: exclusion, ghettoization, expulsion, murder, annihilation, or extermination.

Following closely on the heels of this malady is *scapegoatism*: the refusal or failure to admit to our own mistakes, both individually and collectively. It is easier to blame the other—in this case, the Jews—for our failures at home, in the marketplace, or by the nation-state. The classic example of the latter is, of course, Germany's military failure and defeat in World War I, what was called in German *Dolchstoßlegende* (stab-in-the-back), the notion, widely believed and promulgated in right-wing circles in Germany after 1918, that the German Army did not lose on the battlefield but was instead betrayed by the civilians on the home front, especially the Republicans *and the Jews* who overthrew the monarchy in the German Revolution of 1918–1919. (That a Jewish population of five hundred thousand children, women, and men in Germany—one-half of

1 percent of the people—by the time the Nazis acceded to power in 1933 had such an undue influence is, of course, absurd, but rather evidence in and of itself of centuries-old perpetuating myths of Jewish power.)

Another strong possibility drawn from our sociological understanding of the way in which groups function is that of competitiveness and envy or jealousy, in actuality or in potentiality. Jews have or want to have what others do not or not yet have, or, if they have it, Jews are desirous of taking it away from them. Such thinking and actions relate to the corruptible nature of power itself: once having acquired it, groups are reluctant to surrender it and will, if given the opportunity, behave mercilessly toward those who threaten or are perceived to threaten their hold on power.

Thus, whatever the reasons or explanations for antisemitism—all or some of the factors enumerated above—plus now the psychological and the sociological, it remains an enduring phenomenon on the world's stage and a stain and blight on the world's conscience.

Further Reading

Glock, Charles Y., and Rodney Stark. *Christian Beliefs and Anti-Semitism*. New York: Harper & Row, 1966.

Goldhagen, Daniel Jonah. *The Devil That Never Dies: The Rise and Threat of Global Antisemitism*. New York and London: Little Brown and Company, 2013.

Goldstein, Phyllis. *A Convenient Hatred: The History of Antisemitism*. Brookline, MA: Facing History and Ourselves, 2011.

International Holocaust Remembrance Alliance. "Stockholm Declaration: A Commitment Shared by All Member Countries," www.holocaustremembrance.com/stockholm-declaration.

Jacobs, Steven Leonard, and Mark Weitzman. *Dismantling the Big Lie: The Protocols of the Elders of Zion*. Los Angeles and Jersey City, NJ: Simon Wiesenthal Center and KTAV Publishing House, 2003.

Langmuir, Gavin I. *Toward a Definition of Antisemitism*. Berkeley: University of California Press, 1990.

Marcus, Kenneth. *The Definition of Anti-Semitism*. Oxford and New York: Oxford University Press, 2015.

Nirenberg, David. *Anti-Judaism: The Western Tradition*. New York: W. W. Norton & Company, 2014.

O'Brien, Darren. *The Pinnacle of Hatred: The Blood Libel and the Jews*. Jerusalem: Hebrew University Magnes Press, 2011.

Pearl, Judea. "BDS and Zionophobic Racism," in Andrew Pessin and S. Ben-Atar, eds., *Anti-Zionism on Campus*. Bloomington: Indiana University Press, Ch. 16, pp. 224–235.

xxxvi | Overview

Perednik, Gustavo. "Judeophobia—Anti-Semitism—Jew-Hate and Anti-Zionism," www.zionism-israel.com/Judeophobia.htm.

Prager, Dennis, and Joseph Telushkin. *Why the Jews? The Reasons for Antisemitism.* New York and London: Simon & Schuster, 2003.

Wistrich, Robert S. *A Lethal Obsession: Anti-Semitism from Antiquity to the Global Jihad.* New York: Random House, 2010.

Zakim, Leonard. *Confronting Anti-Semitism: A Practical Guide.* Hoboken, NJ: KTAV Publishing House, 2000.

Chronology

900–500 BCE—(Possible dating of the Book of Exodus)

> 1:8–10: Then a new pharaoh, to whom Joseph meant nothing, came to power in Egypt. "Look," he said to his people, "the Israelites have become far too numerous for us. Come, we must deal shrewdly with them or they will become even more numerous and, if war breaks out, will join our enemies, fight against us and leave the country."

721 BCE—The Ten Northern Tribes are destroyed by Assyria.

596 BCE—The Israelites are exiled to Babylonia.

Mid-fourteenth century BCE—(Possible dating of the Book of Esther)

> 3:8–9: Then Haman said to King Ahasuerus, "There is a particular people that is dispersed and spread among the inhabitants throughout all the provinces of your kingdom whose laws differ from those of all other peoples. Furthermore, they do not observe the king's laws. It is not appropriate for the king to provide a haven for them. If the king is so inclined, let an edict be issued to destroy them. I will pay 10,000 talents of silver to be conveyed to the king's treasuries for the officials who carry out this business."

70 CE—Roman legions destroy the Second Temple in Jerusalem in response to the Jewish rebellion against their oppression and restrictions against their worship practices. "Christian Jews" would later blame this destruction as a result of the Jews' failure to accept the Christ.

628—Muhammad (571–632) defeats a tribe of Jews at the Battle of Khayber and destroys their population.

694—The Visigothic king Egica (610–702) of Spain announces measures to confiscate all Jewish property and baptize all Jewish children.

xxxviii | Chronology

1096—The First Crusade to "save" the Holy Land from the Muslim infidels begins. All along the route, thousands of Jews are put to death, their property confiscated, and their places of residence and worship destroyed.

1144—A young boy, William of Norwich, Great Britain, is found murdered, and the Jews are wrongfully accused of murdering him and draining his blood for ritual purposes. This is the first instance of the so-called blood libel.

1171—The entire Jewish community of Blois, France, is murdered because of a false accusation of blood libel.

1190—Riots break out in York, Great Britain, and 150 Jews commit suicide rather than face certain murder. Fifty-seven Jews are slaughtered in St. Edmund's, Great Britain, as well.

1255—Eighteen Jews are hanged in Lincoln, Great Britain, having been falsely accused of the murder of an eight-year-old boy named Hugh. Though he would later be named Little St. Hugh of Lincoln, the church never officially canonizes him.

1287—Ninety Jewish men, women, and children are murdered in Oberwesel, Germany, after being falsely accused of ritual murder.

1290—King Edward I (1239–1307) of England issues his Edict of Expulsion banishing all Jews from his realm.

1298—Throughout Germany, 120,000 Jews are murdered during the Rintfleisch Massacres.

1306—King Phillip the Fair of France (1268–1314) issues an Edict of Expulsion against all the Jews then living in France, except those willing to be baptized.

1321—In Chinon, France, 160 Jews are burned at the stake after being falsely accused of ritual murder.

1347–1351—The Black Death (bubonic plague) sweeps across Europe, causing the deaths of seventy-five million to one hundred million people. Across the continent, Jews are blamed for its cause, resulting in numerous murders and the destruction of ghettos and other places of residence.

1349—Two thousand Jews are burned alive in Strasbourg, Alsace, after having been falsely accused of poisoning the wells.

1391—The five thousand–member Jewish community of Valencia, Spain, is invaded by rioting mobs. Around 250 Jews are killed, women and girls are raped, and the damage to homes, businesses, and synagogues is extensive. In Barcelona, Spain, two hundred Jews are also murdered.

1478—The Spanish Inquisition is established to brutally root out heresy in the Roman Catholic Church with a focus on insincere converts, the majority of whom were formerly Jews.

1492—Jews are forced to flee Spain under the Edit of Expulsion (the Alhambra Decree) promulgated by King Ferdinand II (1452–1516) of Castile and Queen Isabella I (1451–1504) of Aragon.

1506—One thousand Jews are murdered in Lisbon, Portugal.

1543—Martin Luther (1483–1546) publishes *On the Jews and Their Lies* and *Of the Unknowable Name and the Generations of Christ*, two notoriously and foundational antisemitic texts.

1648—Ukrainian hetman (leader) Bohdan Khmelnytsky (1595–1657) initiates a revolt against Polish nobility that ultimately results in the murders of more than one hundred thousand Jews.

1670—Jews are expelled from Vienna, Austria, by the order of Emperor Leopold I (1640–1705).

1680—Seventy-two persons are accused of being "Judaizers" by the Spanish Inquisition. Eighteen are burned at the stake; fifty-four are sentenced to be galley slaves or to serve life imprisonment.

1768—In Poland, thousands of Jews are slaughtered by Cossacks at the Massacre of Uman.

1840—In Damascus, Syria, Jews are falsely accused by the Islamic leadership of the murder of the Capuchin monk Father Thomas. The synagogue is pillaged, the Jews leaders are arrested and tortured, some leaders are murdered, and the community is subjected to violent, destructive reprisals.

1879—The disgruntled failed journalist Wilhelm Marr (1819–1904) publishes his slanderous *Der Weg zum Siege des Germanenthums über das Judenthum* ("The Way to Victory of Germanism over Judaism") and popularizes the use of the word *Antisemitismus* (antisemitism).

1889—Adolf Hitler is born in Braunau am Inn, Austria. As the result of his political vision, he causes the Holocaust to become a reality in Nazi-dominated Europe during World War II. In 1945, he commits suicide in Berlin, Germany.

xl | Chronology

1889—Captain Alfred Dreyfus (1859–1935) of the French military is falsely accused of both espionage and treason and brought to trial. Found guilty, he is stripped of rank and imprisoned. In 1906, he is officially exonerated and restored to rank.

1903—The Kishinev pogrom breaks out in Moldova. Forty-nine Jews are killed, five hundred are injured, and fifteen hundred homes are damaged, causing worldwide protests against those responsible.

1903–1904—The Russian secret police, Okrana, publishes *The Protocols of the Learned Elders of Zion*, now the world's longest-lived antisemitic forgery of a Jewish conspiracy to rule the world.

1913—Mendel Beilis (1874–1934) is arrested in Kiev, Ukraine, and accused of ritually murdering a young boy. He is later acquitted of this false charge.

1918–1921—During the White Terror in Russia, 100,000–150,000 Jews are murdered.

1920—A pogrom breaks out in Vilna, Lithuania, resulting in the deaths of at least 80 Jews by the Polish Army after the withdrawal of Soviet troops.

1928—In Messena, New York, the small Jewish community is investigated, including the local rabbi, after a little girl disappears. She returns the next day, after having fallen asleep in a wooded area. Rumors of blood libel surface—the only such incident in American history.

1929—Sixty-nine Jews are murdered by Arabs in Hebron, pre-state Israel/Palestine, because of the false rumor of Jews attempting to take over the Temple Mount. Twenty-four of the victims were Jewish seminary students.

1935—The Nuremberg Racial Laws for the Protection of German Blood and Honor are instituted in Nazi Germany, signaling the beginning of the end of Jewish citizenship and worse.

1938, November 9–10—In Germany, 267 synagogues are destroyed, seven thousand Jewish businesses are damaged or destroyed, and thirty thousand Jewish men are arrested, all supposedly in response to the murder of Ernst vom Rath (1909–1938), the third secretary at the German Embassy, in Paris, France, by Herschel Grynszpan (1921–?), in retribution for the Nazis' treatment of his Polish parents and sister.

1939–1945—During World War II, more than six million Jews are murdered throughout Europe by the Nazis and their allies in horrific settings where they were militarily successful. Towns and villages are destroyed and ghettos liquidated. The Jews are subjected to imprisonment in concentration and death camps, torture, starvation, and brutalization, among other atrocities.

1946—In Kielce, Poland, forty-two Jews are killed and more than forty are wounded by Polish soldiers, police officers, and civilians when they attempt to return to their homes in the aftermath of the Holocaust.

1953—Soviet premier Joseph Stalin (1878–1953) has nine doctors, six of whom are Jews, arrested for falsely attempting to poison him in the so-called Doctors' Plot. All are ultimately freed and vindicated because of his untimely death.

1972—Black September Palestinian terrorists invade the Olympic Village in Munich, Germany, and kill eleven Israeli athletes. Five of the eight terrorists are killed as well as a German police officer. Three of the terrorists are captured.

1976—An Air France plane flying from Tel Aviv to Paris is hijacked by Arab terrorists and lands at Entebbe, Uganda. A successful raid to liberate the passengers, including one hundred Jews, results in only one death, the Israeli second-in-command, Yonatan "Yoni" Netanyahu (1946–1976).

1980—A bomb explodes in a synagogue in France, killing four Jews and wounding nine others.

2017—The Unite the Right rally takes places in Charlottesville, Virginia, as neo-Nazis and other haters protest the removal of General Robert E. Lee's statue from a public park. One anti-hater is killed and others are wounded. Both groups clash violently as the haters proclaim, "Jews will not replace us!"

2018—Eleven Jews are murdered at the Tree of Life Synagogue in Pittsburgh, Pennsylvania, by a white supremacist.

2019—A white supremacist invades the Chabad Center in Poway, California, killing one person and wounding three others, including the rabbi, before being arrested.

Adversus Judaeos

Adversus Judaeos refers to a collection of sermons by leading Roman Catholic churchmen of the fourth century. Specifically, it refers to the "Eight Homilies against the Jews" preached by St. John Chrysostom (349–407), the bishop of Antioch, the "golden-mouthed orator," during the years 386–387. Other preachers who were equally venomous against the Jews of the day include Tertullian (155–240), who is sometimes referred to as the "father" of Latin Christianity and the "founder" of Western theology; an unknown author referred to as Pseudo-Tertullian—because of the similarities of his writings and attacks against Marcion (85–160)—who was said to have rejected the God of the Hebrew Bible/Old Testament and was excommunicated from the Church; Pseudo-Gregory of Nyssa, who is reportedly the author of "Testimonies against the Jews" (335–395); the theologian Hippolytus (170–235); Eusebius, the bishop of Caesarea Maritima (265–340); and St. Justin Martyr (100–165).

While debate continues over how antisemitic St. John truly was, with his adversaries condemning his homilies as transparently filled with hatred of the Jews, his scholarly supporters argue that his "over-the-top" comments, in line with normal invective speeches of the day, were, in truth, an attack on those Christians who continued to frequent synagogues and participate in Jewish worship. However, as representative of a type of early antisemitism, his condemnations of Jews included (1) their responsibility for the death of the Christ (deicide), and thus their being cursed and dispersed; (2) their rejoicing in Christ's death; (3) a comparison of the synagogue to a brothel and a cavern of the devil; (4) a claim that the rabbinate was corrupt and that its authority over the Jews could be bought; (5) an accusation that Jews were sexually debauched and regularly engaged in criminal behaviors; (6) a claim that Jews were no longer the chosen people

1

al-Banna, Hassan

of God; and (7) a statement that Jews were "fit for slaughter." During World War II, the Nazis regularly reprinted his homilies as they attempted to win German and other committed Christians to their genocidal agenda.

In his important book *The Conflict of the Church and Synagogue: A Study in the Origins of Antisemitism*, British Anglican theologian and scholar James Parkes (1896–1981) wrote, "In these discourses, there is no sneer too mean, no gibe too bitter for him to fling at the Jewish people. No text is too remote to be able to be twisted to their confusion; no argument is too casuistical, no blasphemy too startling for him to employ" (72).

The same critique could equally be said of those who preached in the same manner and employed the same litany of hate against the Jewish people. Sermons in this vein would be preached up to and including the twentieth century, with Muslim imams doing so as well.

See also: Blood Libel; Crusades; Deicide; Luther, Martin; Martyrdom, Sanctifying the Name of God; Oberammergau Passion Play; Pius XII, Pope; Spanish Inquisition; Usury

Further Reading

Davies, Alan T., ed. *Anti-Semitism and the Foundations of Christianity*. New York: Paulist Press, 1979.

Klein, Charlotte. *Anti-Judaism in Christian Theology*. Philadelphia: Fortress Press, 1978.

Parkes, James. *The Conflict of the Church and Synagogue: A Study in the Origins of Antisemitism*. Philadelphia: Jewish Publication Society, 1934.

Ruether, Rosemary Radford. *Faith and Fratricide: The Theological Roots of Anti-Semitism*. New York: Seabury Press, 1994.

Wilken, Robert L. *John Chrysostom and the Jews: Rhetoric and Reality in the Late 4th Century*. Eugene, OR: Wipf and Stock, 2004. [Reprint]

Williams, A. Lukyn. *Adversus Judaeos: A Bird's Eye View of Christian Apologiae until the Renaissance*. Cambridge, UK: Cambridge University Press, 2012/1935.

al-Banna, Hassan

Hassan al-Banna (1906–1949) was born in Egypt to a conservative imam and scholar of the Hanbali Islamic tradition and is well known today as the founder of the Muslim Brotherhood (*Jamaat al-Ikhwan al-Muslimun*, "Society of the Muslim Brotherhood"/MB, or *Ikwan* for short), whose current iteration, Hamas, remains at war with the State of Israel, as clarified in its 1988 "Covenant of the Islamic Resistance Movement," which calls for the complete destruction of the nation-state. In the covenant, al-Banna's statement, "Israel will exist, and will continue to exist, until Islam abolishes it, as it abolished that which was before it," remains central to that document. The Muslim Brotherhood may be characterized as "a salafi movement, a Sunni path, a Sufi truth, a political organization and social idea" (www.worldbulletin.net). Al-Banna attempted to present to his ever-growing followership a modern ideological interpretation of an all-encompassing understanding of Islam as a counterforce to what he believed to be not only its existing state of corruption but also the domination of the Arab peoples by Western imperialists in Egypt and throughout the Middle East. In 1949, he was perceived as a threat to the Egyptian government and assassinated by its secret police, with many claiming it was done at the instigation of King Farouk (1920–1965).

By al-Banna's own account, in 1928, six unnamed workers at the Suez Canal approached him and complained of injustices at the hands of the British and French. In response, he created an organization called the Muslim Brotherhood, and a decade later, its ranks had swelled to more than five hundred thousand members and expanded into other Arab countries. In addition to writing numerous books, articles, and tracts, al-Banna built his organization based on existing welfare organizations and neighborhood groups and centered them around the mosque itself. Among the issues addressed were (1) colonialism; (2) education; (3) public health; (4) exploitation of natural resources; (5) social inequality; (6) Arab nationalism in and out of Egypt, including the unity of the Arab peoples (*ummah*); (7) the lesser status of the Islamic world internationally; and (8) the growing Arab/Palestinian-Israeli conflict. The Muslim Brotherhood, with al-Banna at its helm, actively supported the 1936–1939 revolts in Palestine and the 1948 Arab-Israeli War, having formally founded a jihadist branch in 1940 to defend Muslims against the Zionist movement in Palestine as well as the British occupation of the Suez Canal. According to Joseph S. Spoerl, writing in the *New English Review* (2012), "al-Banna's worldview may be summarized in four main propositions: first, Islam is a perfect and complete way of life; second, Islam must be the basis of all legislation; third, Western societies are decadent and corrupt; and fourth, God has commanded Muslims to conquer and rule the earth" (www.newenglishreview.org).

The Brotherhood has also been engaged in the Algerian War of Independence (1954–1962), the current conflicts in Afghanistan and Kashmir, and the Arab Spring beginning in 2010. Thus, violence against those perceived as enemies of Islam—especially Jews, Israeli Jews, Zionists and Zionism, and the State of Israel—remains a fundamental and central part of the legacy of al-Banna, as expressed in his 1930 article "On Jihad."

See also: al-Husseini, Amin; BDS (Boycott, Divestment, Sanctions) Movement; Blood Libel; Crusades; Qutb, Sayyid

Further Reading

al-Banna, Hassan. *Five Tracts of Hasan al-Banna (1906–1949)*. Translated by Charles Wendell. Berkley: University of California Press, 1978.

Brynjar, Liz. *The Society of Muslim Brothers in Egypt: The Rise of an Islamic Mass Movement*. Reading, UK: Garnet, 1998.

Esposito, John. *Unholy War: Terror in the Name of Islam*. Oxford and New York: Oxford University Press, 2002.

Farmer, Brian R. *Understanding Radical Islam: Medieval Ideology in the Twenty-First Century*. Bern, Switzerland: Peter Lang, 2007.

Fourest, Caroline. *Brother Tariq: The Doublespeak of Tariq Ramadan*. New York: Encounter Books, 2008.

"Hassan al-Banna, the Founder of Muslim Brotherhood." https://www.worldbulletin.net/this-week-in-history/hassan-al-banna-the-founder-of-muslim-brotherhood-h184669.html

Maréchal, Brigitte. *The Muslim Brothers in Europe: Roots and Discourses*. Leiden, Netherlands: Brill, 2008.

Mitchell, Richard Paul. *The Society of Muslim Brothers*. Oxford and New York: Oxford University Press, 1993.

Spoerl, Joseph S. "The World View of Hasan al-Banna and the Muslim Brotherhood." *New English Review*, 2012. https://www.newenglishreview.org/Joseph_S._Spoerl/The_World_View_of_Hasan_al-Banna_and_the_Muslim_Brotherhood/

Vidino, Lorenzo. *The New Muslim Brotherhood in the West*. New York: Columbia University Press, 2010.

al-Husseini, Amin

Mohammed Amin al-Husseini (1897–1974) was born in Jerusalem to a prominent Palestinian family and was a fierce Arab/Palestinian nationalist and a vehement opponent of Jews and Zionism. He attempted to broker an understanding with Nazi Germany under Adolf Hitler (1889–1945) that the Nazis would export their antisemitism and Final Solution to the Middle East. His family lore was that they were descended from the grandson of the Prophet Muhammad. His aggressive opposition to the Zionist project was already in evidence as early as the 1920s. Appointed as the mufti of Jerusalem (the head of the Muslim Religious Council) in 1923 by Sir Herbert Samuel (1870–1963), the British high commissioner for Palestine, al-Husseini did everything within his power to thwart Jewish immigration, including funding secret, violent groups of Arab nationalists and extremists. Equally, he brooked no disagreements within the Arab-Muslim community in pre-state Israel and would also use violence against his enemies.

In 1942, al-Husseini was already in Berlin, having initially arrived in Italy and held meetings with its Fascist prime minister, Benito Mussolini (1883–1945), who appeared to be supportive of his anti-Zionist and anti-Jewish agenda. Meeting with Hitler that November, he attempted to extract the same support; however, Hitler remained noncommittal due to the war effort. Al-Husseini would then broaden his efforts on two fronts: (1) working for Nazi propaganda radio by broadcasting antisemitic diatribes to his fellow Muslims and Arabs in the Middle East, urging them to make war on the Jews in their midst, and (2) recruiting Arabs to the Nazi cause as soldiers in the Balkans in such places as Albania, Croatia, and Bosnia, in which he had limited success.

At war's end, al-Husseini attempted to flee to Switzerland, but he was detained by the French first, in Germany, and then put under house arrest in Paris, all the while French refusing to turn him over to the British to be tried as a war criminal. In disguise, he would later flee to Cairo, where the Egyptians granted him political asylum. Though initially popular as both a religious and political leader, after the defeat of the combined Arab armies in Israel's 1948 War of Independence and the flight of many Palestinians to the surrounding Arab states, al-Husseini lost much of his status and support.

Al-Husseini died in Beirut, Lebanon, in 1974. He had requested to be buried on the Temple Mount, known in Arabic as the *Haram esh-Sharif* or

6 | Alt-Right

"Noble Sanctuary." Israel, already in control of East Jerusalem as a result of the 1967 Six-Day War, denied the request.

Scholarly opinion remains somewhat divided vis-à-vis the question of al-Husseini's antisemitism in relation to his intense Palestinian nationalism and hatred of Zionism and Zionists. That hatred, however, as evidenced by his desire and willingness to collaborate with the Nazis in their genocidal agenda against Jews speaks for itself.

See also: al-Banna, Hassan; BDS (Boycott, Divestment, Sanctions) Movement; Crusades; Farhud; Martyrdom, Sanctifying the Name of God; Qutb, Sayyid

Further Reading

Elpeleg, Zvi. *The Grand Mufti: Haj Amin al-Husseini, Founder of the Palestinian National Movement.* Translated by David Harvey. London and New York: Routledge, 2007/1993.

Gensicke, Klaus. *The Mufti of Jerusalem and the Nazis: The Berlin Years.* London: Vallentine Mitchell, 2011.

Jbara, Taysir. *Palestine Leader: Hajj Amin Al-Husayni, Mufti of Jerusalem.* London: Kingston Press, 1985.

Pappé, Ilan. *The Rise and Fall of a Palestinian Dynasty: The Husaynis, 1700–1948.* Berkeley: University of California Press, 2011.

Perlman, Moshe. *Mufti of Jerusalem: The Story of Haj Amin el Husseini.* London: Victor Gollanz, 1947.

Schechtman, Joseph B. *The Mufti and the Fuhrer: The Rise and Fall of Haj Amin el-Husseini.* New York: Thomas Yoseloff, 1965.

Alt-Right

The alt-right, an abbreviation of *alternative right*, is a loosely constructed ultraconservative political movement of individuals, groups, and organizations who espouse white nationalism, white supremacy, white separatism, racism, antisemitism, and anti-immigration, primarily in the United States but also having links to similar groupings in Great Britain, France, Germany, Greece, Hungary, New Zealand, and Australia. The full term was first used by retired professor of philosophy and history Paul E.

Gottfried (b. 1941) in November 2008 and later published in December of that year in an article titled "The Decline and Rise of the Alternative Right." Neo-Nazi and white supremacist Richard B. Spencer (b. 1978) has argued that he and Gottfried are the joint authors of the term, though Spencer makes use of the shortened form rather than the full term in both his writings and his speeches. Subsequent to Gottfried, who has since distanced himself from Spencer and others, the term was largely confined to the Internet and various alternative and hate-filled sites and social media, where disgruntled whites, primarily young males, vented their dissatisfactions with where the United States appears to be heading with the influx of immigrants, primarily from Latin America and the Middle East; their own perceived loss of economic and educational opportunities; and their lessening affirmations of both their masculinity and their white identities. It has further blossomed into public spectacles and violent acts and demonstrations, the most well-known being the "Unite the Right" rally in Charlottesville, Virginia, in 2017, where white supremacist James Alex Fields Jr. (b. 1997) drove his car directly into the path of protestors, injuring many and murdering Heather Danielle Heyer (b. 1985–2017). (On June 28, 2019, Fields was sentenced to life in prison for this hate crime.)

Those associated with the alt-right movement also tend to be anti-feminist, in favor of so-called traditional family structures and patriarchy, anti-egalitarian in regard to diverse populations, anti-liberal, and politically anti-interventionist and isolationist in global political and military affairs. Those who espouse antisemitism also argue conspiracy theories, attributing the roots of all the ills in American society to Jews and so-called Jewish power. One prominent alt-right advocate, neo-Nazi, white supremacist, and Holocaust denier Andrew Anglin, the founder of the website the Daily Stormer in 2013, has advocated for the extermination of Jews. Greg Johnson, another prominent alt-righter, has advocated for all Jews leaving the United States and moving, voluntarily and involuntarily, to Israel. This wide spectrum of views may also include those who are antiabortion/pro-life, antigay, and opposed to same-sex marriages. Taken to its perverse conclusion, many of those who identify with the alt-right are articulating what they believe to be "white genocide." With the election of the forty-fifth president of the United States, Donald J. Trump (b. 1946), many members of the alt-right believed that their voices and concerns would now be heard by someone who would champion their causes.

There is no unifying political statement or manifesto for the alt-right, despite the publication in 2016 of Milo Yiannopoulos's (b. 1984)

8 | Alt-Right

cowritten article "An Establishment Conservative's Guide to the Alt-Right." There appears, however, a division or split between those who see themselves as neo-Nazis and white supremacists, who advocate violence in pursuit of their goals, and those who see themselves as white nationalists and more moderate in their views and who reject violence.

In addition to those already named, the following are some of the more prominent persons associated with or identified with the alt-right:

- Steve Bannon (b. 1953): Former executive chairman of Breitbart News and former White House chief of staff.
- Peter Brimelow (b. 1947): British-born American editor and journalist and founder of the webzine *VDare*.
- Mike Cernovich (b. 1977): Right-wing conspiracy theorist, antifeminist, and social media personality.
- David Duke (b. 1950): Former grand wizard of the Ku Klux Klan (KKK) and politician as well as a Holocaust denier and convicted felon.
- Brad Griffin: Owner of the white nationalist blog *Occidental Dissent* and commentator on any and all events happening in the world of the alt-right.
- Matthew Heimbach (b. 1991): Neo-Nazi and founder of the Traditional Workers Party (TWP) and one of the organizers of the "Unite the Right" rally in Charlottesville, Virginia.
- Kevin B. MacDonald (b. 1944): American professor of psychology in California and author of a three-volume text on evolutionary strategy, arguing that Jews are motivated by hatred toward American and Christian cultures and use their intelligence and group ethnocentricity to compete for valuable resources solely for their own group interests.
- Stephen Miller (b. 1985): Senior policy advisor to President Donald Trump and the strongest voice for any and all anti-immigration policies.
- Mike "Enoch" Peinovitch (b. 1977): Neo-Nazi conspiracy theorist, blogger, and founder and host of *The Right Stuff* and *The Daily Shoah*.
- Jared Taylor (b. 1951): White supremacist, editor of *American Renaissance*, and president of the New Century Foundation. Taylor has made it a point of pride that he is not antisemitic and has repeatedly urged Jews to join him in his conservative causes.

Historically, thinkers within the alt-right movement have drawn their inspiration from such prominent Europeans and Americans as Corneliu Condreanu (1899–1938), a Romanian politician and founder of the antisemitic Iron Guard, which was active during World War II; Julius Evola

(1898–1974), who was once described as the leading philosopher of the European neofascist movement; Henry Louis (H. L.) Menken (1880–1956), an American journalist, satirist, isolationist, racist, and antisemite; and Oswald Spengler (1880–1936), a German philosopher and historian whose 1918 book *The Decline of the West* argues that Western civilization is in decline due to inroads made by other non-European cultural groups.

See also: Barnes, Harry Elmer; Carto, Willis; Christian Identity; Duke, David; Icke, David; Pierce, William Luther; Proud Boys; White Supremacy; World Church of the Creator; Yockey, Francis Parker

Further Reading

Fang, Lee. *The Machine: A Field Guide to the Resurgent Right.* New York and London: New Press, 2013.

Hawley, George. *Making Sense of the Alt-Right.* New York: Columbia University Press, 2017.

Lyons, Matthew N. *Insurgent Supremacists: The U.S. Far Right's Challenge to State and Empire.* Oakland, CA: PM Press, 2018.

Malice, Michael. *The New Right: A Journey in the Fringe of American Politics.* New York: All Point Books, 2019.

Nagle, Angela. *Kill All Normies: Online Culture Wars from 4chan and Tumblr to Trump and the Alt-Right.* Winchester, UK, and Washington, DC: Zero Books, 2017.

Niewert, David. *Alt-America: The Rise of the Radical Right in the Age of Trump.* London and New York: Verso, 2017.

Stern, Alexandra Minna. *Proud Boys and the White Ethnostate: How the Alt-Right Is Warping the American Imagination.* Boston: Beacon Press, 2019.

Wendling, Mike. *Alt-Right: From 4chan to the White House.* London: Pluto Press, 2018.

B

Barnes, Harry Elmer

Harry Elmer Barnes (1889–1968) was an American historian who earned his PhD from Columbia University, studying the history of crime and punishment and the prison system, in 1918, and taught there until 1929. Subsequently, he would only be an adjunct (temporary) instructor at several smaller institutions of higher learning.

Dissatisfied with what he regarded as the "wrong" understanding of World War I, which saw Germany as the aggressor, Barnes concluded that Great Britain, France, Italy, Japan, Soviet Russia, and the United States were responsible—though the Axis powers of Germany, Austria-Hungary, the Ottoman Empire, and Bulgaria bore some measure of responsibility. He published his findings in *The Genesis of the World War: An Introduction to the Problem of War Guilt* in 1926. In the process of his work and writings, Barnes became increasingly both isolationist, in regard to U.S. involvement in European affairs, and a Germanophile. His cantankerous and argumentative personality did not acquit him well; throughout his career, he continued to attack, at times viciously, those who did not agree with him or accord him the honor and respect he felt he deserved.

Barnes continued this orientation through his many books and articles, and by the end of the World War II, he was more than willing to lessen both Germany's responsibilities throughout the period and, collaterally, diminish not only the numbers themselves but the actual atrocities associated with the Holocaust, arguing that all sides involved in the conflict bore equal measures of guilt and responsibility. As academic and other publishers distanced themselves from him and refused to continue to publish his work, Barnes even went so far as to accuse "the Jews" of a plot against him and the lawyer involved in a libel suit of being an "Anti-Defamation League stooge."

Following World War II, Barnes further argued that the plight of ethnic Germans and their expulsion from both Czechoslovakia and Poland, at times brutally so, was worse than that of the Jews who lost their lives at the hands of the Nazis. Having befriended and mentored a younger scholar by the name of David L. Hoggan (1923–1988), a Harvard PhD and already an antisemite, and, like Barnes, very much a Germanophile, Barnes persuaded him to publish his dissertation in Germany in 1955 as *Der erzwungene Kreig* ("The Forced War"), which blamed a British-Polish alliance for World War II. A highly negatively critical review of that text in the prestigious *American Historical Review* (AHR) in 1962 by the German American historian Gerhard Weinberg (b. 1928) and a flurry of letters in response by both Barnes and Hoggan led to the AHR ceasing to continue the disagreement in its pages. The book would later be published in 1989 in English as *The Forced War: When Peaceful Revision Failed* by the Holocaust denialist Institute for Historical Review in California. (Hoggan would go on to anonymously write the notorious *The Myth of the Six Million* published by the Noontide Press, an arm of the IHR.)

At about this same time, Barnes befriended the Frenchman Paul Rassinier (1906–1967), who has been labeled "the father of Holocaust denial." Barnes also attacked the reparations agreement between the Federal Republic of Germany and the State of Israel, arguing that it was based on the "theory" of supposedly six million Jewish deaths rather than facts, and he went so far as to critique West Germany for apologizing for the Holocaust. He equally rejected any and all Jewish claims of victimization for antisemitism throughout the centuries. American historian Deborah Lipstadt (b. 1947), in her book *Denying the Holocaust: The Growing Assault on Truth and Memory*, states that Barnes was the link between the revisionism of the 1920s vis-à-vis German responsibility for World War II and the Holocaust denialism of the 1950s. Historian Lucy Dawidowicz (1915–1990) held a similar position somewhat earlier.

To date, there has been no academically creditable book-length study of Barnes or his voluminous writings, though two articles worth noting are those by Justus D. Doenecke (1978) and Roy Turnbaugh (1978). The only book thus far published is that of Arthur Goddard, ed., *Harry Elmer Barnes: Learned Crusader* in 1968, though the publisher has long been identified with right-wing causes and founded by American revisionist historian and Holocaust denialist James J. Martin (1916–2004).

In 1994, Wills Carto (1926–2015), a political activist, antisemitic conspiracy theorist, and Holocaust denialist, and his Liberty Lobby launched

BDS (Boycott, Divestment, Sanctions) Movement

a new magazine titled *The Barnes Review* (TBR), which is "dedicated to historical revisionism and Holocaust denial" and named for Barnes. Among its many antisemitic articles are "Adolf Hitler—An Overlooked Candidate for the Nobel Prize," "Treblinka Was No Death Camp," and "In Defense of Adolf Hitler." In recent years, it has also been promoting the virulently antisemitic Christian Identity movement, which claims that Jews are the "spawn of Satan." TBR continues to be published today and is now owned by the Foundation for Economic Liberty Inc. It also publishes additional antisemitic works (e.g., *The March of the Titans: A History of the White Race*; *Cultural Insurrections: Essays on Western Civilization, Jewish Influence, & Anti-Semitism*); hosts a bookstore on its website; and hosts an annual conference. In 2003, anti–Vatican II Roman Catholic Hutton Gibson (b. 1918), the father of American actor Mel Gibson (b. 1956), was featured.

See also: Alt-Right; Carto, Willis; Christian Identity; Duke, David; Icke, David; Pierce, William Luther; Proud Boys; White Supremacy; World Church of the Creator; Yockey, Francis Parker

Further Reading

Barnes, Harry Elmer. *The Genesis of the World War: An Introduction to the Problem of War Guilt.* New York: Alfred A. Knopf, 1926.

Dawidowicz, Lucy. *The Holocaust and the Historians.* Cambridge, MA: Harvard University Press, 1981.

Doenecke, Justus D. "Harry Elmer Barnes." *Wisconsin Magazine of History* 56, no. 4 (1978): 311–323.

Goddard, Arthur, ed. *Harry Elmer Barnes: Learned Crusader.* Colorado Springs: Ralph Myles, 1968.

Lipstadt, Deborah. *Denying the Holocaust: The Growing Assault on Truth and Memory.* New York: Free Press, 1993.

Turnbaugh, Roy. "Harry Elmer Barnes and World War I Revisionism: An Absence of Dialogue." *Peace & Change* 5, nos. 2–3 (1978): 63–69.

BDS (Boycott, Divestment, Sanctions) Movement

The Boycott, Divestment, and Sanctions (BDS) movement is an international and global movement—originally begun by Palestinians—to exert

BDS (Boycott, Divestment, Sanctions) Movement | 13

continuing pressure, ostracism, marginalization, and isolation upon the State of Israel to end what it perceives to be an apartheid state comparable to South Africa and a colonialist regime under the control of the United States. The BDS movement claims Israel is continually disenfranchising the Palestinian people and thus should be isolated from the family of nations. Some have argued that the BDS movement arose in response to or in conjunction with the Second Intifada of 2000, but others have argued that its true origins were with the Arab League boycotts of the 1940s and their goal of frustrating "further Jewish development in Palestine by means of boycotts against Zionist products." (*Intifada* is an Arabic word that literally means "tremor," "shivering," or "shuddering." It is derived from the Arabic term *nafada*, which means "to shake," "shake off," or "get rid of," and is a key concept in contemporary Arabic usage, referring to a legitimate uprising against oppression, in this case the Palestinian perceptions of Israeli hegemony. It is often rendered into English as "uprising," "resistance," or "rebellion.") Such efforts are understood by Israel and its supporters as transparent attempts to demonize and delegitimize the state. Furthermore, those who support the BDS movement regard the "occupation" of the West Bank, now more than six decades on, and formerly that of Gaza, prior to Israel's withdrawal in 2005, as consistent with what they perceive to be Israel's expansionist agenda and its continuing violations of international and humanitarian law.

An additional stated goal of the BDS movement is to dismantle the Israeli security fence—initially constructed in 2003—which divides the Palestinian people and their families, communities, and lands and prevents their economic success, but it refuses to give the barrier any credibility whatsoever for the decrease in suicide bombings of Israelis and their families throughout Israel since its inception. It has also called for a democracy of total equality between Israeli Jews and Israeli Arabs/Palestinians, knowing that by doing so Israel would lose its "Jewish character." The BDS movement has also vehemently called for the right of all those Arab/Palestinian families (and their descendants if the previous generation is no longer alive) to return to their former places of residence before their relocation in 1948 because of the Israeli War of Independence and to be appropriately compensated. Such a call, however, continues to ignore the historical reality that many of those who left did so at the behest of Arab military and governmental leaders in Egypt, Jordan, and other countries, who vowed a quick end to the newly created State of Israel and their immediate victorious return. A recent U.S. response to this tactic has been

14 | BDS (Boycott, Divestment, Sanctions) Movement

the creation of the Academic Engagement Network (AEN) of American faculty, whose stated goal is "to counteract the Boycott, Divestment, and Sanctions (BDS) movement on campuses and to affirm the key values of academic freedom and free speech" and "seeking to facilitate intelligent, constructive and civilized discourse about Israel, including criticism" (www.academicengagement.org). Today, the issue of the status of Palestinian refugees, however defined, with the ongoing support of the United Nations Relief and Works Agency (UNRWA), remains both a political football and unresolved.

From its original goals, the BDS movement has further expanded its call for the rejection of all Israeli-made products and companies and those of the nation-states outside of Israel doing business with them, all academic cooperations with Israeli universities and their faculties, and all invitations to Israeli cultural contributions throughout the world (e.g., participation in music, song, film, and athletic festivals). Throughout the world, actors, artists, and writers, like others, have come down both in support of the BDS movement and in opposition to it, but not the forced exodus of Jewish communities throughout the Middle East.

The BDS movement has also publicly asked nation-states throughout the world to place both sanctions and embargoes on Israel and its productive capacities and capabilities. In line with its divestment efforts, it has continually asked/demanded of companies, businesses, churches, and governments that they divest from their investment portfolios both Israeli stocks and bonds and companies continuing to do business with Israel (e.g., Caterpillar, Hewlett-Packard, IBM, Motorola, and Microsoft in the United States and Volvo in Sweden). Churches with Middle Eastern constituencies—Presbyterian, Methodist, United Church of Christ, Roman Catholic, Evangelical Lutheran Church in America—have specifically been targeted. Some have passed resolutions detrimental to Israel and divested part of their economic portfolios; others have not. To date (2018), it should also be noted, twenty-one states in the United States have passed anti-BDS legislation (in order of passage): Tennessee, South Carolina, Illinois, Alabama, Colorado, Indiana, Florida, Virginia, Arizona, Georgia, Iowa, New York, New Jersey, California, Pennsylvania, Ohio, Michigan, Texas, Minnesota, Nevada, Kansas, North Carolina, Maryland, and Wisconsin.

The BDS movement's proponents deny any link whatsoever with any forms of antisemitism, though avowed antisemites are found within their ranks; instead, they argue that their anti-Zionist agenda is solely politically motivated. Some of their more radical voices have called for the total

BDS (Boycott, Divestment, Sanctions) Movement | 15

dismantling of the State of Israel itself. It has attracted adherents both from the political left and the political right on both the European (Eastern and Western) and North American continents. Throughout the Arab Middle East and elsewhere, the BDS movement has found numerous supporters, including Arab governments and UN non-governmental organizations (NGOs) and even rabbis and Jewish radical activists in the United States as well. The BDS movement can, however, be legitimately critiqued for its highly one-sided and biased approach to the complexity of issues involved in the ongoing Arab/Palestinian-Israeli/Middle East conflict.

In 2017, the Israeli government published a "BDS blacklist" of those organizations whose activist members would be barred from entering the country—not without both internal and external controversy to be sure. The eighteen included, in Europe, Association France Palestine Solidarité, BDS France, BDS Italy, European Coordination Committee and Associations for Palestine, Friends of al-Aqsa, Ireland Palestinian Solidarity Campaign, Palestine Committee of Norway, Palestine Solidarity Association of Sweden, and BDS Kampagne; (2) in the United States, American Friends Service Committee (AFSC) (which, ironically, helped Jews during the Holocaust/*Shoah*), American Muslims for Palestine, Code Pink, Jewish Voices for Peace (JVP), National Students for Justice in Palestine, and U.S. Campaign for Palestinian Rights; and (3) others, such as BDS Chile, BDS South Africa, and BDS National Committee.

On balance, in the areas where BDS activists have placed their ongoing energies, their successes have been overwhelmingly limited and momentary: Israel has not been politically isolated, having relationships with more than one hundred countries; its gross domestic product (GDP) has showed annual growth as has, ironically, its Palestinian population; and its exports continue, seemingly unabated, throughout the world. However, warning signs of concern continue to present themselves. For example, if the nation-state of Palestine is recognized and accepted into the family of nations, it could then bring its case for criminal liability to the International Criminal Court (ICC) in The Hague, Netherlands (though Israel has not signed the ICC Statutes for precisely this reason). The specific charge would be violation of the 1976 International Convention on the Suppression and Punishment of the Crime of Apartheid. Then, too, some Israelis—present and former government officials, academics, active and retired military, and the like—have, at times, had to curtail their overseas trips in response to pressures on their hosts to disinvite them or face the public consequence of disruptive demonstrations.

16 | Beilis Affair

See also: al-Banna, Hassan; al-Husseini, Amin; Crusades; Farhud; Qutb, Sayyid

Further Reading

Babbin, Jed, and Herbert London. *The BDS War against Israel: The Orwellian Campaign to Destroy Israel through the Boycott, Divestment and Sanctions Movement.* Scotts Valley, CA: CreateSpace, 2014.

Dershowitz, Alan. *The Case against BDS: Why Singling Out Israel for Boycott Is Anti-Semitic and Anti-Peace.* Scotts Valley, CA: CreateSpace, 2018.

Nelson, Cary R., ed. *Dreams Deferred: A Concise Guide to the Israeli-Palestinian Conflict and the Movement to Boycott Israel.* Bloomington: Indiana University Press, 2016.

Nelson, Cary R., Gabriel Noah Brahm, and Russell Berman, eds. *The Case against Academic Boycotts of Israel.* New York: Modern Language Association, 2014.

Pessin, Andrew, and Doron S. Ben-Atar, eds. *Anti-Zionism on Campus: The University, Free Speech, and BDS.* Bloomington: Indiana University Press, 2018.

Beilis Affair

Menachem Mendel Beilis was born in 1874 and worked as the superintendent in a brick factory in Kiev, Ukraine, which was part of Russia. Born into a Hasidic religious family, he was somewhat indifferent to his religious Jewish identity and went so far as to work on the holy Sabbath, Saturday, and other festivals and holidays. He was also an ex-soldier and father of five children.

On March 12, 1911, the mutilated body of a thirteen-year-old boy, Andrei Yushchinsky, was found in a cave near the brick factory. Although there was no evidence whatsoever tying Beilis to the crime—the actual murderers are believed to be members of a criminal gang headed by Vera Cherberyak, who wanted to keep Yushchinsky quiet, after he heard of their plans through his friendship with Cherberyak's son—he was charged with the murder that July and languished in horrific prison conditions for more than two years before being brought to trial, all the while protesting his innocence.

The trial took place from September 25 through October 28, 1913. The thrust of the prosecution's case was that of ritual murder, the notorious *blood libel* or *blood accusation*—the draining of Yuschinsky's blood in preparation for the making of the *matzot* (unleavened squares) associated with the festival of Passover—and that theory was advanced as "scientific" evidence by an antisemitic Roman Catholic priest and professor, Justinas Pranaitis (1861–1917), the author of the notorious tract *Talmud Unmasked: The Secret Rabbinical Teachings Concerning Christians*. The case was complicated by Beilis's own lack of religiosity, however, as well as the ease with which the defense team, only one of whom was Jewish, Oscar Gruzenberg (1866–1940), demonstrated Pranaitis's total ignorance of Jewish matters after the stirring testimony of the chief rabbi of Moscow, Yaakov Mazeh (1859–1924). After more than seven hours of deliberation, the jury of relatively undereducated peasants, in a split decision, six to six (which according to Russia law mandated acquittal)—despite their own antisemitic proclivities and those of the prosecutors and their experts and witnesses as well as the country itself—found the evidence insufficient and forced the judge to declare him not guilty, though the judge did sustain the argument that the death was indeed a ritual murder.

Beilis tried returning to the brick factory to support his family but was unable to do so because of his notoriety. He initially left Russia for Palestine, but he was unsuccessful there as well. In 1920, he immigrated to the United States, where he had no better luck despite his fame and initial support, including financial, by the American Jewish community during the years of his imprisonment and trial. Beilis died somewhat unexpectedly on July 7, 1934, and was buried in the Mount Carmel Cemetery, Glendale, Queens, New York. Ironically, it is the same cemetery where Leo Frank (1884–1915) and the much-lauded Yiddish author and playwright Sholem Aleichem (1859–1916) are also buried.

See also: Blood Libel; Deicide; Dreyfus Affair; Frank Trial and Lynching

Further Reading

Beilis, Mendel. *Scapegoat on Trial: The Story of Mendel Beilis*. New York: CIS Publishers, 1992.

Gottheil, Richard, Hermann L. Strack, Joseph Jacobs. "Blood Accusation," *Jewish Encyclopedia*, 1906. www.jewishencyclopedia.com

18 | Blood Libel

Leikin, Ezekiel, ed. *The Beilis Transcripts: The Anti-Semitic Trial That Shook the World*. Northvale, NJ: Jason Aronson, 1993.

Levin, Edmund. *A Child of Christian Blood: Murder and Conspiracy in Tsarist Russia: The Beilis Blood Libel*. New York: Schocken Books, 2014.

Lindemann, Albert S. *The Jew Accused: Three Anti-Semitic Trials: Dreyfus, Beilis, Frank, 1894–1915*. Cambridge, UK, and New York: Cambridge University Press, 1991.

Samuel, Maurice. *Blood Accusation: The Strange History of the Beiliss Case*. New York: Alfred A. Knopf, 1966.

Weinberg, Robert. *Blood Libel in Late Imperial Russia: The Ritual Murder Trial of Mendel Beilis*. Bloomington: Indiana University Press, 2013.

Blood Libel

The blood libel—also sometimes referred to as the blood accusation—is, perhaps, among the most notorious of antisemitic charges against both the Jewish people and Judaism (however, the latter is interpreted and understood). It falsely purports to accuse both of requiring the blood of a religious Christian, usually a naïve, young, and innocent child (male more so than female), to be drained and used in the preparation of the *matzot*—the flat, unleavened squares—associated with the festival of Passover (in Hebrew, *Pesach*). Equally and perversely, it is also associated with the Easter celebration of the resurrection of the Christ in the destruction of the sacramental wafer (which, according to legends, spouts the blood of Jesus as Jews attempt its destruction) and further perpetuates the notion of the Jews as a deicide people (i.e., "God killers") mocking the death of Jesus and symbolically desecrating his memory. Its falsity is easily called into question not only by the Torah/Hebrew Bible/Old Testament and its strong avoidance of blood (see, for example, Leviticus 3:17, 7:26, 17:10–14 and Deuteronomy 12:15–16 and 20–24) but also the postbiblical rabbinic literature, both of which strongly advise against contact with human and animal blood, ritually and ceremonially.

Most historians date the beginnings of this vile charge to the murder of William of Norwich in England in 1144. Yet, already in the early twentieth century, scholars revisited such texts as Josephus's (37–100) *Contra Apionem* (though the original text of the Egyptian antisemite Apion (30/20 BCE–45/48 CE) to which he responded has been lost), the earlier Greek writer Democritus (460–370 BCE), Greek philosopher Socrates's (469–399 BCE) *Ecclesiastical History*, and the writings of Bishops Agobard of Lyon (779–850 CE) and Bernard of Clairvaux (1090–1153), among others, and all of which contain references, however false, to Jews wantonly murdering Christians for either ritual purposes or simply out of contempt and disrespect for Christians and Christianity. Be that as it may, the 1906 *Jewish Encyclopedia* (www.jewishencyclopedia.com) lists more than 120 such reported accusations between the years 1144 and 1900 (and more since!) throughout every country on the European continent, Russia included, which oftentimes resulted in mass violence against vulnerable Jewish communities. Sadly, and tragically, Jewish converts to Roman Catholicism throughout the middle Dark Ages aided in the perpetuation of this lie and further added to it a hateful litany of accusations of sorcery and licentiousness. It must also be said, however, that some secular rulers and some princes of the church decried and rejected these accusations and attempted to protect "their Jews" from the mobs, oftentimes with little power or ability to do so.

In the first part of the twentieth century, the Nazis made propagandistic use of the blood libel, most notoriously in Julius Streicher's (1885–1946) newspaper *Der Stürmer* (*The Stormer* or *The Attacker*), which was replete with graphic portrayals of Jews executing young German males and virginal young females and draining their blood. After the end of World War II, in Kielce, Poland, forty-two Jews were murdered and forty injured when an eight-year-old boy went missing and the Holocaust survivors were accused of the crime. Even the United States was not spared from this libel. In 1928, in Massena, New York, a four-year-old girl went for a walk and seemingly disappeared, only to return a day later because she had fallen asleep (though the rumor persisted that she had been rescued by an anonymous benefactor). The rabbi of the small synagogue along with other Jewish communal leaders were interrogated by the police and questioned as to whether Jews had in the past used human blood for ritual purposes. Although the mayor of the town would ultimately apologize, there were citizens who remained convinced that only her "rescue" thwarted an attempt at ritual murder. In January 2005, twenty members of the Russian *Duma* (the lower house of

20 | Blood Libel

the Russian Federation Parliament) publicly accused Jews of blood libels against the Russian people.

The blood libel remains a staple today not only of Western antisemites but Middle Eastern, primarily Arab, foes of Israel. On a regular ongoing basis, political cartoons appear in Arab nation-state newspapers depicting Israelis replete with Stars of David on military uniforms dripping with the blood of innocent Palestinians, especially children. And according to the Middle East Media Research Institute (MEMRI, https://www.memri.org/reports/antisemitic-cartoons-arab-and-iranian-press), supposed reputable scholars and imams continue to perpetuate the lie of the blood libel. In 1983, for example, Mustafa Tlass (1932–2017), the former Syrian minister of defense (1972–2004), published his libelous *The Matzah of Zion*, which is replete with all the previously held antisemitic tropes, including this one, and attempts to address the notorious Damascus Affair of 1840, when thirteen leaders of that Jewish community were charged with the murder of French Franciscan monk Father Thomas and his assistant and were arrested, tortured, indicted, and imprisoned, with some being murdered. International pressure and negotiations secured the release and exoneration of nine of the leaders; four had already died as the result of their wounds.

In sum, the very longevity of this libel in the minds of many attests to the enduring antisemitic hatred of Jews and Judaism regardless of locale, education, political leaning, economic standing, or religious affiliation. Its many virulent expressions testify to its crudity, its graphic appeal to violence, and the willingness of some to both believe and accept this most outrageous of accusations against this minority people and their religious faith.

See also: *Adversus Judaeos*; Beilis Affair; Deicide; Dreyfus Affair; Frank Trial and Lynching; Martyrdom, Sanctifying the Name of God; Oberammergau Passion Play

Further Reading

Dundes, Alan. *The Blood Libel Legend: A Casebook in Anti-Semitic Folklore.* Madison: University of Wisconsin Press, 1991.

Johnson, Hannah. *Blood Libel: The Ritual Murder Accusation at the Limit of Jewish History.* Ann Arbor: University of Michigan Press, 2012.

O'Brien, Darren. *The Pinnacle of Hatred: The Blood Libel and the Jews.* Jerusalem, Israel: Hebrew University Magnes Press, 2011.

Rose, E. M. *The Murder of William of Norwich: The Origins of the Blood Libel in Medieval Europe*. Oxford and New York: Oxford University Press, 2015.

Winter, Ofir. "Antisemitic Cartoons in the Arab and Iranian Press." Inquiry and Analysis Series No. 38, MEMRI, 2007. https://www.memri.org/reports/antisemitic-cartoons-arab-and-iranian-press

C

Carto, Willis

Willis Allison Carto (1926–2015) was a self-perceived Jeffersonian Democrat who fought in World War II in the Philippines, for which he received a Purple Heart. He is better known, however, as the primary promoter of antisemitic and Holocaust-denying materials through the newspapers he published and, more importantly, through his founding of the Institute for Historical Review in Torrance, California. During his long career, he also came to be identified with segregationist politics, white supremacism, the Ku Klux Klan (KKK), and the Christian Identity movement.

Carto also saw himself as a devotee of the American fascist and antisemitic thinker Francis Parker Yockey (1917–1960), a former prosecutor at the Nuremberg Trials of the Nazi leadership, whose book *Imperium: The Philosophy of History and Politics* (1948) was rife with antisemitism, support for the National Socialist (Nazi) Movement, white nationalism, and other right-wing political causes. Carto also visited him in prison prior to Yockey's suicide. Carto's own book *Profiles in Populism* (1962) included such figures as Detroit auto manufacturer Henry Ford (1863–1947); the publisher of the American edition of the *Protocols of the Learned Elders of Zion*, together with the extensive four-volume commentary *The International Jew*; and Roman Catholic radio priest and purveyor of antisemitism Father Charles Coughlin (1891–1979), a supporter of Adolf Hitler (1889–1945) and Benito Mussolini (1883–1945).

In 1955, Carto founded the Liberty Lobby as a politically conservative and anti-Communist action committee and began publishing its newspaper, the *Spotlight*. He remained at its helm until its bankruptcy in 2001. In 1966, he acquired the newspaper the *American Mercury*, which he continued to publish until 1980. Both publications would evolve from right-wing politics and focus more and more on both antisemitism and Holocaust denial as well as attacks on the United States' so-called liberal agenda as anti-American.

In 1968, in support of Alabama governor George Wallace's (1919–1998) unsuccessful presidential run, Carto ran a group called the National Youth Alliance. Among those he recruited was the American academic William Pierce (1933–2002), who would recreate that organization as the National Alliance, the largest neo-Nazi, white supremacist, and antisemitic organization in the United States for more than three decades. (Pierce was also a supporter of George Lincoln Rockwell (1918–1967), the founder of the American Nazi Party.)

To further his own agenda, eleven years later, in 1979, he would found the Institute for Historical Review (IHR) in California along with its publishing company, Noontide Press, and annual conferences that brought together leading antisemites and Holocaust deniers from the United States and abroad (e.g., David Irving (b. 1938) from England and Robert Faurisson (1929–2018) from France). Carto would go on to lose control of the organization because of an internal political struggle in 1993. In the aftermath of his loss of the IHR, he began publishing the *Barnes Review* to promote his own views as well as those of the late Harry Elmer Barnes (1889–1968), an American academic and historical revisionist who opposed the United States' entry into World War II and a Holocaust denier.

Summarily, we may characterize Carto's ideas, organizations, and publications into four categories:

1. Jewish world domination and conspiracy
2. White racial and cultural superiority
3. Extreme anti-Communism
4. Decline and decay of Western civilization

Willis Carto died of a heart attack in 2015, and one year later, he was buried with full military honors in Arlington National Cemetery. KKK and Christian Identity pastor Thomas A. Robb (b. 1946) officiated at his funeral.

See also: Alt-Right; Barnes, Harry Elmer; Christian Identity; Duke, David; Icke, David; Faurisson, Robert; Irving, David; Ku Klux Klan; Pierce, William Luther; Proud Boys; Rassinier, Paul; Rockwell, George Lincoln; White Supremacy; World Church of the Creator; Yockey, Francis Parker

24 | Christian Identity

Further Reading

Coogan, Kevin. *Dreamer of the Day: Francis Parker Yockey and the Postwar Fascist International.* Brooklyn, NY: Autonomedia, 1999.

Lyons, Matthew N., and Chip Berlet. *Right-Wing Populism in America: Too Close for Comfort.* New York: Guilford Press, 2000.

Michael, George. *Confronting Right Wing Extremism and Terrorism in the USA.* New York and London: Routledge, 2012.

Michael, George. *Willis Carto and the American Far Right.* Gainesville: University Press of Florida, 2008.

Mintz, Frank. *The Liberty Lobby and the American Right: Race, Conspiracy and Culture.* Westport, CT: Greenwood Press, 1985.

Christian Identity

The Christian Identity movement is an antisemitic movement in the United States that grew out of either British Israelism or Anglo-Israelism, a minority variation of Protestantism within the Church of England. It was originally a pseudohistorical and theological attempt to explain what happened to the original Ten Lost Tribes of Israel that were defeated by the Assyrians in 721 BCE and fully absorbed into that cultural and religious community. However, the claim was made that they had survived, migrated westward, and settled in England, which was first proposed in the book *Lectures on Our Israelitish Origins* in 1840 by John Wilson. The actual author of the term *Christian Identity* was Howard B. Rand (1889–1991), who first proposed that the Jews were not descended from the tribe of Judah but, rather, descended from Isaac's older brother, Esau, and were Canaanites.

Transported to the United States in the early part of the twentieth century, Christian Identity was embraced by the likes of Wesley Swift (1913–1970), a former Methodist minister and founder of the Church of Jesus Christ Christian; William Dudley Pelley (1890–1965), the founder of the fascist paramilitary Silver Legion of America, better known as the Silver Shirts; Reuben H. Sawyer (1866–1962), a KKK leader and minister; Gerald L. K. Smith (1898–1976), the founder of the Christian Nationalist Crusade and the America First Party; William Potter Gale (1917–1988, whose own father had abandoned his Jewish identity), the founder of the Posse Comitatus, a far-right populist movement; Bertrand Comparet (1910–1983), a Christian Identity minister and lawyer; George Lincoln Rockwell (1918–1967), the founder of the American Nazi Party; and Richard Girnt Butler (1918–2004), a white supremacist minister. Another person associated with the origins of Christian Identity is William Cameron (1878–1955), the editor of Henry Ford's *Dearborn Independent* and the person responsible for its publication of the *Protocols of the Learned Elders of Zion*.

Collectively, these men and their followers subscribed to the "two-house" or "two-seed" theology: the belief that the above-mentioned tribes were the ancestors of the superior white ("Aryan") Europeans from Adam and Eve—the "true Israelites"—and Jews were the descendants of the tribes of Judah and Benjamin, inferiors who had come from Eve's mating with the snake (Satan) in the Garden of Eden. These Jews, in turn, were also the masters of Africans, or "mud peoples," and thus a race war was already in the making from which the Jews would be defeated or exterminated. Christian Identity followers would emerge victorious with the return of Jesus Christ. The potential for violence by members of the different subgroups that identify with Christian Identity—for example, the Phineas Priesthood (an allusion to the biblical priest Phineas who slew an Israeli and his Midianite mistress for engaging in sexual intercourse in public according to the Book of Numbers) and those who still identify with the so-called militia movements—is an ongoing concern for law enforcement officials as well as Jewish and African American organizations.

The primary locations for Christian Identity followers are the Pacific Northwest and Midwest of the United States; however, in terms of actual numbers, Christian Identity appears to be in something of a downward spiral. Those who identify with the radical right find its theological underpinnings far less convincing, and many of the original clergy leaders are now dead. However, they still maintain that the U.S. government has been taken over by Jews and refer to it by the acronym ZOG (Zionist Occupation Government).

See also: Alt-Right; Barnes, Harry Elmer; Carto, Willis; Christian Identity; Duke, David; Ku Klux Klan; Pierce, William Luther; Proud Boys; Rockwell, George Lincoln; White Supremacy; World Church of the Creator; Yockey, Francis Parker

26 | Coughlin, Charles E.

Further Reading

Aho, James. *The Politics of Righteousness: Idaho Christian Patriotism*. Seattle: University of Washington Press, 1990.

Barkun, Michael. *Religion and the Radical Right: The Origins of the Christian Identity Movement*. Chapel Hill: University of North Carolina Press, 1997.

Jeansonne, Glen. *Gerald L. K. Smith: Minister of Hate*. Baton Rouge: Louisiana State University Press, 1997.

Kaplan, Jeffrey. *Radical Religion in America: Millenarian Movements from the Far Right to the Children of Noah*. Syracuse, NY: Syracuse University Press, 1997.

Levitas, Daniel. *The Terrorist Next Door: The Militia Movement and the Radical Right*. New York: St. Martin's Press, 2004.

Quarles, Chester L. *Christian Identity: The Aryan American Bloodline Religion*. Jefferson, NC: McFarland Publishing, 2004.

Coughlin, Charles E.

Charles Edward Coughlin (1916–1979) was a Canadian-born Roman Catholic priest at the Shrine of the Little Flower in Oak Park, Michigan. He is infamously remembered not only for his exploitation of the radio airwaves to the tune of forty million weekly Sunday listeners, his growing political isolationism during World War II even after the Japanese attack at Pearl Harbor in 1941, his opposition to President Franklin Delano Roosevelt (1882–1945), and his support for Italian fascism and Nazi national socialism but also for his virulent antisemitism.

Educated at St. Michael's College in Toronto, Canada, that was run by the Congregation of St. Basil, Coughlin entered their seminary and prepared for ordination as a Basilian priest. It is important to note that, among its orientations, the seminary had a strict opposition to usury (lending money at unreasonably high rates of interest), an antisemitic charge long associated with Jews since the Middle Ages. Coughlin would come to disagree with other tenants of the group (chastity, poverty, and obedience), and, in 1923, he was reordained in the Roman Catholic Archdiocese of Detroit, Michigan, by Bishop Michael

Gallagher (1886–1937) and then tasked with growing the small, newly founded Shrine of the Little Flower, named for the French Saint Thérèse of Lisieux (1873–1897), where he would remain until his retirement in 1966 and death in 1979.

In 1926, Coughlin began broadcasting on radio, focusing primarily on Catholic religious teachings and items of interest to children, largely to an Irish Catholic audience, and going so far as to condemn the burning of a cross by the Ku Klux Klan (KKK) on the grounds of the church. (His now well-known moniker the "radio priest" is a tribute to his early realization of the power of this new medium and especially to its potential for evangelism.) Three years later, with his oratorical skills along with the commanding presence of his voice, he focused more and more on his concerns about the political and social issues of the day. Increasingly, his "sermons" devolved into strident attacks against capitalism, socialism, and Soviet Communism, all of which he saw as opponents of the working man. In one of his broadcasts in 1930, he referenced both Jesus's supposed attack on the "money changers in the Temple" in the New Testament and the "Shylocks" of modern capitalism, a reference to Shakespeare's villainous Jewish character in *The Merchant of Venice*. Originally supportive of Franklin Roosevelt during his bid for the presidency during the Great Depression in 1929, five years later, paralleling his founding of the National Union for Social Justice (NUSJ), he would publicly declare his opposition to FDR, believing that his monetary policies would lead the United States to ruin, in part because of the supposed manipulation of Jewish conspirators. Some have argued that the basis of Coughlin's opposition was his failure to secure a position of prominence or influence within the Roosevelt administration.

By 1936, Coughlin's antisemitism was publicly transparent. He accused Jews of backing the Russian Revolution of 1917, going so far as to state that "when he got through with the Jews in America, they'll think the treatment they received in Germany was nothing." In 1938, he published the notoriously antisemitic *Protocols of the Learned Elders of Zion* in installments in his weekly magazine *Social Justice*. The antisemitic organization Christian Front, active from 1938 to 1940, stated that it was inspired by Coughlin's sermons and the need for a "crusade against the anti-Christian forces of the Red Revolution." Slowly but surely, especially after the death of Bishop Gallagher in 1937 and his replacement by the bishop and later cardinal Edward Aloysius Mooney (1882–1958),

28 | Coughlin, Charles E.

opposition to Coughlin began to grow not only from radio stations, which began refusing to air his broadcasts, but also from members of the Catholic hierarchy, including the archbishop of Cincinnati, Ohio, and the papal nuncio to the United States. In 1940, in an agreement between the federal government and the church to avoid charges of sedition and a trial against Coughlin, he agreed to discontinue his political activities and public broadcasts, but he remained as the parish priest of the Shrine of the Little Flower until his retirement in 1966. Coughlin's FBI files are presently housed at Wayne State University in Detroit, Michigan, though many of his personal and other files were previously destroyed.

Coughlin also authored numerous publications with such titles as *The New Deal in Money, Money: Questions and Answers, God or Democracy,* and *Bishops versus the Pope* as well as periodically publishing his radio sermons. Especially relevant was his 1939 *"Am I an Anti-Semite?": 9 Addresses on Various "-isms," Answering the Question, Nov. 6, 1938–Jan. 1, 1939.* He was also a central character in both Arthur Miller's (1915–2005) novel *Focus* (1945) and Phillip Roth's (1933–2018) novel *The Plot against America* (2004).

See also: Barnes, Harry Elmer; Carto, Willis; Christian Identity; Deicide; Icke, David; Pius XII, Pope; *Protocols of the Learned Elders of Zion*; Rockwell, George Lincoln; Yockey, Francis Parker

Further Reading

Athans, Mary Christine. *The Coughlin-Fahey Connection: Father Charles E. Coughlin, Father Denis Fahey, C.S.Sp. and Religious Anti-Semitism in the United States, 1938–1954.* New York: Peter Lang Publishing, 1991.

Brinkley, Alan. *Voices of Protest: Huey Long, Father Coughlin, and the Great Depression.* New York: Alfred A. Knopf, 1982.

Carpenter, Ronald H. *Father Charles E. Coughlin: Surrogate Spokesman for the Disaffected.* Westport, CT: Greenwood Publishing Group, 1988.

Davis, Richard Akin. *Radio Priest: The Public Career of Father Charles Edward Coughlin.* Chapel Hill: University of North Carolina Press, 1975.

Lee, Alfred McClung, and Elizabeth Briant Lee, eds. *The Fine Art of Propaganda: A Study of Father Coughlin's Speeches.* New York: Harcourt Brace and Company, 1939. [An important historical source; still available.]

Marcus, Sheldon. *Father Coughlin: The Tumultuous Life of the Priest of the Little Flower.* New York: Little, Brown, and Company, 1972.

Tull, Charles J. *Father Coughlin, the New Deal, and the Election of 1936.* Notre Dame, IN: University of Notre Dame Press, 1962.

Tull, Charles J. *Father Coughlin and the New Deal*. Syracuse, NY: Syracuse University Press, 1965.

Warren, Donald. *Radio Priest: Charles Coughlin: The Father of Hate Radio*. New York: Free Press, 1996.

Crusades

The Crusades continue to remain a source of both historical and religious fascination for people today, most especially for Christians, Jews, and Muslims, who view the events through radically different religious and theological lenses. As such, the events themselves remain on the table, so to speak, in any honest, open, and continuing dialogue/trialogue among these three constituencies.

The Crusades were a series of religious military journeys inspired by papal pronouncements during the eleventh century and later, whose announced goal was to retake the holy city of Jerusalem from its Muslim overseers ("infidels") and thus ensure continued access to all sites holy to Christianity. Prior to the onset of the Crusades, however, reports were being sent back to European cities that access was being obstructed or denied by *both Muslims and Jews*, further setting the scene for the violence to come. While many who chose to join this pilgrimage of faith did so with the best of intentions, convictions, and commitments, others included peasants and criminals with little or nothing to lose, various European nobles who saw opportunities for increasing their economic coffers and eliminating whatever debt they had accrued from Jewish moneylenders, and religionists intent on vanquishing enemies to their faith.

Less well known, however, was the destruction caused to Jewish communities throughout Europe and the concomitant loss of Jewish life, most particularly during the First Crusade of 1096, the Second Crusade of 1145–1147, and the Third Crusade of 1189–1190. It was during this same period of intense violence that the Judaic idea of martyrdom—*al K'dushat Ha-Shem* (those who died for the sanctification of the Holy Name of God)—came to the fore as rabbis and laity, together with their families, chose to die by their own hands rather than permit themselves to be

30 | Crusades

slaughtered by the soldiers and peasants, stirred up by their priests, who were prepared to mercilessly cut down these "enemies of God," who were falsely perceived as being responsible for the death of their Lord (i.e., Jesus Christ). In addition, the relative social cohesion and relative tranquility of relationships between Jews and Christian throughout Europe prior to the Crusades—not without periods of disturbance and violence—were disrupted to the point of far-reaching consequences for much subsequent history.

First Crusade (1096)

In 1095, Pope Urban II (1042–1099) called for a retaking of the Holy Land at a conciliar meeting in France. Those who responded affixed crosses to their garments (*croises* or *crociati*, hence "crusaders"). Arriving first in the Rhenish area of Germany where the various Jewish communities were economically successful, the Crusaders were incensed that these "murderers of Christ" thrived and sought to put an end to their status before moving eastward. Thousands of Jews lost their lives before the Crusaders departed; their communities were devastated, some never recovering. Prior to the Crusaders' departures, however, some Jews were given the option of forced conversion or death and chose to convert, only later to return to their ancestral faith.

Second Crusade (1145–1147)

Inspired by Pope Eugene III (1080–1153), the scenario from the First Crusade would repeat itself. And, again, like the First Crusade, the Jews of Germany would suffer a far worse fate than the Jews of France and England.

When Saladin (1137–1193) retook Jerusalem in 1187, Jews throughout Europe suffered the tragic consequences of the Crusader defeats, as they were again murdered and their villages destroyed.

Third Crusade (1189–1190)

Ironically, during the Third Crusade, the Jewish communities in England would suffer the most tragic of events, in part as the direct result of the participation of Richard the Lion-Hearted (1157–1199) in the Crusade and his need to fund and sustain his journey east. Jewish communities were, again, destroyed and Jews murdered or forcibly converted.

Because of all three ventures, Jews continued to find themselves vulnerable, and their ability to survive was now placed in the hands of the Roman Catholic Church and the various kingdoms and dukedoms, who were regularly unable to do so or who sought financial recompense either prior to an attack or in the aftermath of an attack. Legal restrictions against Jews also increased during and after the Crusades, culminating, perhaps, in the Fourth Lateran Council of 1215, which merged Roman Catholic religious restrictions with (secular) Roman law. However, some historians have suggested that, ultimately, this sense of vulnerability is not fully borne out by the facts themselves, as Jews rebuilt their communities; their numbers increased, as did their economic viability; and Jewish learning flourished throughout Europe. And yet, the unease of the Jews never fully left them and remains reflected in the various liturgical poems (in Hebrew, *piyyutim*) that were incorporated into *Siddurim* (Sabbath and Festival prayer books), *Makhzorim* (High Holy Day prayer books), and *Haggadot* (Passover prayer books) today. Then, too, discrimination against Jews in various forms (political, economic, social) became the order of the day throughout the continent, and while there were subsequent Crusades as well (1202–1204, 1208, 1212, 1218–1221, 1228–1229, 1248–1254, and 1270), it was during first three that the major damage was done to the Jews and their Jewish communities.

It was also both tragically and perniciously during this same period that the relationship between Jews and Christians took a decidedly overtly antisemitic turn with the charge of the *blood libel* (also known as the *blood accusation*) appearing, first in England (1144) and then throughout Europe, whereby both individual Jews and Jewish communities were false accused of kidnapping Christian children, murdering them, and draining their blood to be used in the preparation of the *matzot* (unleavened cakes) associated with the festival of Passover.

Finally, it is important to note that there are any number of important Jewish sources that detail the horrific events that befell their communities. Among the most important are the following:

- *The Chronicle of Simon bar Simpson* (1140) details the destruction of the Jewish community of Mainz, Germany, in 1096.
- *The Chronicle of Rabbi Eliezer bar Nathan* (mid–twelfth century) further elaborates on the events in Germany.

Crusades

- *The Narrative of the Old Persecutions* (fourteenth century), author unknown, adds even more details.
- *Sefer Zekhirah of Rabbi Ephraim (Book/Scroll of Remembrance*, twelfth century) is an eyewitness account of the Second Crusade.

See also: *Adversus Judaeos*; Blood Libel; Deicide; Luther, Martin; Martyrdom, Sanctifying the Name of God; Oberammergau Passion Play; Usury

Further Reading

Chazan, Robert. *European Jewry and the First Crusade*. Berkeley: University of California Press, 1996.

Chazan, Robert. *From Anti-Judaism to Anti-Semitism: Ancient and Medieval Christian Constructions of Jewish Identity*. Cambridge, UK: Cambridge University Press, 2016.

Chazan, Robert. *God, Humanity, and History: The Hebrew First Crusade Narratives*. Berkeley: University of California Press, 2000.

Chazan, Robert. *In the Year 1096: The First Crusade and the Jews*. Philadelphia: Jewish Publication Society, 1996.

Cohen, Jeremy. *Sanctifying the Name of God: Jewish Martyrs and Jewish Memories of the First Crusade*. Philadelphia: University of Pennsylvania Press, 2004.

Eidelberg, Shlomo. *The Jews and the Crusades: The Hebrew Chronicle of the First and Second Crusades*. Hoboken, NJ: KTAV Publishing House, 1996.

Maalouf, Amin. *The Crusades through Arab Eyes*. Translated by Jon Rothschild. New York: Schocken Books, 1984.

Nirenberg, David. *Communities of Violence: Persecution of Minorities in the Middle Ages*. Princeton, NJ, and London: Princeton University Press, 2015.

D

Deicide

Deicide (literally "the killing of the god") exists in numerous cultures (Egyptian, Greek, Norse, Japanese, Hawaiian, and Aztec) but has particular resonance in an antisemitic context, where it refers to the New Testament charge that the Jews in Roman-occupied and Roman-controlled Palestine were the primary culprits responsible for the murder of Christ Jesus, the "son of God." It is found in the Gospel of Matthew, chapter 27, where the Jews are assembled in the courtyard outside of the Roman procurator Pontius Pilate's (d. ca. 36–39 CE) home prior to Passover. Pilate, in a supposed expression of goodwill toward his subjects, offers to release one of two captives, either Barabbas (in Aramaic, *Bar Abbas*, "son of the father") or Jesus:

> Now it was the governor's custom at the festival to release a prisoner chosen by the crowd. At that time they had a well-known prisoner whose name was Jesus Barabbas. So when the crowd had gathered, Pilate asked them, "Which one do you want me to release to you: Jesus Barabbas, or Jesus who is called the Messiah?" For he knew it was out of self-interest that they had handed Jesus over to him. While Pilate was sitting on the judge's seat, his wife sent him this message: "Don't have anything to do with that innocent man, for I have suffered a great deal today in a dream because of him." But the chief priests and the elders persuaded the crowd to ask for Barabbas and to have Jesus executed. "Which of the two do you want me to release to you?" asked the governor. "Barabbas," they answered. "What shall I do, then, with Jesus who is called the Messiah?" Pilate asked. They all answered, "Crucify him!" "Why? What crime has he committed?" asked Pilate. But they shouted all the louder, "Crucify him!" When Pilate saw that he was getting nowhere, but that instead an uproar was starting, he took water and washed his hands in front of the

34 | Deicide

> crowd. "I am innocent of this man's blood," he said. "It is your responsibility!" All the people answered, "His blood is on us and on our children!" Then he released Barabbas to them. But he had Jesus flogged, and handed him over to be crucified. (Matthew 27:15–26)

(The accounts found in the Gospels of Mark and Luke are modifications, but this scenario does not appear in the Gospel of John, though the latter does provide the rationale for the Romans putting Jesus to death by arguing that the Jewish leaders had no power to do so (John 18:31).)

The important Roman Catholic theologian St. John Chrysostom (349–407 CE), the archbishop of Constantinople, Turkey, known far and wide for the power of his oratory, was the first to accuse the Jews of the murder of Jesus and incorporate it into his theology, arguing that no forgiveness or pardon was possible for this sin. The first time the word *deicide* appears in Latin—*deicidas*—is in a sermon by the bishop of Ravenna, Italy, Peter Chrysologus (380–450 CE).

Subsequently, for the last two thousand plus years, especially in the West more so than in the East, Jews have been consistently vilified as the enemies of God and subject to various forms of violence against them—murders, pogroms, ghettoizations, expulsions, and forced conversions. Eastertide, particularly in Europe and especially during the Middle Ages, was particularly frightful, as the largely illiterate crowds were whipped up akin to a religious frenzy as the priests retold the story of Jesus's death to dramatic effect, after which the angry peasants would break into the Jewish ghettos and murder the inhabitants therein. This charge of deicide has remained part and parcel of Christianity, especially Roman Catholicism and later Protestantism, since its inception and is still found today in some of the more fundamentalist Christian communities who regard the events as depicted in Matthew as literally true.

The year 1965 would, however, mark a significant change in this understanding with the passage of the Roman Catholic document *Nostre Aetate* (*In Our Time*) in the closing days of Vatican II (1962–1965), largely exonerating Jews for whatever participation they may have engaged in (i.e., Sadducean complicity rather than Pharisaic), rejecting the idea of any passing on of the sins of the past to the present and future generations, and rejecting as thoroughly anti-Christian any and all forms of antisemitism. Various expressions of Protestant Christianity (e.g., Anglican, Methodist, Lutheran, Presbyterian) rather quickly followed suit, leading to a flowering of Jewish–Christian dialogue, especially in the United States.

Although there is no historical basis for this false charge—none whatsoever!—the Talmud in Sanhedrin 43a maintains that Jesus was put to death by a Jewish court for sedition and sorcery. The "alternative biography" of Jesus known an *Toledot Yeshu* (*Generations of Jesus*), a satiric text, appearing as early as the fourth century, of unknown authorship and origin and possibly even written or edited by non-Jews and found in a number of different versions, maintains that Jesus was born of a Jewish mother and Roman father and a maker of miracles. Among those various texts were those that also maintain that the Jewish court of the time was responsible for his death. Both the Talmud and *Toledot Yeshu* would go on to become weapons in the arsenals of Jew-haters, despite all such fraudulent claims being thoroughly debunked by sound historical scholarship as well as public pronouncements by all religious denominations.

See also: *Adversus Judaeos*; Blood Libel; Crusades; Luther, Martin; Martyrdom, Sanctifying the Name of God; Oberammergau Passion Play; Spanish Inquisition; Usury

Further Reading

Civan, Judith. *Abraham's Knife: The Mythology of Deicide in Antisemitism.* Bloomington, IN: Xlibris, 2004.

Cohen, Jeremy. *Christ Killers: The Jews and the Passion from the Bible to the Big Screen.* Oxford and New York: Oxford University Press, 2007.

Davis, Frederick B. *The Jew and Deicide: The Origin of an Archetype.* Lanham, MD: University Press of America, 2003.

Tomson, Peter J. *Presumed Guilty: How the Jews Were Blamed for the Death of Jesus.* Translated by Janet Dyk. Minneapolis, MN: Fortress Press, 2005.

Dreyfus Affair

Captain Alfred Dreyfus of the French Army was born in 1859 in Alsace to a wealthy Jewish family highly assimilated into French culture and religiously nonobservant. A graduate of the Ecole Polytechnique as an engineer, he entered the military and was attached to the general staff in Paris,

36 | Dreyfus Affair

the only Jew in such a position (though other Jews did achieve officer rank in the French Army).

In 1894, a supposedly treasonable document—the so-called *bordereau*—offering to give or sell weapons secrets to Germany was found in the wastebasket of the German military attaché. The handwriting on the spurious document was said to resemble that of Dreyfus, and he was brought to trial that same year, found guilty by a court of military conservatives and monarchists—in violation of standard legal protocols—stripped of rank, publicly humiliated, and sentenced to life at Devil's Island, off the coast of South America.

The hue and cry and protestations regarding his innocence, his own included, led to a second trial in 1899, and he was again found guilty and returned to Devil's Island. During the years between, the French military intelligence officer Georges Picquart (1854–1914), who would himself suffer exile to Africa after an initial imprisonment, concluded that the forged document was the work of the French officer and adventurer Ferdinand Walsin Esterhazy (1847–1923) with additional forged documents by a Colonel Hubert-Joseph Henry (1846–1898), who committed suicide in prison after his arrest.

By the turn of the twentieth century, the case had become a cause célèbre not only in France but internationally as well, with many voices calling for yet another trial and Dreyfus's acquittal. Most notable among them was the premier French litterateur of the day Emile Zola (1840–1902), whose scathing front-page editorial "J'Accuse" in the newspaper *L'Aurore* accused not only the military but the government and the Roman Catholic Church of an orchestrated cover-up.

In 1906, twelve years after Dreyfus was first brought to trial and found guilty, he was finally exonerated, restored to rank but elevated to major, fought for France in World War I, and retired with the rank of lieutenant-colonel. He died in 1935.

The consequences of this entire affair are notable. First, it exposed the deep-seated antisemitism of the French people, military, and government and saw the increasing prominence of journalist and antisemite Eduard Drumont (1844–1917), whose book *La France juive* (*Jewish France*) went through numerous reprintings. Second, covering that trial the Viennese journalist Theodor Herzl (1860–1904), who was so appalled by the public spectacle of antisemitism on a daily basis outside the courtroom that, upon his return to Austria, he concluded that the only solution to this enduring problem was for the Jewish people to have a nation-state of their own. He wrote his tract *Der Judenstaat* (*The State of the Jews*) and, given both his charismatic personality and organizational abilities, became the "Father of Modern Political Zionism," predicting a Jewish state—Israel—fifty years after his death in 1904. Third, and of equally important significance, it revealed to the world the power of political antisemitism not only to rally the masses but to accomplish whatever right-wing goals were important to both those in power and those aspiring to achieve it. The Nazis, under Adolf Hitler (1889–1945), would learn this lesson well and take it to its most perverse conclusion, which we know today as the Holocaust.

See also: Beilis Affair; Blood Libel; Frank Trial and Lynching; National Socialism/Nazism; Nationalism

Further Reading

Begley, Louis. *Why the Dreyfus Affair Matters*. New Haven, CT, and London: Yale University Press, 2009.

Bredin, Jean-Denis. *The Affair: The Case of Alfred Dreyfus*. London: Sidgwick & Jackson, 1986.

Chapman, Guy. *The Dreyfus Trials*. London: Batsford, 1972.

Lindemann, Alfred S. *The Jew Accused: Three Anti-Semitic Affairs: Dreyfus, Beilis, Frank, 1894–1900*. Cambridge, UK: Cambridge University Press, 1991.

Duke, David

After the deaths of William Luther Pierce (1933–2002), the founder of the National Alliance and a longtime mentor, and George Lincoln Rockwell (1918–1967), the founder of the American Nazi Party, David Duke (b. 1950) remains the most visible and well-known white supremacist, nationalist, separatist, conspiracy theorist, antisemite, anti-Zionist, and Holocaust denier. He is also a past grand wizard of the Ku Klux Klan, a convicted felon, and a politician from Louisiana with only one successful campaign to his credit—one term in the Louisiana House of Representatives—and a host of failed ones. (His felony conviction for defrauding his political base of funds to use for his own personal interests, especially his gambling,

38 | Duke, David

resulted in a fifteen-month prison term in Texas.) He has unsuccessfully run for the Louisiana State Senate, Louisiana governor, U.S. House of Representatives and Senate, and the Democratic candidacy for president in 1988 and Republican candidacy for president in 1992.

On a national level, Duke's opposition is to the Federal Reserve banking system and the media, both of which he argues are controlled by Jews, as well as abolishing the Internal Revenue System (IRS). He also argues for racial separation and traditional "Christian" family values (though he has long been accused of using Christianity exploitatively) and is anti-Communist and against "white genocide," this last being a plot of the Jews.

Duke first came to national attention during his student days at Louisiana State University in Baton Rouge, where he was often photographed protesting in a Nazi uniform as well as hosting parties on Adolf Hitler's (1889–1945) birthday (April 20). After graduating from LSU in 1947, he founded the Knights of the Ku Klux Klan (KKKK). His first unsuccessful political campaign took place a year later when he ran as a Democrat for the Louisiana Senate, where he received one-third of all votes cast (11,079). Four years later, he ran for the Tenth District Senate seat and finished second (9,897 votes) in a three-way tie. In 1988, now a Republican, he finished first (3,395) in the primary from Metairie and went on to defeat the Democrat by a margin of 50.7 percent–49.3 percent (8,459–8,232 votes). His one term in office was undistinguished, and all but one of the legislative offerings he proposed were rejected.

In 1990, Duke went on to found the National Association for the Advancement of White People (NAAWP), a direct slap at the National Association for the Advancement of Colored People (NAACP). Attempting to falsely argue that he had reformed his views—he was not a racist but rather an advocate for white majoritarian rule—in 1991, he unsuccessfully ran for governor of Louisiana and, along the way, gave further voice to his Holocaust denialism. In that election, he received 38.8 percent of the vote versus 61.2 percent for Edward Edwards.

By 2004, Duke had effectively removed himself from the political arena only briefly, but after Pierce's death, he was apparently bothered by the fragmentation of the various white nationalist groups in the United States. Hosting a "European Nationalist" conference put on by his newly founded Euro-American Unity and Rights Organization (EURO) in Kenner, Louisiana (Duke often refers to himself as a Euro-American) punctuated throughout by overt public statements of antisemitism, he got those in attendance to sign the New Orleans Protocol with its three provisions:

1. Zero tolerance for violence.
2. Honorable and ethical behavior in relations with other signatory groups. This includes not denouncing others who have signed this protocol. In other words, no enemies on the right.
3. Maintaining a high tone in our arguments and public presentations.

In 2004, Duke received a doctoral degree from the Ukrainian Interregional Academy of Personnel Management (MAUP), an unaccredited institution, with a dissertation entitled *Zionism as a Form of Ethnic Supremacism*. He has also taught classes at that same institution, which itself has a long history of hate and antisemitism. Two years later, he traveled to Iran, where he participated in a Holocaust denial conference at the invitation of its then president Mahmoud Ahmadinejad (b. 1956).

In 2015, Duke resumed his political activities, seemingly endorsing then candidate and now president Donald J. Trump (b. 1945), who would reject that endorsement, and, in 2016, he announced that he would run for the Republican Senate seat from Louisiana; he received only 3 percent of the vote.

Duke has also self-published two books, *My Awakening: A Path to Racial Understanding* (1998)—which he claims has sold more than 580,000 copies worldwide—and *Jewish Supremacism: My Awakening to the Jewish Question* (2001), both of which clearly spell out his racism and antisemitism. The second has been translated in Russian with the title *The Jewish Question through the Eyes of an American*. He continues to maintain his own website to promote the sale of his books and other paraphernalia as well as his other writings.

Among Duke's more brazen statements are the following:

Our clear goal must be the advancement of the white race and separation of the white and black races. This goal must include freeing the American media and government from subservient Jewish interests. (1978)

These Jews who run things, who are producing this mental illness— teenage suicide—all these Jewish sicknesses. . . . That's nothing new. The Talmud's full of things like sex with boys and girls. (1985)

The Jews are trying to destroy all other cultures . . . as a survival mechanism. . . . The only Nazi country in the world is Israel. (1991)

40 | Duke, David

We shall not surrender our freedom and our very existence to Jewish or any other power. (1998)

See also: Barnes, Harry Elmer; Carto, Willis; Christian Identity; Faurisson, Robert; Irving, David; Ku Klux Klan; National Socialism/Nazism; Pierce, William Luther; *Protocols of the Learned Elders of Zion*; Proud Boys; Rassinier, Paul; Rockwell, George Lincoln; White Supremacy; Yockey, Francis Parker

Further Reading

Bridges, Tyler. *The Rise of David Duke*. Jackson: University of Mississippi Press, 1995.

Maginnis, John. *Cross to Bear*. Baton Rouge, LA: Darkhorse Press, 1992.

Powell, Lawrence N. *Troubled Memory: Anne Levy, the Holocaust, and David Duke's Louisiana*. Chapel Hill: University of North Carolina Press, 2000.

Rose, Douglas D., ed. *The Emergence of David Duke and the Politics of Race*. Chapel Hill: University of North Carolina Press, 1992.

Sims, Patsy. *The Klan*. Lexington: University Press of Kentucky, 1996.

Swain, Carol M., and Russel Nieli. *Contemporary Voices of White Nationalism in America*. Cambridge, UK: Cambridge University Press, 2003.

Wise, Tim. *Great White Hoax: Responding to David Duke and the Politics of White Nationalism*. Seattle, WA: Northwest Coalition for Human Dignity, 2003.

Zatarain, Michael. *David Duke: Evolution of a Klansman*. Gretna, LA: Pelican Press, 1990.

F

Farhud

Farhud, Arabic for "violent dispossession," references a pogrom against the Jews of Baghdad, Iraq, in the aftermath of the British victory in the so-called Anglo-Iraqi War, which took place in 1941. The Farhud, however, can be neither seen nor understood apart from the Holocaust of the Second World War II (1939–1945). At its conclusion, nearly two hundred Jews were killed, as were three hundred to four hundred rioters, and more than one thousand Jews were injured. In addition, almost one thousand Jewish homes were destroyed. All these figures are inexact, and there remains something of a controversy even today regarding the actual numbers in all categories.

Occurring in June 1941, the two-day riot fell on the Jewish holy day of Shavuot (meaning either "Oaths" or "Weeks"), seven weeks after the holy Passover period. Prior to the Farhud, relations between the Jews and their neighbors, both Muslims and Arabs, had been reasonably positive for generations. The Jewish community understood itself as the descendants of the original Jews who had gone into exile after the Babylonian conquest of ancient Israel in 586 BCE and had welcomed their neighbors into their homes.

That relationship began to change with the ascension of Adolf Hitler (1889–1945) to the chancellorship of Nazi Germany in 1933. The German Embassy in Baghdad, under the leadership of Dr. Friz Grobba (1886–1973), in the decade prior to the Farhud, began a steady stream of antisemitic propaganda in the media, going so far as to purchase the newspaper *Al-Alam Al-arabi* (*The Arab World*) and publishing an Arabic translation of Hitler's *Mein Kampf* (*My Fight* or *My Struggle*). That same year, Grobba, already fluent in both Arabic and Turkish as a result of his service in both Palestine and Afghanistan and committed to ousting the British

42 | Farhud

from the Middle East, convinced the then king Ghazi I (1912–1939) to send a contingent of Iraqi military officers to Germany for additional training and to allow a similar advisory contingent of German military officials to come to Iraq. Upon their return, a successful military coup took place in 1941, fully supported by Grobba and Nazi Germany. The military leadership was equally anti-British and attempted to remove the British from Iraq, where it had long held the reins of power and control over the vast oil reserves. An additionally significant "player" in the tense relationship was Haj Amin al-Husseini (1895–1974), the mufti of Jerusalem, who had arrived in Baghdad in 1939 after the unsuccessful Palestinian revolt of 1936–1939. Notoriously antisemitic and anti-Zionist, al-Husseini later traveled to Berlin, where he was welcomed by Hitler, pensioned, and then broadcast a continuous stream of hate-filled invectives to rid the Middle East of its Jews on Berlin radio.

In the month prior to the Farhud, the British had had enough and successfully launched the Anglo-Iraqi War, toppling the government of Rashid Ali (1892–1965) and returning the monarchy to power under Abd al-Ilah of Hejaz (1913–1958), the first cousin and brother-in-law of King Ghazi I. Thus, in part, the Farhud must be seen as resulting from the failure and humiliation of the Iraqis at having lost their war at the very same time Hitlerite Germany was stepping up and expanding its objectives in the Middle East. In the process, Jews were falsely accused of civic disloyalty and aiding the British—not unlike the Nazi claim after Germany's losses in World War I. Those in power further accused the entire Jewish community of actively being Zionists and thus working in opposition to the Iraqi government and the Palestinian people. Both ideological attacks were spurred on by German Nazi supporters.

Somewhat disputed as to the actual causes that began the Farhud—an attack on a Jewish delegation to the new king and a series of antisemitic sermons in the main Baghdad mosque—violence against the Jews broke out on June 1–2, 1941, and it ultimately fell to the British to restore order. Over the years, varied numbers have been suggested for all casualties: 180–800 killed, 1,000–2,000 Jews injured, 600 Jewish-owned businesses destroyed, 100–1,000 Jewish homes destroyed, and 300–400 rioters also killed.

In the aftermath of the Farhud, the Jewish community of Iraq came to realize its own vulnerability and became more politicized, especially among the younger generation. Shortly after the birth of the State of Israel in May 1948, during the years 1950–1951, Iraqi Jews began an exodus, in part, rejecting the possibility of any successful reintegration of its community fully into Iraqi civic, cultural, and economic life. Fear of the future was heightened by the government's increasing restrictions on Jewish life. Today, its remnant Jewish community remains small and isolated but relatively secure, even if vulnerable. The U.S. invasions of Afghanistan (2001) and Iraq (2003) have done little if anything to shore up their security. In the aftermath of the latter invasion, a treasure trove of historical Jewish artifacts has been unearthed (collected by Saddam Hussein's (1937–2006) government). The current government wants the artifacts returned, claiming they are the cultural property of Iraq. The Jews who fled, and currently largely reside in both Israel (120,000 Iraqi Jews were brought to Israel between 1950 and 1952 under Operation Ezra and Nehemiah) and the United States, have collectively argued that they are the property of the Jewish people and belong in Israel. Attempts to return them to Iraq by the United States in 2018 met with a storm of protests.

In Ramat Gan, Israel, a monument to those Jews killed in the Farhud and afterward was erected. On June 1, 2015, the United Nations acknowledged the first International Farhud Day over the objections of the Iraqi delegation.

See also: al-Banna, Hassan; al-Husseini, Amin; Blood Libel; Martyrdom, Sanctifying the Name of God; Qutb, Sayyid

Further Reading

Baskin, Orit. *New Babylonians: A History of the Jews of Modern Iraq.* Stanford, CA: Stanford University Press, 2012.

Black, Edwin. *The Farhud: Roots of the Arab-Nazi Alliance in the Holocaust.* Washington, DC: Dialog Press, 2010.

Gat, Moshe. *The Jews Exodus from Iraq, 1948–1951.* London: Frank Cass, 1997.

Meir-Glitzenstein, Esther. *Zionism in an Arab Country: Jews in Iraq in the 1940s.* London and New York: Routledge 2004.

Farrakhan, Louis

Louis Farrakhan (b. Eugene Louis Wolcott, 1933) is the leader/minister of the Nation of Islam (NOI) and has long been associated with public

44 | Farrakhan, Louis

remarks against Jews, whites, and members of the LGBTQ+ communities. His latest affirmation (2018) was to claim that he was not an antisemite but an "anti-termite"—knowing full well that such a derogatory term has historically been associated with the Nazis of World War II, who labeled and libeled Jews as "vermin."

Farrakhan, whose names in Arabic means "the criterion," began his public career as a singer and musician, but the chance encounter with the then leader of the NOI, Elijah Muhammad (1897–1975), saw him turn from that vocation to willingly embrace the values and lifestyle of members of the NOI. Initially, he was given the name Louis X (the X signifying to members and others the lost names of their African ancestral roots) and appointed by Muhammad as the NOI's national representative because of his commanding presence and oratorical skills. Upon Muhammad's death in 1975, his designated successor was his son Wallace, who changed his own name to Warith Deen Mohammed (1933–2008) and came to reject many of his father's teachings—specifically the separation of the black and white races and the deification of the founder of the NOI, the somewhat shadowy figure of Wallace D. Fard (1877–ca. 1934)—and turned his followers toward a more mainstream embrace of Sunni Islam, including its Five Pillars (faith, prayers, charity, fasting, and pilgrimage). He also welcomed whites into worship and began building bridges toward other faith communities.

At first, Farrakhan following Warith's teachings and directions, but three years later, in 1978, he broke with him and, together with his own followers, returned to the original teachings of Elijah Muhammad. As his following increased so too did Warith Mohammad's following shrink, and by the early 1980s, Farrakhan was in charge and the acknowledged leader of the NOI, which continues today despite various medical setbacks due to prostate cancer.

The highpoint of Farrakhan's success came in 1975 when he led the Million Man March in Washington, DC, and while his public pronouncement of its success in saying more than two million men participated in this rally to affirm traditional values of male responsibility as husbands and fathers, the National Park Service has put those in attendance at no more than 440,000.

More problematic, however, has been the cloud of suspicion surrounding Farrakhan regarding the assassination of Malcolm X (1925–1965), himself originally a follower of Elijah Muhammad. After his journey to the Middle East and his own *haj* (pilgrimage to Mecca), Malcolm X broke with Muhammad and embraced a more traditional Islamic observance and faith. Like Warith Mohammad, he also began to reach out to non-Muslims as well. In a 2000 interview on the television program *60 Minutes*, Farrakhan acknowledged that his own rhetoric may have contributed to the assassination, but he denied that he had ordered it.

Both the Anti-Defamation League (ADL) in New York and the Southern Poverty Law Center (SPLC) in Montgomery, Alabama, have long tracked Farrakhan's public speeches, in which he has consistently condemned Jews; argued for their participation in political and other governmental conspiracies; denied the historical accuracy vis-à-vis the Holocaust; condemned Israel and Zionism and Zionists; and, most especially, condemned Jews for their factually incorrect supposed disproportionate involvement in the slave trade. (NOI has now published a three-volume text, *The Secret Relationship between Blacks and Jews*, volume 1 (1991), volume 2 (2010), and volume 3 (2016).) Farrakhan has also condemned the white race, the U.S. government, all manner of homosexual persons, and "mainstream" blacks who accept and participate in a racially oppressive and divided nation. As he ages, according to some, his followers continue to decrease in number. Whether he will continue to manifest a national presence is open to question.

See also: al-Banna, Hassan; al-Husseini, Amin; BDS (Boycott, Divestment, Sanctions) Movement; Blood Libel; Deicide; Qutb, Sayyid; Usury

Further Reading

Alexander, Amy, ed. *The Farrakhan Factor: African American Writers on Leadership, Nationhood, and Minister Louis Farrakhan*. New York: Grove Press, 1997.

Berg, Herbert. *Elijah Muhammad and Islam*. New York: New York University Press, 2009.

Brackman, Harold. *Ministry of Lies: The Truth behind the Nation of Islam's "The Secret Relationship between Blacks and Jews."* New York: Four Walls Eight Windows Publishers, 1994.

Curtis, Edward E., IV. *Black Muslim Religion in the Nation of Islam*. Chapel Hill: University of North Carolina Press, 2006.

Evanzz, Karl. *The Messenger: The Rise and Fall of Elijah Muhammad*. New York: Pantheon Books, 1999.

Gardell, Mattias. *In the Name of Elijah Mohammed: Louis Farrakhan and the Nation of Islam, 1960–1975*. Durham, NC: Duke University Press, 1996.

46 | Fascism

Gibson, Dawn-Marie. *A History of the Nation of Islam: Race, Islam, and the Quest for Freedom*. Santa Barbara, CA: Praeger. 2012.

Lincoln, C. Eric. *The Black Muslims in America*. Grand Rapids, MI: William B. Eerdmans, 1994.

Magida, Arthur J. *Prophet of Rage: A Life of Louis Farrakhan and His Nation*. New York: Basic Books, 1996.

Weitzman, Steven, and Sylvester Johnson. *The FBI and Religion: Faith and National Security before and after 9/11*. Berkeley: University of California Press, 2017.

Fascism

Fascism, as a political governing philosophy, is usually identified as being to the right of center, conservative thinking, and, historically, most associated with the rise of Benito Mussolini (1883–1945) in Italy prior to and during the World War II. Among its primary characteristics are the following:

1. Radical authoritarianism
2. Ultra-nationalism, and understanding the nation-state as an organic unity best populated by one dominant and superior people and possessors of past historical rights
3. Dictatorial power in the hands of a charismatic leader
4. One-party politics and government
5. Suppression of opposition and oftentimes minorities
6. Racism and hierarchies of various racial groupings, oftentimes between "superiors" and "inferiors"
7. Rejection of egalitarianism—the doctrine that all people are equal and deserve equal rights and opportunities
8. Commitment to the myth of the rebirth of society from its present cultural, religious, and social decadence and political decline
9. Strong regimentation of society
10. Economic self-sufficiency bordering on political isolationism
11. Strong military as an expression of masculinity coupled with traditional views of family structures and femininity (i.e., marriage and family)
12. Pervasive use of "romantic" historical symbols

13. Legitimation of violence to solve social, economic, and political problems as seen and understood through the lens of a Social-Darwinist theory of the survival of the fittest and the purging of the physically and mentally weak and socially undesirable elements
14. Imperialism—extending a country's power and influence through diplomacy or military force

It must be noted, however, that not all these characteristics always apply to all nation-states labeled as Fascistic or in one or more specific geographic locales. (The U.S. Holocaust Memorial Museum in Washington, DC, in a recent exhibit, recategorized these characteristics as the following: (1) power and continuing nationalism, (2) disdain for human rights, (3) identification of enemies as a unifying case, (4) supremacy of the military, (5) rampant sexism, (6) controlled mass media, (7) obsession with national security, (8) religion and government intertwined, (9) corporate power protected, (10) labor power suppressed, (11) disdain for intellectuals and the arts, (12) obsession with crime and punishment, and (13) rampant cronyism and corruption.)

Many scholars and others view the National Socialism/Nazism of Germany under Adolf Hitler (1889–1945) as the most extreme expression of Fascism in the modern era. Both movements—Mussolini's Fascism and Hitler's Nazism—coexisted in the middle of the twentieth century and remain somewhat viable even in the present twenty-first century, though in significantly diminished forms and numbers. Initially, at least in the case of Mussolini, antisemitism—hatred of the Jews and Judaism—was not part of his original attack on liberal democracy in his 1932 text "The Doctrine of Fascism," though it would evolve toward it but to a much lesser degree that Hitler's Nazism, where from the outset it remained central to its entire program, resulting in the wanton murders of more than six million Jewish children, women, and men and untold others in the Holocaust. In 1938, however, Mussolini's Italy adopted its own antisemitic laws, and he argued that antisemitism had always been an integral part of Fascism.

Historically, Fascism arose in Italy in the aftermath of World War I, in which both Mussolini and Hitler fought, and coalesced into movements opposed not only to liberalism but also to the Marxism of the Communists in their own revolution between 1914 and 1917 and the anarchic chaos that followed the defeat of both countries. All three societies—Germany, Italy, and Russia—as well as other nation-states (Great Britain, France, the

48 | Fascism

United States) were now forced to confront mass death on an unprecedented scale, the ever-increasing use of new technologies of death, the intertwining of industrial output and economic realities during wartime as never before, and the surrendering of distinctions between civilian noncombatants and the military on both the fields of battle and the home front.

From 1923, the year after Mussolini assumed power, until 1932, Italian troops waged a war against rebel forces in areas of Libya under its control, which included mass killings, the use of concentration camps, forced starvation, and ethnic cleansing and expulsion of the native and "inferior" populations—all tools that Hitler would use against the Jews. The Great Depression of the 1930s that affected every European country was seen and understood by the Fascists as the result of a "Judeo-Masonic-Bolshevik conspiracy," more so in Germany than Italy. Other nation-states that also embraced Fascism included Spain under Francisco Franco (1882–1975), Argentina under Juan Peron (1895–1974), and Portugal under Antonio de Oliveira Salazar (1889–1979). Close examination of their regimes also reveals a strong antisemitic component.

In the United States, many of the historical characteristics of European Fascism as outlined above have been and are present in American history, for example, intense nationalism, racism and antisemitism, and economic self-sufficiency. However, other factors, such as authoritarian/dictatorial leadership, one-party government, necessity of societal emergence from a degraded present, a too-powerful military, and the legitimation of violence as a solution to society's problems, have never held sway and have never assumed a dominant place in the country. Representative democracy as practiced in the United States has continued to prove a bulwark against those oftentimes vocal opponents of the American way of life and provided a home to a continually diverse population that includes Jews, Asians, Hispanics, and blacks, denying a foothold to Fascism as has been the case throughout Europe.

See also: al-Husseini, Amin; Alt-Right; Kristallnacht; National Socialism/Nazism; Nationalism; Social Darwinism

Further Reading

Albright, Madeleine. *Fascism: A Warning.* New York: HarperCollins, 2018.

Burley, Shane. *Fascism Today: What It Is and How to End It.* Chico, CA: AK Press, 2017.

Fogarty, Brian E. *Fascism: Why Not Here?* Washington, DC: Potomac Books, 2009.

Goldberg, Jonah. *Liberal Fascism: The Secret History of the American Left, from Mussolini to the Politics of Change*. New York: Crown Forum, 2009.

Gregor, A. James. *The Search for Neofascism: The Use and Abuse of a Social Science*. Cambridge, UK: Cambridge University Press, 2006.

Gross, Bertram. *Friendly Fascism: The New Face of Power in America*. Montreal, QC: Black Rose Books, 1980.

Hanebrink, Paul. *A Specter Haunting Europe: The Myth of Judeo-Bolshevism*. Cambridge, MA, and London: Harvard University Press, 2018.

Paxton, Robert O. *The Anatomy of Fascism*. New York: Vintage Books/Random House, 2004.

Seldes, George. *Facts and Fascism*. New York: In Fact, 2009/1947.

Stanley, Jason. *How Fascism Works: The Politics of Us and Them*. New York: Random House, 2018.

Traverso, Enzo. *The New Faces of Fascism: Populism and the Far Right*. Translated by David Broder. London and New York: Verso, 2019/2017.

Faurisson, Robert

Along with Paul Rassinier (1906–1967), Robert Faurisson (1929–2018) was, perhaps, France's most infamous Holocaust denier, but one with impressive academic credentials. He received his PhD in 1972 while teaching high school and later became a professor of French literature at the University of Lyon (1973–1990). In 1991, he was fined and dismissed from his post after being found guilty of violating the Gayssot Act of 1990, which made it an offense in France to question the existence or size of the category of crimes against humanity as defined in the London Charter of 1945, the basis upon which the Nazi leaders were convicted by the International Military Tribunal at Nuremberg in 1945–1946.

Faurisson's Holocaust denialism began in 1972 with a lengthy letter to Yad Vashem, Israel's official memorial to the victims of the Holocaust in Jerusalem, outlining several arguments based on his own interpretations of archival documents that there was no genocide against the Jews during World War II. He then aligned himself with the denialist Institute for Historical Review in Torrance, California, lecturing at their annual conferences and writing numerous articles for their *Journal of Historical Review*. Three of his most well-known articles are "The 'Problem' of the Gas

Faurisson, Robert

Chambers" (1980); "Is *The Diary of Anne Frank* Genuine?" (1982); and "My Life as a Revisionist (September 1983 to September 1987)" (1989). In 1980, he published *Memory in Defense of Those Who Accuse Me of Falsifying History: The Question of the Gas Chambers in France*, with a preface by American linguist, philosopher, cognitive scientist, historian, political activist, and social critic Noam Chomsky (b. 1928) entitled "Some Elementary Comments on the Rights of Freedom of Expression." (Chomsky later admitted he had not read the work but was upholding the principle of free speech.) In 1989, Faurisson was attacked and badly beaten by three assailants who claimed to be from the Sons of the Memory of the Jews, an organization about which nothing was known then or now. The assailants were never found.

In 2004, Faurisson was the recipient of a volume honoring him on his seventy-fifth birthday by the denialist Theses & Dissertations Press in Chicago, Illinois, an imprint of the denialist Castle Hill Publishers in England. Eight of his fellow denialists contributed to that volume, including Arthur Butz (b. 1933), Germar Rudolf (b. 1964), and Ernst Zündel (1939–2017). In 2012, Faurisson received an award from the denialist and then president of Iran Mahmoud Ahmadinejad (b. 1956). Faurisson died in 2018 at the age of eighty-eight.

See also: Barnes, Harry Elmer; Carto, Willis; Coughlin, Charles E.; Duke, David; Farrakhan, Louis; Holocaust, Denial of; Irving, David; Pierce, William Luther; Rassinier, Paul; Rockwell, George Lincoln; Yockey, Francis Parker

Further Reading

Gottfried, Ted. *Deniers of the Holocaust: Who They Are, What They Do, Why They Do It*. Brookfield, CT: 21st Century Books, 2001.

Kahn, R. A. *Holocaust Denial and the Law: A Comparative Study*. New York: Palgrave Macmillan, 2004.

Lipstadt, Deborah. *Denying the Holocaust: The Growing Assault on Truth and Memory*. New York: Free Press, 1993.

Stern, Ken. *Holocaust Denial*. New York: American Jewish Committee, 1993.

Vidal-Naquet, Pierre. *Assassins of Memory: Essays on the Denial of the Holocaust*. New York: Columbia University Press, 1993.

Zimmerman, John C. *Holocaust Denial: Demographics, Testimonies, and Ideologies*. Lanham, MD: University Press of America, 2000.

Frank Trial and Lynching

Leo Max Frank was born in Texas in 1884 to Jewish immigrant parents and died after being lynched in Milledgeville, Georgia, in 1915 by a conspiratorial mob, many of whom were identified many years later as prominent citizens and politicians dissatisfied with the commutation of his life sentence after having been falsely convicted of the rape and murder of a fourteen-year-old girl, Mary Phagan, in the factory at the National Pencil Company owned by Frank's uncle, where he was the plant superintendent. Both the police investigation and the prosecution and trial were seriously flawed. Frank's murder led to two important results in American history, one positive and one negative. The negative one was the revival of the racist and antisemitic Ku Klux Klan (KKK) that resulted from the rampant antisemitism that surrounded the trial and was ramped up by politician Tom Watson (1856–1922) in his *Jeffersonian Magazine*. Watson would serve in both the U.S. House of Representatives (before Frank) and the Senate (afterward). In addition, after the trial, the prosecutor, Hugh Dorsey (1871–1948), was elected and reelected as governor of Georgia.

The positive result was the founding of the Anti-Defamation League in 1913—the year Mary Phagan's body was found in the basement of the factory—whose mission, according to its website (www.adl.org), is "to stop the defamation of the Jewish people, and to secure justice and fair treatment to all." Additionally, it has been estimated that after the trial and Frank's conviction, more than half of the Jews in Georgia left the state.

Mary Phagan's body was found on April 27, 1913, and Frank was arrested and charged with her murder in August that same year. After a three-week trial, he was convicted, and his lawyers repeatedly filed a series of appeals all the way to the U.S. Supreme Court, which turned the case down in April 1915. Four months later, Frank was taken from his prison cell and lynched. His original sentence of death was commuted by then governor John Slayton (1886–1955), who later left Georgia with his wife for a decade out of fear for his personal safety.

In 1986, the Georgia State Board of Pardons "pardoned" Leo Frank, citing judicial irregularities without addressing the question of his innocence. (The pardon is said to have largely resulted from the death-bed confession of Alonzo Mann in 1982, who had worked at the factory as a child and had said that he saw the black janitor Jim Conley—the original suspect and long suspected by historians of being the murderer—carrying Phagan's body and had sworn him to secrecy on pain of his own death.

52 | Frank Trial and Lynching

When Mann told his own mother what he had seen, she, too, had insisted on his silence, fearing for his safety as an African American and telling him that no good would come from his admission.) In 2008, the Georgia Historical Society and the American Society for Historic Preservation jointly erected a marker near the building in Marietta where Frank was lynched.

Leo Frank's body was transported rather quickly after the lynching and buried in the Mount Carmel Cemetery in Glendale, Queens, New York, on August 20, 1915.

See also: Beilis Affair; Blood Libel; Christian Identity; Dreyfus Affair; Ku Klux Klan

Further Reading

Bernstein, Matthew H. *Screening a Lynching: The Leo Frank Case on Film and Television.* Athens: University of Georgia Press, 2009.

Dinnerstein, Leonard. *The Leo Frank Case.* Revised edition. Athens: University of Georgia Press, 2008.

Golden, Harry. *A Little Girl Is Dead.* Cleveland, OH: World Publishing Company, 1985.

Lindemann, Albert S. *The Jew Accused: Three Anti-Semitic Trials: Dreyfus, Beilis, Frank.* New York: Cambridge University Press, 1991.

Melnick, Jeffrey. *Black-Jewish Relations on Trial: Leo Frank and Jim Conley in the New South.* Jackson: University Press of Mississippi, 2000.

Oney, Steve. *And the Dead Shall Rise: The Murder of Mary Phagan and the Lynching of Leo Frank.* New York: Pantheon, 2003.

Phagan, Mary. *The Murder of Little Mary Phagan.* Far Hills, NJ: New Horizon Press, 1987. [NB: The author is the great-niece of the victim.]

G

Goldstein, Baruch*

Baruch "Benji" Koppel Goldstein (1956–1994) was an American Israeli physician and discipline of the late rabbi Meir Kahane (1932–1990). (Kahane was an American Israeli ultranationalist Orthodox rabbi and the founder of the American Jewish Defense League and the Israeli *Kach* Political Party; he was assassinated by an Arab gunman in New York City in 1990.)

In 1994, Goldstein murdered 29 Palestinian worshippers at the Cave of the Patriarchs and wounded 125 others before being beaten to death by the survivors. (No criminal charges were filed against them.) This act of murder may possibly be understood as his personal response to those he perceived to be the ultimate antisemitic enemies of Judaism, the Jewish people, and the holy land of Israel rather than the secular state. His grave remains today something of a shrine to his fellow right-wing religionists, who both venerate his memory and applaud his act. On a plaque near his grave are the words "He gave his life for the people of Israel, its Torah and land." However, rejected for burial in a consecrated Jewish cemetery, Goldstein is buried across from the Meir Kahane Memorial Park. More than ten thousand people have visited the site. Certain ultra-Orthodox rabbis (e.g., Yaacov Perrin, Samuel HaCohen, and Dov Lior (b. 1933)) at his funeral praised both him and his act.

Born in Brooklyn, New York, Goldstein was educated at the Yeshiva of Flatbush and the Albert Einstein School of Medicine and immigrated to Israel in 1983. After military service, he lived in Kiryat Arba, near Hebron, and worked as an emergency room physician. However, he refused to treat Arab patients, even those serving in the Israel Defense Force

---

* This entry also appears in a somewhat different form in Michael Jerryson, ed., *Religious Violence Today: Faith and Conflict in the Modern World* (Santa Barbara, CA: ABC-CLIO, 2020).

54 | Goldstein, Baruch

(IDF)—including the Druze, arguing (falsely) that it was contrary to Jewish law—and equally compared Israel's democracy to Germany under Nazism, oftentimes wearing a yellow star with the word "Jude" ("Jew" pejoratively) on it. Some have debated whether these latter claims are untrue.

The murders took place on February 25, 1994, at the Cave of the Patriarchs, also known as the Ibrahimi Mosque inside the Cave. Among those murdered were six boys fourteen years old or younger, which causes serious questions about his rationale. The question remains about whether Goldstein's act was revenge for Kahane's murder, as he had often spoken of doing so. The year before, the police had identified Goldstein as having engaged in acts of desecration by pouring acid and damaging the prayer rugs inside the mosque. Additionally, Goldstein was already known from years before to Israel's internal security service, the Shin Bet, as someone with a potential for doing serious violence.

It is of significance that Goldstein's act of murder took place during the holiday of Purim, celebrating the victory of the Jews against the genocidal intent of the Persian Prime Minister Haman according to the biblical Book of Esther. Goldstein saw the Arab people in that same mind-set: wanting to murder any and all Jews and destroying Judaism and, by extension, the holy and sacred land of Israel. From his own perspective, his action was one of preventing genocide.

After the massacres, riots broke out: forty-one Palestinians were killed and more than 120 injured. Suicide bombings took place inside Israel, with fourteen Israelis murdered and eighty-five injured. In the United States, in 1994, a Lebanese immigrant attacked a van carrying Chabad Orthodox Jewish students, killing one and injuring three in retaliation.

Goldstein's act was condemned by the majority of Israelis, including its then prime minister Yitzhak Rabin (1922–1995), who would himself be assassinated by a right-wing yeshiva student. Jews in the United Kingdom and United States and the United Nations condemned him as well.

In his book *Terror in the Mind of God: The Global Rise of Religious Violence*, Mark Juergensmeyer offers the following assessment:

> Though these defenders of the acts of Baruch Goldstein want to portray him as a kind of Jewish patriot defending his community's rights, they cannot escape the implications of his and other Jews militants' acts in precipitating Muslim violence on the other side, both in imitation and revenge. . . . On the Jewish side, the death of their leader radically

changed Kahane's movement: some followers sought revenge for his assassination, and this motive, along with Kahane's anti-Arab ideology, compelled his disciple, Goldstein, to attack Muslim worshippers in the shrine of the Tomb of the Patriarchs in Hebron. (Juergensmeyer 2017, 65 and 66)

See also: al-Banna, Hassan; al-Husseini, Amin; BDS (Boycott, Divestment, Sanctions) Movement; Farhud; Martyrdom, Sanctifying the Name of God; Qutb, Sayyid

Further Reading

Horowitz, Elliott. *Reckless Rites: Purim and the Legacy of Jewish Violence.* Princeton, NJ, and London: Princeton University Press, 2008.

Juergensmeyer, Mark. *Terror in the Mind of God: The Rise of Global Religious Violence.* 4th edition. Berkeley: University of California Press, 2017.

Lustick, Ian S. *For the Land and the Lord: Jewish Fundamentalism in Israel.* Washington, DC: Council on Foreign Relations, 1988.

Sprinzak, Ehud. *Brother against Brother: Violence and Extremism in Israeli Politics from Altalena to the Rabin Assassination.* New York: Free Press, 1999.

Holocaust*

The Problem of Definition

In truth, there is no one single word to define the horrendous and murderous deaths of nonmilitary combatants by the Nazis and their allied minions during World War II and largely the result of the implementation of a Hitlerian ideology that blamed the Jews not only for Germany losing World War I—the so-called *Dolchstoßlegende* (the "stab-in-the-back" myth)—but also for all the supposed ills that afflicted Western civilization. The English word *Holocaust*, derived from the Greek word *holocaustos*—referring to animal offerings totally consumed by fire by the priests to the God of ancient Israel—indirectly suggests the religious aspects or dynamics of what transpired and, perversely, may even play into the justifications of those who would argue that the Nazi were doing the "will of God" as priestly agents of the Divine. The Hebrew word *Shoah* (destruction or devastation) only refers to Jews, as does the Yiddish word *Khurbn*. The Sinti/Roma word *Porajmos* (devouring) refers only to their tragedy. None of these words, however, addresses the fate of innocent civilians throughout Europe who were subjected to Nazi tyranny, hegemony, or worse, nor homosexual persons, Jehovah's Witnesses, political dissidents, or so-called asocials. The following two definitions—one by a recognized scholar of the Holocaust only recently posited and the second by the author—focus on different aspects of the event.

The first is that of Michael Marrus (b. 1941), a retired professor of the University of Toronto:

---

* This entry appears in a somewhat different form in Michael Jerryson, ed., *Religious Violence Today: Faith and Conflict in the Modern World* (Santa Barbara, CA: ABC-CLIO, 2020).

The brutalization of men, women, and children across Europe, in a sinister racially inspired scheme of wiping millions of Jews off the face of the earth; rounding them up everywhere they could be found, often after murderous attacks; exposing them to disease, cold, hunger, and other degrading conditions, robbing, torturing them, beating them, shooting them, and in some cases murdering them by gassings in trucks or in specially constructed gas chambers, and by the killing of many hundreds of thousands, amounting to *close to* six million in all. (Marrus 2016, 4)

The following definition is used in an undergraduate course taught by the author entitled the Holocaust in Historical Perspective and has evolved over years of teaching and is further unpacked below:

The *Shoah*/Holocaust is the historically validated, legalized, bureaucratic marriage of technology and death, directed primarily against the Jewish People and Judaism by the Nazis of Germany and their non-German allies on the European continent between the years 1939 and 1945, and which resulted in the murderous deaths of *more than* six million Jewish persons, children, women and men.

Thus, the keys to understanding and unpacking this latter definition are described in the following paragraphs.

Historically validated: Despite the claims of so-called Holocaust revisionists (more accurately described as "Holocaust denialists"), the overwhelming abundance of documents (official governmental materials), films and photographs, memoirs, and eyewitness accounts of both victims and perpetrators, and the like, situate the events within a historical context.

Legalized: With the passage of a whole host of discriminatory legislation and laws by the Nazi government of Germany, its allies, and those formerly independent and sovereign states that fell to its power and might, laws were put in place that disadvantaged (and worse!) the Jews within their ever-expanded orbit. Examples include the Law for the Protection of German Blood and German Honor and the Reich Citizenship Law, both enacted Septembers 15, 1935.

Bureaucratic marriage of technology and death: To murder such large populations on so vast a scale required an organizational apparatus second to none, beginning in Germany itself, and integration into its various structures (political, military, economic, academic, etc.) and its scientific

58 | Holocaust

communities (medical, biological, physiological, genetic, etc.) the goal of the extermination/annihilation of the Jews. Those organizations included the *Sturmabteilung* (SA, Storm Troopers), *Geheime Staatspolizei* (*Gestapo*, secret state police), *Schutzstaffel* (SS, protection squad), the *Sicherheitsdienst des Reichführers SS* (SD, Security Service), and the various departments and branches of the German government and its ministries. In addition, one must also include German society as being either complicit in these crimes or indifferent to the fate of their Jewish friends and neighbors, and oftentimes their own family members, as numerous works indicate. Today, significantly, German governmental and citizen acceptance of the reality of the Holocaust is officially and publicly acknowledged, and education about the Holocaust is a mandated part of the national curricula.

By the Nazis of Germany and their non-German allies: The Holocaust/*Shoah* could not have been accomplished solely by the Nazis themselves. It relied on the willing complicity of populations found in those nation-states that came into the Nazi orbit: Poland, Lithuania, Latvia, the Baltic States, Romania, Czechoslovakia, and Ukraine, among others. Those already predisposed to implementing their antisemitic agendas now found themselves having the power to do so, and others, whether for personal or professional goals, were all too easily co-opted and complicit in the murders of their Jewish friends, neighbors, family members, and those whom they did not know.

On the European continent: It is now the scholarly consensus that, had the Nazis been successful both in their military conquests throughout the period of World War II and the implementation of the Holocaust/*Shoah* on the European continent, they would have taken their two goals worldwide, opting for both political sovereignty on other continents (North America, South America, Australia, Asia, and Africa) and implementation of their Final Solution to the Jewish Question (*die Endlösung der Judenfrage*) to exterminate/annihilate all Jews worldwide.

Directed primarily against the Jewish people and Judaism: The goal of the Nazis was not only the obliteration of the Jewish people physically but also the evisceration of their centuries-old religious tradition known as Judaism; its cultural production (books, music, newspapers, etc.), including its physical institutions (synagogues); and its plethora of communal organizations.

Between the years 1939 and 1945: Except for Kristallnacht (the pogrom of November 9–10, 1938), the Nazis and their allies commenced their journey to death and destruction with the beginning of World War II on September 1, 1939, and the invasion of Poland and ceased their operations with V-E (Victory over Europe) Day on May 8, 1945 (after the apparent suicide of Adolf Hitler (1889–1945) on April 30 or May 1). However, others have argued for a beginning date of January 30, 1933, with the assumption of Hitler's appointment as chancellor of Germany, and encompassing the entire twelve-year period of *das Dritte Reich* ("the Third Reich"). Still others have argued for an even earlier date, suggesting that with the end of World War I (November 11, 1918); the formation of the German Workers Party (DAP, January 5, 1919), which would subsequently become the National Socialist German Workers Party (NSDAP, acronym "Nazi") once Hitler claimed its leadership; and the signing of the Versailles Treaty (June 28, 1919) along with the onerous burden of financial restitution, the march to the Holocaust had begun.

More than six million Jewish persons, children, women, and men: Conclusively accurate figures remain difficult to come by, and ranges of deaths appear more appropriate, as noted below. With the opening of the archives after the collapse of the Soviet Union in 1991, it now appears that whatever understandings and figures were previously agreed upon, they will have to be revised upward rather than downward. But this much is certain: more than one million of those murdered Jews were children up to age twelve, and five hundred thousand children were between the ages of twelve and eighteen. In total, whatever the number, the losses themselves represent more than one-third of all Jews alive at the beginning of the twentieth century (sixteen million to eighteen million), two-thirds in Europe alone, and are a net loss from which the Jewish People will never recover. Additionally, the present demographic realities (Jews in Israel ~6,000,000–7,000,000; in the United States ~6,000,000+; in the former Soviet Union ~3,000,000; and in the rest of the world ~3,000,000) equate to a potential future growth and loss of approximately 50 percent of Jewry (i.e., victims included girls who never reached the age of maturity; girls and women who never married; those who married but were murdered prior to giving birth or were murdered with their children; and families who never achieved their desired number of children or were murdered with them or whose surviving children were less than the total number birthed).

And yet, while this author's own definition addresses many salient concerns, it does not include the overall historical context(s), the locales of death and destruction, or the manners of those murders, which are discussed below.

60 | Holocaust

Historical Context, Locales, and Manner of Murders

Historical context(s): Since the fall and destruction of the Second Temple by the Romans in the year 70 CE, two thousand years ago, the Jewish people have been a vulnerable, wandering minority throughout primarily Western Europe, a population whose very safety, security, and survival were dependent upon those holding the reins of political, economic, religious, and social power. The early rise of Christianity, which saw the destruction as payback for the failure of the Jews to recognize and accept their long-sought-for Messiah in the person of Jesus Christ, coupled with the alliance of Roman and later Protestant Christianity with the nation-state, up until the Enlightenment and Protestant Reformation—both of which severed the church-state marriage—only increased that vulnerability. With the power to restrict the Jews came the implementation to do so.

Thus, a fertile ground was prepared for the active antisemitism upon which the Nazis were able to draw, given the reality of a negative Western assessment of the Jewish people and Judaism. That "journey of antisemitism" may thus be described as follows: (a) social-cultural dislike, (b) religious-theological dislike, (c) the merging of the two, and (d) racial-biological dislike, the Nazi contribution. In every historical period, Jews were subjected to discrimination, repression, and violence, and Judaism itself was subjected to various forms of discrimination.

Locales: Although places of Jewish internment were initially established in Germany, with Dachau being the site of the incarceration of more than ten thousand Jewish men after Kristallnacht (November 9–10, 1938), the primary locale for the construction and location of the *Konzentrationslagers* (concentration camps), *Arbeitslagers* (work camps), and *Vernichtungslagers* (extermination camps) was Poland; other Eastern European countries also found themselves home to such sites. In Poland, six primary killing centers were established: Chelmno (Kulmhof), Belzec, Sobibor, Treblinka, Maidanek, and Auschwitz. Additionally, the major concentration camps were Ravensbruck, Neuengamme, Bergen-Belsen, Sachsenhausen, Gross-Rosen, Buchenwald, Theresienstadt, Flossenburg, Natzweiler-Struthof, Dachau, Mauthausen, Stutthof, and Dora/Nordhausen. More than 3,500,000 Jews met their end in these factories of death. All told, the actual number of these sites have been estimated to have been *more than* forty thousand; for example, thirty thousand slave labor camps in the occupied countries, one thousand concentration camps (with numerous subcamps), and one thousand prisoner-of-war camps.

Manners of murders: It is important to realize that the systemic murder of the Jews of Europe was an evolving process that included the *Einsatzgruppen* (mobile killing squads), which consisted of four units of approximately up to 1,500 men following the invasion of the Soviet Union (Operation Barbarossa, beginning June 22, 1941), who entered eastern villages and then corralled and slaughtered more than 1,300,000 Jews; removing Jews from civil society through restrictive legislation (e.g., Nuremberg Racial Laws of September 1935); ghettoization; death from carbon monoxide poisoning in large vans with capacities of up to one hundred persons (perhaps as many as 500,000 persons were murdered this way); and, finally, the various camps and subcamps leading to all manner of brutalities, starvation, disease, beatings, and, ultimately, death due to Zyklon B gas in gas chambers and body disposal in oven crematoria. Additionally, horrific pseudoscientific medical experiments were performed on any number of unwilling prisoners (disease injections, high-altitude and seawater immersions, amputations, drug testing, sterilizations, infliction of simulated battle wounds, etc.) that regularly resulted in death. In terms of the number of murdered, the following numbers give some indication of the horrific scale of these crimes (80%–90% of these victims were Jews):

Auschwitz-Birkenau	1,000,000
Treblinka	870,000–925,000
Belzec	434,000–600,000
Chelmno	152,000–320,000
Sobibor	170,000–250,000
Majdanek	79,000–255,000
Total	**2,705,000–3,350,000**

Once the war ended, some perpetrators—but not all, including the Nazi leadership—were brought to various trials (e.g., International Military Tribunal (1945–1946); Doctors' Trials (1946–1947); Dachau Trials (1945–1947); Auschwitz Trial (1947); and the Buchenwald Trial (1945–1948)). Ultimately, only a relatively small number of perpetrators out of a total of perhaps two hundred thousand men and women were prosecuted and punished, including death for some, for their crimes. Many escaped punishment by hiding in Germany; the Middle East, especially

62 | Holocaust

Egypt and Syria; or South America (e.g., Argentina, Brazil, Paraguay, and Uruguay). Others returned home to be reintegrated into their respective societies without discrimination.

For the Jewish survivors, however, including those who survived the death marches (estimated at more than 250,000), the trauma of the Holocaust/*Shoah* remains to this day. Many have shared their stories of survival with their immediate families and the public at large. Unable to return to their countries of origin—no longer in possession of their homes or assets—they left the graveyards of Europe to build new lives in Israel, the United States, Australia, Canada, and elsewhere, leaving behind much smaller and devastated populations in France, England, and Eastern Europe.

It should also be noted that the great myth/lie of the Holocaust/*Shoah* remains that the Jews, willingly or unwillingly, went to their deaths "like lambs to the slaughter," when the reality was that various forms of resistance broke out in many of the places of their incarcerations, including the ghettos (e.g., the Warsaw Ghetto uprising of April 1943) and the camps (the Sobibor uprising in October 1943). There was also active participation of somewhere between twenty thousand and thirty thousand Jews in partisan anti-Nazi insurgencies (e.g., the Bielski brothers and partisans in Poland beginning in 1941).

Finally, with the passing of the survivors, the aging of the second generation" (their children), and the coming-of-age of the third generation" (their grandchildren), issues of memory and historically accurate retellings of the events appear to gain increasing prominence, as do questions of uniqueness versus unprecedentedness and the place of the Holocaust within the larger discussions of genocide. Thus, there is no indication whatsoever that Holocaust-related issues will disappear from the world stage anytime soon.

See also: al-Husseini, Amin; Barnes, Harry Elmer; Coughlin, Charles E.; Duke, David; Farhud; Farrakhan, Louis; Fascism; Faurisson, Robert; Holocaust, Denial of; Irving, David; Kristallnacht; National Socialism/Nazism; Nationalism; Pius XII, Pope; Rassinier, Paul; Rockwell, George Lincoln; Social Darwinism; Wagner, Richard

Further Reading

Black, Jeremy. *The Holocaust: History & Memory*. Bloomington: Indiana University Press, 2016.

Cesarani, David. *Final Solution: The Fate of the Jews, 1933–49*. New York: Macmillan, 2016.

Dwork, Debórah, and Robert Jan van Pelt. *Holocaust: A History*. New York and London: W. W. Norton & Company, 2012.

Gerlach, Christian. *The Extermination of the European Jews*. Cambridge, UK: Cambridge University Press, 2016.

Hayes, Peter. *Why? Explaining the Holocaust*. New York and London: W. W. Norton & Company, 2017.

Longerich, Peter. *Holocaust: The Nazi Persecution and Murder of the Jews*. Oxford and New York: Oxford University Press, 2010.

Marrus, Michael. *Lessons of the Holocaust*. Toronto, ON and London: University of Toronto Press, 2016.

Pine, Lisa, ed. *Life and Times in Nazi Germany*. London: Bloomsbury Academic, 2016.

Rees, Laurence. *The Holocaust: A New History*. New York: Public Affairs, 2017.

Holocaust, Denial of

Holocaust Denialism is the antisemitic attempt by a minority of so-called scholars, the majority of whom lack proper academic credentials as historians or in related disciplines, to question the historical veracity of the Holocaust by (1) focusing on specific details that legitimate scholars continue to discuss (e.g., the lack of a specific document signed by Adolf Hitler (1889–1945) to mandate the extermination of the Jews, dismissing his numerous speeches); (2) arguing that the figure of six million Jewish deaths is far more inaccurate than the one hundred thousand *at most* who (unfortunately) perished during wartime from incarceration, disease, or as collateral military damage (accurate figures, however, put those tragic murders at somewhere between 5,933,000 and 5,967,000, though with the opening of the Soviet archives these figures may very well be revised upward); (3) arguing that the concentration camps, labor camps, and extermination camps were constructed not to murder Jews but to save and protect them from various European populations who may or may not have been antisemitic; and (4) continuing to affirm that the "Holohoax" is a nefarious plot on the part of Jews worldwide—specifically American and Israeli Jews—to financially continue to ruin not only Germany and its World War II allies through reparation payments but also the West, all in

64 | Holocaust, Denial of

support of the nation-state of Israel. The French term for such pseudohistory is *négationnisme* (negationism). Those who advocate this distortion of history argue that they are "historical revisionists" in keeping with the sound academic practice of revising our understandings of the past as new documents and other materials (e.g., archaeological evidence) surface and mandate both revising and rewriting our knowledge. These ongoing efforts at Holocaust denialism cannot be divorced from various antisemitic conspiracies theories against the Jewish people, most notably the *Protocols of the Learned Elders of Zion* of the early twentieth century, which remains current.

Such denialism obviously started with the Nazis. During the last days of the Third Reich, Heinrich Himmler (1900–1945, the *Reichsführer* of the *Schutzstaffel* (SS, protection squadron) and a leading member of the Nazi Party (NSDAP))—the "architect" of the Nazi genocide—gave orders to destroy evidence of their crimes (unearthing bodies and reducing them to ash, destroying camp buildings and records, etc.). Even before, Himmler and others made much use of coded language and concealment about their crimes, the most obvious being *die Endlösung der Judenfrage* (the Final Solution to the Jewish Question). In the aftermath of World War II, American professor Harry Elmer Barnes (1889–1968), who taught at Columbia University in New York (1918–1929), came to question the Holocaust, as did French political activist and author Paul Rassinier (1906–1967), who, ironically, had spent time in both Buchenwald and Mittelbau-Dora as a member of the French Resistance. Rassinier is still considered by many today, both his supporters and critics, as "the father of Holocaust denial."

In 1978–1979, American antisemite Willis Carto (1926–2015) founded the Institute for Historical Review in California as well as its publishing house, Noontide Press, and began to publish the *Journal of Historical Review*, all blatant attempts to foist Holocaust denialism on the unsuspecting by lending it an aura of supposed academic legitimacy, including a series of annual conferences at which speakers attempted to debunk historical scholarship on the Holocaust. Today, the ease of use vis-à-vis the Internet continues to provide numerous forums, websites, and the like, for such denialists worldwide to post unsubstantiated and false historical claims, including books and other documents. To combat Holocaust denialism online, the Nizkor Project (from the Hebrew for "we will remember," www.nizkor.org) was founded by Ken McVay and gifted to B'nai B'rith of Canada in 2010.

Holocaust, Denial of | 65

Among the most well-known and infamous Holocaust denialists are the following:

- Mahmoud Ahmadinejad (b. 1956) was the sixth president of Iran (2005–2013). During his term in office, he hosted the denialist International Conference to Review the Global Vision of the Holocaust (2006), and after leaving office, he sponsored the International Holocaust Cartoon Competition (2015).
- Austin App (1902–1984) was a German American professor of medieval English literature who taught at the University of Scranton and La Salle University. App defended Germans and Nazi Germany during World War II. He is known for his work denying the Holocaust, and he has been called the first major American Holocaust denier.
- Andrew Anglin (b. 1984) is an American neo-Nazi, white supremacist, and Holocaust denier who hosts a website and message board that continue to advocate for genocide against Jews.
- Don Black (b. 1953) is the founder and webmaster of the antisemitic, neo-Nazi, white supremacist, Holocaust denialist, and racist *Stormfront* Internet forum. He was a grand wizard in the Ku Klux Klan (KKK) and a member of the American Nazi Party in the 1970s.
- Pat Buchanan (b. 1938) is an American paleoconservative political commentator who has in the past unsuccessfully run for office. He is an author, syndicated columnist, politician, and broadcaster who continues to challenge accepted facts of Holocaust history and make overtly antisemitic statements.
- Arthur Butz (b. 1933) was an associate professor of electrical engineering at Northwestern University and is best known for his Holocaust denialist views and as the author of *The Hoax of the Twentieth Century*, a Holocaust denial publication that argues that the Holocaust was a propaganda hoax.
- Roger Garaudy (1913–2012) was a French philosopher, resistance fighter, and a prominent communist author who converted to Islam in 1982. In 1998, he was prosecuted for Holocaust denial under French law for claiming that the death of six million Jews was a myth.
- Hutton Gibson (b. 1918) is the father of the American actor Mel Gibson (b. 1956). In a 2003 interview, he questioned how the Nazis could have disposed of six million bodies during the Holocaust and claimed that the September 11, 2001, attacks were perpetrated by remote control. He has also been quoted as saying the Second Vatican Council (1962–1965), which rejected Jewish responsibility for the death of the Christ and repudiated antisemitism as anti-Christian, was "a Masonic plot backed by the Jews."

Holocaust, Denial of

- Michael A. Hoffman II (b. 1950) is an American denier and conspiracy theorist and is also known for his attacks on Orthodox Judaism, the Talmud, and Zionism. Hoffman published one book on the Zündel trial in Canada, arguing that Zündel's case was that of free speech and that, legally, he should be allowed to publish whatever he chooses. He also worked for a time as the assistant director of the Institute for Historical Review in California, and his newsletter *Revisionist History* regularly publishes Holocaust-denying materials.

- Fred A. Leuchter (b. 1943) is an American Holocaust denier who is best known as being the author of the "Leuchter Reports," pseudoscientific documents that allege there were no gas chambers at Auschwitz-Birkenau. Leuchter's work is often presented by Holocaust deniers as scientifically based evidence for Holocaust denial, despite his research methods and findings having been widely discredited on both scientific and historical grounds.

- Gemar Rudolf (b. 1964) is a German chemist and convicted Holocaust denier in Germany and the author of numerous publications attempting to repudiate the Holocaust.

- Bradley R. Smith (1930–2016) was the founder of the Committee for Open Debate on the Holocaust (CODOH). He attempted to place controversial advertisements in college and university newspapers under such titles as "A Revisionist Challenge to the US Holocaust Memorial Museum" and "The Holocaust Controversy: The Case for Open Debate." Under the guise of free speech, more than 350 student newspapers published the ads.

- Ernst Zündel (1939–2017) was the publisher of denialist literature in Canada. He was brought to trial in the 1980s and jailed several times both in Canada and in Germany. After his release, he remained in Germany until his death.

In September 1996, David Irving filed a libel suit against American professor Deborah Lipstadt of Emory University, in Atlanta, Georgia, and her publisher, Penguin Books, for her characterization of Irving as a Holocaust denier, falsifier of history, and bigot/racist in her book *Denying the Holocaust: The Growing Assault on Truth and Memory* (1994). Because British law—unlike American law—places the burden of proof on the defendant rather than the plaintiff, Lipstadt assembled not only an excellent legal team but a group of scholars who thoroughly eviscerated Irving's protestations. Judge Charles Gray, finding for Lipstadt, ordered Irving to pay the publisher's costs, which amounted to more than GBP$3,000,000 (USD $2,000,000), causing Irving to file for bankruptcy and lose his home, but this did not prevent him from writing, traveling, and lecturing in support of his continuing denialist falsehoods. The case also became the subject of the 2016 film *Denial*.

See also: al-Husseini, Amin; Barnes, Harry Elmer; Carto, Willis; Coughlin, Charles E.; Duke, David; Farhud; Fascism; Faurisson, Robert; Holocaust; Icke, David; Irving, David; Kristallnacht; National Socialism/Nazism; Pierce, William Luther; Pius XII, Pope; Rassinier, Paul; Rockwell, George Lincoln; Social Darwinism; Wagner, Richard; Yockey, Francis Parker

Further Reading

Evans, Richard J. *Lying about Hitler: History, Holocaust, and the David Irving Trial*. New York: Basic Books, 2002.

Gottfried, Ted. *Deniers of the Holocaust: Who They Are, What They Do, Why They Do It*. Brookfield, CT: 21st Century Books, 2001.

Gray, Charles. *The Irving Judgment*. New York: Penguin Books, 2000.

Guttenplan, D. D. *The Holocaust on Trial*. New York: Norton, 2002.

Kahn, R. A. *Holocaust Denial and the Law: A Comparative Study*. New York: Palgrave Macmillan, 2004.

Lipstadt, Deborah. *Denying the Holocaust: The Growing Assault on Truth and Memory*. New York: Plume, 1994.

Lipstadt, Deborah. *History on Trial: My Day in Court with a Holocaust Denier.* New York: Harper Perennial, 2006.

Stern, Ken. *Holocaust Denial*. New York: American Jewish Committee, 1993.

van Pelt, Robert Jan. *The Case for Auschwitz: Evidence from the Irving Trial*. Bloomington: Indiana University Press, 2016.

Zimmerman, John C. *Holocaust Denial: Demographics, Testimonies, and Ideologies*. Lanham, MD: University Press of America, 2000.

I

Icke, David

David Icke (b. 1952) is a former soccer player and sports commentator in Great Britain and also a New Age conspiracist with an international following who continues to deny both his antisemitism and his Holocaust denialism—despite the evidence in his writings. He maintains that he underwent a spiritual experience in which beings spoke to him, and a psychic later informed him that he would bring an important message to the world but would face difficulties getting it accepted. He has dabbled in British politics, but he resigned from the Green Party, which found his radical views in conflict with their own. He has also claimed to be a "Son of the Godhead" on several occasions.

A well-known and controversial British author and lecturer, Icke maintains an Internet following of supposedly more than several hundred thousand who seemingly accept his understanding of a reality of reptilelike aliens mating with humans, various classes of beings, and a hidden agenda to rule the world. He has endorsed the notorious antisemitic forgery the *Protocols of the Learned Elders of Zion* in two of his books, *The Robots' Rebellion* (1994) and *And the Truth Shall Set You Free* (1995), though he discounts its authorship as not Jewish but "Zionist." Icke has also courted far-right and neo-Nazi types to his banner and has spoken at several of their conferences and published some of his work in their periodicals.

According to American journalist Yair Rosenberg, writing in the online periodical *Tablet Magazine*, who has closely examined Icke's writings, he categorizes and quotes from *And the Truth Shall Set You Free* as follows:

- The Talmud is "among the most appallingly racist documents on the planet."
- B'nai B'rith, the world's oldest Jewish service organization, was behind the slave trade.

Racist far-right groups are Jewish fronts.
Jews are behind antisemitic attacks.
Jews bankrolled their own extermination in the Holocaust.
Schools should teach the controversy about whether the Holocaust really happened.

Among Icke's supporters in the United States is novelist and poet Alice Walker (b. 1944), the author of the 1982 novel *The Color Purple*, whose own antisemitic writings and promotion of Icke have yet to be addressed.

See also: Barnes, Harry Elmer; Carto, Willis; Duke, David; Faurisson, Robert; Holocaust; Holocaust, Denial of; Irving, David; Pierce, William Luther; Rassinier, Paul; Rockwell, George Lincoln; Yockey, Francis Parker

Further Reading

Barkun, Michael. *Chasing Phantoms: Reality, Imagination, and Homeland Security since 9/11.* Chapel Hill: University of North Carolina Press, 2011.

Barkun, Michael. *A Culture of Conspiracy: Apocalyptic Visions in Contemporary America.* Berkeley: University of California Press, 2003.

Roberson, David G. *UFOs, Conspiracy Theories and the New Age.* London: Bloomsbury Publishing, 2016.

Ronson, Jon. *Them: Adventures with Extremists.* London: Simon & Schuster, 2001.

Rosenberg, Yair. "The *New York Times* Just Published an Unqualified Recommendation for an Insanely Anti-Semitic Book." Tablet, December 17, 2018. https://www.tabletmag.com/scroll/277273/the-new-york-times-just-published-an-unqualified-recommendation-for-an-insanely-anti-semitic-book

Intersectionality

Intersectionality is both a theory that suggests that prejudices against either individuals or groups cannot be reduced to only one factor but remain largely the interplay of several factors clustered together (e.g., class/social-economic standing, race, gender, sexual orientation, religion, creed) and an

70 | Intersectionality

analytical tool with which to "unweave the strands" of those various interconnected factors. Conceptually, it has also maintained that any such discussion and analysis cannot be divorced from addressing the realities of power—who holds it and what methods and techniques are used to deprive others of it. Politically, it may be characterized as both left leaning and left of center. Historically, it has been most identified with a 1989 paper/presentation delivered by professor of law at both UCLA and Columbia University Kimberlé Crenshaw (b. 1959) entitled "Demarginalizing the Intersection of Race and Sex: A Black Feminist Critique of Antidiscrimination Doctrine, Feminist Theory and Antiracist Politics" at the Chicago Legal Forum. In that paper and subsequently, Crenshaw suggests and continues to maintain that such "intersectionality"—she was the first person to use that specific term, though the concept of multiple factors in addressing prejudice and hate has been around far longer—must be viewed through three lenses, (1) structurally, (2) politically, and (3) representationally, all of which have been shown and proven disadvantageous to black women. While her specific focus was to address the different realities vis-à-vis areas of oppression of black women in contradistinction to white women and the failure of feminist thought to address that distinction in a more carefully nuanced way, as intersectionality has evolved, it has unleashed a significant strain that can only be described as both antisemitic and anti-Zionist.

Building on Crenshaw's work, Patricia Hill Collins (b. 1948), a professor of sociology at the University of Maryland, has further suggested that there are three areas worthy of study: (1) background, ideas, issues, conflicts, and debates; (2) an analytical strategy to examine various social institutions; and (3) a critique of social justice initiatives and how they may be bettered to bring about positive social change. Some proponents of this last area have focused on the plight of the Palestinians in Israel as they understand it as one of continuing oppression and subjugation and have further committed themselves to activism against Israel by aligning themselves with the Boycott, Divestment, and Sanctions (BDS) movement and other anti-Israel organizations. (The plight of other subject peoples throughout the Middle East—e.g., women in Saudi Arabia or the ongoing persecution of Christian minorities—do not appear to be part of these discussions or concerns.) Others have even gone so far as to argue that "Jewish success," at least in the United States—despite both historical and contemporary evidences of antisemitism—is indicative of Jewish "whiteness" and collaboration with those in power to their own betterment and the detriment of the less fortunate.

Two of the most vocal Jewish critics of intersectionality have been professor of law emeritus Alan Dershowitz (b. 1938) of Harvard University and professor of social psychology Jonathan Haidt (b. 1963) of New York University. The former continues to critique intersectionality as prioritizing identity over everything else, overlooking both historical contexts and contemporary realities, and all too often choosing to align with groups and ideologies that work against their own stated goal of relieving oppression. Dershowitz likewise argues that intersectionality is "pseudo-academic," anti-American, and anti-Western.

For Haidt, the teaching of intersectionality is to be critiqued because it (1) focuses on conflict rather than reconciliation and, possibly, even forgiveness; (2) emphasizes tribalistic differences rather than commonalities; (3) seemingly rejects the United States and American values; (4) privileges identity and identity politics above all else; (5) is contrary to the best efforts of liberal arts education, which emphasizes reasoning, critical thought, and the quest for truth in favor of power and social justice activism; (6) comes perilously close to thinking far too narrowly (i.e., black vs. white) rather than on the complexities of both contemporary reality and historical circumstance. In his 2017 Wriston Lecture for the Manhattan Institute entitled "The Age of Outrage," Haidt goes on to declare rather stridently, "This is not education. This in induction into a cult, a fundamentalist religion, a paranoid worldview that separates peoples from each other and sends them down the road to alienation, anxiety, and intellectual impotence" (https://www.city-journal.org/html/age-outrage-15608.html).

Further critiques of intersectionality have focused on the Women's March (WM) and particularly its leaders, Linda Sarsour (b. 1980), who was born to Palestinian parents and has been an outspoken critic of both Israel and the American Jewish community and Zionism in general, and Tamika Mallory (b. 1980), who has refused to publicly condemn openly antisemitic religious leader the Rev. Louis Farrakhan (b. 1933) of the Nation of Islam and is also politically active in the Black Lives Matters (BLM) movement. Because many of those associated with both the Women's March and Black Lives Matter are persons of color (POC), especially women of color (WOC), some in both movements have strongly suggested that Jews need to mute their criticisms of such persons because of their own perceived benefits in American society. Thus, at the present time, the "situation" of American Jews and their relationship to both WM and BLM remain highly problematic, with some calling for their supportive acceptance into both, others saying that far more education is needed vis-à-vis the Jewish story and journey, and others going so far as to say that Jews have no place within either. Additionally, while the Holocaust/*Shoah* remains central to present-day Jewish identity, Jews find that others' concerns often dismiss it as history with little contemporary value or irrelevant to their concerns, thus heightening Jewish distance rather than involvement.

Finally, Jewishly, it must be recognized and accepted that, except in the case of the stridently Orthodox, who are distinguished by their closed-in communities and distinctive apparel, Jews have all too often been seen and understood as white, even by themselves, and benefited from that whiteness and privilege and, at times, functioned in the roles of powerbrokers and oppressors, though this last acknowledgment pertains only to relatively few within the larger American Jewish community.

See also: Alt-Right; Farrakhan, Louis

Further Reading

Chaout, Bruno. *Is Theory Good for the Jews? French Thought and the Challenge of the New Antisemitism.* Liverpool, UK: Liverpool University Press, 2017.

Haidt, Jonathan. "The Age of Outrage." 2017. https://www.city-journal.org/html/age-outrage-15608.html

Irving, David

David Irving (b. 1938) is a British Holocaust denier who brought a libel lawsuit against American academic Deborah Lipstadt of Emory University, in Atlanta, Georgia, in 1996 for defaming him in her book *Denying the Holocaust: The Growing Assault on Truth and Memory* and her publisher, Penguin Books. Judge Charles Gray ruled against him in a 335-page judgment in 2000 and labeled him not only a denier and antisemite but also a distorter and falsifier of history and a racist. Forced to pay court costs, Irving filed for bankruptcy, but he has continued to lecture and maintain a website. He also continues to maintain that he is the subject of an international Jewish conspiracy to silence and discredit him and his work. The case was the subject of the movie *Denial* released in 2016.

Although originally respected as a nondegreed historian because of his linguistic fluency in the German language as well as his sleuthing ability to find previously unknown documents in various archives, Irving discredited himself for accepting the "scientific" conclusions of fellow denier Fred Leuchter (b. 1943) vis-à-vis the gassings at Auschwitz and later reversing himself as to the factuality of the "Hitler diaries," which he, too, originally labeled as fiction—a conclusion in agreement with the majority of the world's scholarly investigators.

Irving's arguments against the Holocaust are based on the lack of a physical document whereby Adolf Hitler (1889–1945), the chancellor of Germany, ordered the extermination or annihilation of the Jews, disregarding his numerous speeches as campaign and political rhetoric. He has also argued that his defense of Hitler stems from the "cartoonish" way he and the Third Reich have been characterized by the British press and other historians. He went so far as to post a reward of GBP$1,000 to anyone who could furnish such a document. His first book, *The Destruction of Dresden* (1963), was a best seller and, at least initially, established his reputation as a creditable historian. In his 1977 book *Hitler's War*, he also claimed that Anne Frank's (1929–1945) diary was a forgery, the result of a collaboration between the American writer Meyer Levin (1905–1981) and her father, Otto Frank (1889–1980). His 1981 book *Uprising!* characterized the 1956 revolt in Hungary as an anti-Jewish one, as the Communist regime was, according to Irving, largely controlled by Jews.

By the 1980s, Irving was already in the camp of Holocaust denialism. He began associating with the Institute for Historical Review in Torrance, California, and befriended the Canadian German Holocaust denier Ernst Zündel (1939–2017). He has also argued in his speeches/lectures that the Allies—specifically the United States and Great Britain—were equally guilty of war crimes and that the number of Jewish deaths, greatly exaggerated, were primarily the result of Allied bombing campaigns. Between 1963 and 2002, Irving has published more than twenty-five books in English along with additional monographs, translations, and numerous articles in both German and English.

See also: al-Husseini, Amin; Alt-Right; Barnes, Harry Elmer; Carto, Willis; Duke, David; Faurisson, Robert; Holocaust; Holocaust, Denial of; Icke, David; Pierce, William Luther; Rassinier, Paul; Rockwell, George Lincoln; Yockey, Francis Parker

74 | Irving, David

Further Reading

Evans, Richard J. *Lying about Hitler: History, Holocaust and the David Irving Trial*. New York: Basic Books, 2002.

Gottfried, Ted. *Deniers of the Holocaust: Who They Are, What They Do, Why They Do It*. Brookfield, CT: 21st Century Books, 2001.

Gray, Charles. *The Irving Judgment*. New York: Penguin Books, 2000.

Guttenplan, D. D. *The Holocaust on Trial*. New York: Norton, 2002.

Kahn, R. A. *Holocaust Denial and the Law: A Comparative Study*. New York: Palgrave Macmillan, 2004.

Lipstadt, Deborah. *Denying the Holocaust: The Growing Assault on Truth and Memory*. New York: Plume, 1994.

Lipstadt, Deborah. *History on Trial: My Day in Court with a Holocaust Denier,* New York: Harper Perennial, 2006.

Stern, Ken. *Holocaust Denial*. New York: American Jewish Committee, 1993.

van Pelt, Robert Jan. *The Case for Auschwitz: Evidence from the Irving Trial*. Bloomington: Indiana University Press, 2016.

Zimmerman, John C. *Holocaust Denial: Demographics, Testimonies, and Ideologies*. Lanham, MD: University Press of America, 2000.

K

Kristallnacht

Kristallnacht (German for Night of the Broken Glass/Crystal and also called the November Pogrom in Europe) has come to be regarded as the first major act of violence against Germany's Jews since Adolf Hitler's (1889–1945) assumption of the chancellorship on January 30, 1933, and in advance of Germany's invasion of Poland on September 1, 1939. The overall lack of world response would come to be interpreted as a lack of caring about the fate of the Jews and further prepared the Nazis for what would ultimately become the Final Solution of the Holocaust and the wanton murders of more than six million Jewish children, women, and men throughout Europe. In two days—November 9–10, 1938—throughout Germany, ninety-one Jews were murdered and many more injured; 267 synagogues were destroyed and upward of more than one thousand damaged; seventy-five hundred Jewish businesses were damaged, including twenty-nine department stores; and thirty thousand Jewish men, ages sixteen to sixty, were arrested and incarcerated in Dachau, Sachsenhausen, and Buchenwald. Jewish schools, cemeteries, and hospitals were also damaged. At its end, though German insurance firms initially attempted to cover some of the damage done to Jewish institutions and businesses, the Jews of Germany were forced by the Nazi leadership to pay a fine in the amount of one billion Reichsmarks, the *Judenvermögensabegabe* (equaling ~USD \$5.5 billion in today's currency but the equivalent of USD\$4 billion at the time), not only for the murder of vom Rath (detailed below) but for physical damage to German properties as well. Following these two days and nights of terror, more than one hundred thousand Jews left Germany for Great Britain, France, the United States, Palestine, and as far away as Shanghai, China.

It must also be noted that the date, November 9, happened to coincide with the anniversary of the 1923 Beer Hall Putsch (also known as the

76 | Kristallnacht

Munich Putsch, the Hitlerputsch, the Hitler-Ludendorff-Putsch, the Bürgerbräu-Putsch, and *Marsch auf die Feldherrnhalle* (March on the Field Marshals' Hall)), the failed attempt of the National Socialists to seize power in Munich, Bavaria, and effectively launched Hitler's career after his release from Landsberg Prison.

The alleged trigger for this supposed spontaneous and violent demonstration was the murder in Paris, France, of the third secretary at the German Embassy, Ernst vom Rath (1909–1938)—not the intended victim (the ambassador) and who himself was opposed to Nazism—by seventeen-year-old Herschel Grynszpan (1921–?), a Polish Jew, whose parents and sister, along with twelve thousand other Polish Jews, had been forcibly relocated to the German-Polish border area, the so-called Polenaktion, neither country willing to take them. Scholarly investigation, however, has confirmed that the demonstration was more carefully planned and orchestrated than heretofore believed, and the incident of vom Rath's death provided the cover to put it into place. Joseph Goebbels (1897–1945), the Reich minister for propaganda, was the presence behind the scene and the organizational head responsible for Kristallnacht. Somewhat ironically, Hermann Goering (1893–1945), the president of the Reichstag and having the responsibility for Germany's economic policies, was highly critical of what took place after the fact because of its destruction of material resources advantageous and necessary to the Nazi state.

Grynszpan was initially arrested by the French police. He had refused to flee, hoping for a public trial that would bring the plight of the Jews to the world's attention. He was later turned over the German authorities after the fall of France, who imprisoned him after transporting him to Berlin, Germany. They, too, at Hitler's expressed wish, hoped to stage a show trial as evidence of Jewish perfidy but never did so. Once theory for having no trial was that, at some point—perhaps on the advice of his attorneys—he intimated that the act was not a political one but, rather, in response to a failed homosexual relationship, the knowledge of which would have embarrassed the German Nazi government. He was never seen again and is presumed to have been murdered by the end of the war.

The events of Kristallnacht were not, however, without opposition. Numerous examples of protest by both clergy and laypeople were reported and published in local newspapers, but the various Catholic and Protestant hierarchies largely remained silent. More pointedly, Bishop Martin Sasse of the Evangelical Lutheran Church in Thuringia and a leader of the Nazi German Christians published a collection of Martin Luther's (1483–1546) writings, noting that the event occurred on his birthday (November 10) and calling him "the greatest antisemite of his time."

Internationally, protests were launched by various governments and embassies, but only the United States recalled its ambassador. Its protest did not, however, result in an increase in the number of refugees admitted to the United States nor ease the restrictions on those entering or refusing entry into the country.

Finally, the term itself—*Kristallnacht*—was given by Walther Funk (1890–1960), the Reich minister for economic affairs, and intended as a negative and derisive satiric word to describe the loss of Jewish property.

Kristallnacht remains, however, the first bitter salvo in the Nazi agenda of the physical destruction of the Jewish people throughout the European continent, the success of which, in the aftermath of World War II, would have taken that plan around the world, wherever Jews lived, and sought their ultimate extermination and annihilation.

See also: Fascism; Holocaust; Holocaust, Denial of; National Socialism/Nazism; Nationalism; Social Darwinism

Further Reading

Bard, Mitchell G. *48 Hours of Kristallnacht: Night of Destruction/Dawn of the Holocaust*. Lanham, MD: Lyons Press, 2010.

Gerhardt, Uta, and Thomas Karlauf. *The Night of Broken Glass: Eyewitness Accounts of Kristallnacht*. Malden, MA, and London: Polity, 2012.

Gilbert, Martin. *Kristallnacht: Prelude to Destruction*. New York: HarperCollins, 2006.

Koch, Stephen. *Hitler's Pawn: The Boy Assassin and the Holocaust*. New York: Counterpoint, 2019.

Pehle, Walter H., ed. *November 1938: From "Reichskristallnacht" to Genocide*. New York: Berg Books, 1991.

Read, Anthony. *Kristallnacht: The Nazi Night of Terror*. New York: Times Books, 1989.

Schwab, Gerald. *The Day the Holocaust Began: The Odyssey of Herschel Grynszpan*. Westport, CT: Praeger, 1990.

Steinweis, Alan E. *Kristallnacht 1938*. Cambridge, MA: Harvard University Press, 2009.

Weiner Library. *Pogrom November 1938: Testimonies from "Kristallnacht."* London: Souvenir Press, 2106.

Wiviott, Meg. *Benno and the Night of Broken Glass*. Kensington, MD: Kar-Ben Copies, 2014. [Children's book]

Ku Klux Klan

The Ku Klux Klan (KKK) is, perhaps, the most historically and contemporarily well-known racist, white supremacist, anti-Catholic, and antisemitic hate group in the United States, having gone through two remakes after its original founding in 1865 in the immediate aftermath of the American Civil War (1861–1865). Its current splintering into a variety of different groups sharing the label—which the Southern Poverty Law Center estimates at more than fifty such groups—collectively appear to have little overall influence in the various hate movements despite their history and propensity for violence. Different estimates of its total memberships range from approximately three thousand to six thousand. Its most well-known and distinctive garb—white robes and masked conical white hoods—is a product of its second reincarnation and was designed to strike fear primarily among members of the African American community and largely confined to the American South. This second group also garnered much publicity for its burning of large crosses on private property. While its various members, in the main, seek to align themselves with a narrowly conservative and fundamentalist Protestant form of Christianity, all the major mainstream denominations continue to denounce the KKK.

The KKK began in December 1865, when six former Confederate Army officers met in Pulaski, Tennessee, to supposedly found a fraternal social club. Its first "grand wizard" was Confederate general Nathan Bedford Forrest (1821–1877), who is buried in Pulaski and whose grave remains a site of pilgrimage by members of the KKK today. It spread quite rapidly throughout the South and became largely identified as a group opposed not only to Reconstruction but to Northerners coming south (carpetbaggers) and the early rise of black equality, both civilly, especially in politics, and in business. Its overall successes were somewhat limited despite its ongoing violence against both blacks and whites, especially assassinations of those involved in politics. By 1872, it had already largely lost is way as its continuing violence spawned harsh responses up to and including federal legislation, most noticeably the Civil Rights Act of 1871, also known as the Ku Klux Klan Act, signed by president and former Union general Ulysses S. Grant (1822–1885).

A KKK revival took place in 1915, started by William Joseph Simmons (1880–1945), outside of Atlanta, Georgia, and largely in response to the wildly popular D. W. Griffith film *The Birth of the Nation* based on the book by Thomas Dixon Jr. entitled *The Clansman*, both of which romanticized Southern "nightriders" attempting to maintain white supremacy after the Civil War. Simmons was further aided by the tragic case of Jewish businessman Leo Frank (1884–1915), who was falsely accused of raping and murdering fourteen-year-old Mary Phagan and later taken from his prison cell and murdered in Milledgeville, Georgia. For Simmons and those who flocked to his banner of hate, the enemies were now the Roman Catholic Church, the Jews, blacks, and immigrants (Italians, Russians, Lithuanians). During this same period, the KKK also came out against birth control and the teaching of evolution in the public schools.

The KKK was supposedly founded as a men's fraternal organization with a women's component. At its height, it had more than four million members in various chapters throughout the United States, moving beyond the South to the Midwest, noticeably Indiana, and the West. As the group grew, it supported Prohibition and opposed Russian Communism and what it perceived to be a dramatic decline in American morality. In August 1925, sixty thousand white-robed Klansmen marched in Washington, DC. By the 1940s, however, its membership had dwindled to insignificance.

In the late 1950s and early 1960s, in opposition to the civil rights movement, various groups throughout the South sought to revive the KKK, especially in Alabama and Mississippi, and, again, used violence to promote the goal of white supremacy. Further adding to all the other hatreds, they now included homophobia as well. Its most well-known activities were the bombing of the Sixteenth Street Baptist Church in Birmingham, Alabama, in 1963, which killed four black girls and wounded a fifth, the sister of one of the victims, and the deaths of three civil rights workers in Mississippi in 1964. Other murders would follow in their wake.

Today, as noted, the label KKK is used by more than fifty such groups without any attempt at coordination or organizational unity, and it no longer represents the threats it once did. Although its activities have somewhat diminished, two new forms of hate have sprouted: the use of the Internet and social media and the use of one-page fliers left on doorsteps and cars both in neighborhoods and on college campuses championing their causes. Even the attempts of some of these organizations to align themselves with other neo-Nazi groups, both nationally and internationally, appear to have met with little success. A fitting description of the KKK is from the Southern Poverty Law Center: "The Klan's long history is intrinsically tied to violence and soaked in the blood of thousands of innocent victims" (https://www.splcenter.org/sites/default/files/Ku-Klux-Klan-A-History-of-Racism.pdf).

80 | Ku Klux Klan

See also: Alt-Right; Carto, Willis; Christian Identity; Coughlin, Charles E.; Duke, David; Pierce, William Luther; Proud Boys; Rockwell, George Lincoln; Social Darwinism; White Supremacy; World Church of the Creator

Further Reading

Baker, Kelly J. *The Gospel According to the Klan: The KKKs Appeal to Protestant America, 1915–1930*. Lawrence: University of Kansas Press, 2011.

Blee, Katherine M. *Women of the Klan*. Berkeley: University of California Press, 1992.

Chalmers, David M. *Hooded Americanism: The History of the Ku Klux Klan*. Durham, NC: Duke University Press, 1987.

Cunningham, David. *Klansville, USA: The Rise and Fall of the Civil Rights–Era Ku Klux Klan*. New York: Oxford University Press, 2013.

Dobratz, Betty A., and Stephanie L. Shanks Meile. *The White Separatist Movement in the United States*. Baltimore, MD, and London: Johns Hopkins University Press, 2000.

Gordon, Linda. *The Second Coming of the KKK: The Ku Klux Klan of the 1920s and the American Political Tradition*. New York and London: Liveright, 2017.

Harcourt, Felix. *Ku Klux Kulture: America and the Klan in the 1920s*. Chicago and London: University of Chicago Press, 2017.

Nelson, Jack. *Terror in the Night: The Klan's Campaign against the Jews*. New York: Simon and Schuster, 1993.

Newton, Michael, and Judy Ann Newton. *The Klan: An Encyclopedia*. New York and London: Garland Publishing Corporation, 1991.

Sanchez, Juan O. *Religion and the Klan: Biblical Appropriation in Their Literature and Songs*. Jefferson, NC: McFarland Publishing, 2016.

Southern Poverty Law Center. "Ku Klux Klan: A History of Racism and Violence." 2011. https://www.splcenter.org/sites/default/files/Ku-Klux-Klan-A-History-of-Racism.pdf

Thompson, Jerry. *My Life in the Klan*. New York: Putnam, 1982.

Wade, Wyn Craig. *The Fiery Cross: The Ku Klux Klan in America*. New York: Oxford University Press, 1998.

L

Luther, Martin

Martin Luther (1483–1546), the "Father of the Protestant Reformation" and, more specifically, the founder of what would later be called the Lutheran religious tradition, was a German Roman Catholic professor of theology, a priest, a monk, and a composer of liturgical hymns. Propelled by his sharp intellect coupled with a confrontational personality, his initial agendas may be said to have been threefold: (1) winning those who were not yet committed to the Christ to become so; (2) reforming what he regarded as a major violation of Catholic morals and ethics, selling of indulgences by priests and bishops (payments to the Catholic Church that purchased an exemption from punishment (penance) for some types of sins); and (3) reaching out the hand of friendship and love to Jews with the desire to convert them to Christianity. His unrelenting critiques of the Catholic Church ultimately led to his excommunication in 1521, which was largely the result of the publication of his "Ninety-Five Theses," the original title of which was the "Disputation of Martin Luther on the Power and Efficacy of Indulgences." (The historicity of Luther supposedly nailing the theses to the front door of the church at Wittenberg, Germany, cannot be supported.)

Luther's continuing failures to covert Jews—even after the initial publication of his favorable text "That Jesus Christ Was Born a Jew" in 1523—resulted to two overtly antisemitic texts, "On the Jews and Their Lies" (a sixty-five thousand–word treatise) and "Of the Unknowable Name and the Generations of Christ" in 1543, three years before his death. Although he had hoped for their ultimate conversion, he had long believed the Jews guilty of the death of the Christ, and thus their history of suffering and worse, and his personal contact with Jews, including rabbis, was minimal. The former text has served as a hateful source for antisemitism ever since,

82 | Luther, Martin

up to and including the period of Nazi terror and the Holocaust during World War II. After its initial publication, it evoked both popular support and scholarly condemnation. His final sermon series, delivered three days before his death, also included an attack on the stubbornness of the Jews and his call to have them expelled from German lands; it was entitled "Admonition against the Jews." Those who continue to reject this idea of Luther's antisemitism as foundational to all subsequent expressions of it argue regularly that his strong disagreements with Jews were theological and not the racial hatred to which antisemitism would evolve.

The most well-known excerpt of "On the Jews and Their Lies" remains his seven recommendations:

> First to set fire to their synagogues or schools and to bury and cover with dirt whatever will not burn so that no man will ever again see a stone or cinder of them.
>
> Second, I advise that their houses also be razed and destroyed.
>
> Third, I advise that all their prayer books and Talmudic writings, in which such idolatry, lies, cursing and blasphemy are taught, be taken from them.
>
> Fourth, I advise that their rabbis be forbidden to teach henceforth on pain of loss of life and limb.
>
> Fifth, I advise that safe conduct on their highways be abandoned completely for Jews.
>
> Sixth, I advise that usury [the action or practice of lending money at unreasonably high rates of interest] be prohibited to them, and that all cash and treasure of silver and gold be taken from them and put aside for safekeeping.
>
> Seventh, I commend putting a flail, an ax, a hoe, a spade, a distaff, or a spindle into the hands of young, strong Jews and Jewesses and letting them earn their bread in the sweat of their brow, as was imposed on the children of Adam. [Genesis 3:19: By the sweat of your brow will you have food to eat until you return to the ground from which you were made.]

As a thinker strongly committed to his faith, Luther's belief was that salvation through faith in the Christ was an act of grace, and no work, no matter how positive or benevolent, could alter that reality. One consequence of that commitment was his rejection of the pope as the only authoritative interpreter of the Old and New Testaments. For Luther, neither the pope nor the church were infallible. In 1525, he found himself in opposition to the Peasants War and wrote "Against the Murderous,

Thieving Hordes of Peasants?" because of their numerous acts of violence. That opposition caused him to lose the support of many, even as his notoriety as an important religious person was growing. Two years before, in 1523, he had married former nun Katharina von Bora, having long condemned celibacy. The year before, in 1522, he had published his German translation of the New Testament, and the year after, along with his collaborators, he published his translation of the Old Testament, acknowledging all the while that his Hebrew language skills were rather poor at best and his Greek little better, forcing him in both cases to rely on others as collaborators.

Since the 1980s, however, the various international Lutheran denominations have repudiated Luther's antisemitism and sought both forgiveness and reconciliation with Jews for his sins, noting consistently that his hateful rhetoric has never been part of official Lutheran theological or liturgical texts.

See also: *Adversus Judaeos*; Blood Libel; Crusades; Deicide; Holocaust; Martyrdom, Sanctifying the Name of God; Oberammergau Passion Play; Spanish Inquisition; Usury

Further Reading

Edwards, Mark U. *Luther's Last Battles: Politics and Polemics, 1531–46*. Ithaca, NY: Cornell University Press, 1983.

Gritsch, Eric W. *Martin Luther's Anti-Semitism: Against His Better Judgment*. Grand Rapids, MI: William B Eerdmans, 2012.

Kaufman, Thomas, and Lesley Sharpe. *Luther's Jews*. Translated by Jeremy Noakes. Oxford and New York: Oxford University Press, 2017.

Michael, Robert. *Holy Hatred: Christianity, Antisemitism, and the Holocaust*. New York: Palgrave Macmillan, 2006.

Nichols, William. *Christian Antisemitism: A History of Hate*. Northvale, NJ: Jason Aronson, 1995.

Oberman, Heiko. *The Roots of Anti-Semitism: In the Age of Renaissance and Reformation*. Philadelphia: Fortress Press, 1984.

Probst, Christopher J. *Demonizing the Jews: Luther and the Protestant Church in Nazi Germany*. Bloomington: Indiana University Press, 2012.

Stiegmann-Gall, Richard. *The Holy Reich: Nazi Conceptions of Christianity, 1919–1945*. Cambridge, UK: Cambridge University Press, 2003.

Tjernagel, Neelak S. *Martin Luther and the Jewish People*. Milwaukee, WI: Northwestern Publishing House, 1985.

Marr, Wilhelm

Wilhelm Marr (1819–1904), whom Israeli scholar Moshe Zimmerman (b. 1943) labels the "patriarch" of antisemitism, is best known for his use of the German word *Antisemitismus* as opposed to its previous iteration of *Judenhaas* ("Jew-hatred"), giving it a veneer of academic and scientific respectability. The term was supposedly derived from an earlier analysis of languages into so-called Aryan languages (German, English) and "Semitic" languages (Hebrew, Arabic, Amharic). Equally, Marr is well known for his 1879 pamphlet *Der Weg zum Siege des Germanenthums über das Judenthum* ("The Way to Victory of Germanism over Judaism") but far less so for his early "A Mirror to the Jews" or his later "Testament of an Antisemite." Somewhat ironically, Marr's first two wives were Jewish; his third wife was the product of a mixed Jewish–non-Jewish marriage; and his fourth wife at the time of his death was not at all Jewish.

Marr was born in the town of Magdeburg to a father who was a well-known actor and stage director and for whom he briefly apprenticed. Later, in Vienna, he worked for two Jewish firms but was let go, for which he claimed unjustly so. Politically, he turned increasingly to the left, adding to his credentials as both an atheist and an anarchist. Given his recognized writing talents, it is not surprising that he became a journalist, going so far as to publish the satirical magazine *Mephistopheles* from 1847 to 1852. After the failure of the March Revolution of 1848, Marr, like so many others, turned increasingly to the right and began advocating for German-Prussian unification. After a brief, unsuccessful trip to Costa Rica, Marr returned to Hamburg, Germany, and was elected to the Hamburg Parliament in 1859. His attacks on Jewish members of the Parliament for not committing themselves to democracy but exploiting their emancipation for their own financial purposes proved too controversial, and he was not reelected in 1862.

Already a decade before and increasingly, Marr's writings and speeches smacked of antisemitism, and they were especially heavily influenced by the nineteenth-century *Burschenschaft* student movement, which advocated German unification without the participation of Jews and other minorities. Significantly, Marr was also influenced by Social Darwinist and eugenicist Ernst Haeckel (1834–1919), whose beliefs in German racial superiority and purity later provided a foundation for similar Nazi thinking, especially in the person of its leading theoretician, Alfred Rosenberg (1892–1946).

In 1862, Marr wrote and published *Der Judenspiegel* ("A Mirror to the Jews"), which rather quickly went through five editions. Originally intended to be a defense of Reform or Liberal Judaism against that of Orthodox Judaism, it quickly evolved into an attack on religion in general as well as those opposed to the democratization of Germany (meaning Jews). Marr coupled that attack with what he perceived as Jewish particularism and exclusivity, which, according to him, was a misread of their own history, being first, last, and always a mixed people and, most assuredly, a mixed race of people. And although he granted them certain civil rights, he excluded Jews from holding any governmental offices whatsoever. Seventeen years later, he fully expanded on his ideas in *Der Weg zum Siege des Germanenthums über das Judenthum*. (By that time, *Der Judenspiegel* was already in its twelfth edition.) That same year, in Berlin, he founded *Antisemiten-Liga* (Antisemitic League or League of Antisemites), a somewhat futile attempt to translate his beliefs into a politically active movement. That "success" would fall to others, for example, Adolf Stoecker (1835–1909), the Christian court chaplain to Kaiser Wilhelm I (1797–1888), and his Christian Social Party.

In his more well-known text, Marr argues that Jews had, for the last almost two thousand years, been engaged in a conspiracy to undermine the Western world and were on the verge of success. As he wrote in the preface, "I wish two things for this pamphlet: 1. That Jewish critics will not hush it up. 2. That it will not be disposed of with the usual, smug commentary. . . . I shall announce, loudly and without any attempt to be ironic, that Judaism has triumphed on a worldwide historical basis." He also went on to argue that Jews and Germans were engaged in a historical and longstanding conflict that would not be resolved by the assimilation of Jews into German society because of their fundamental racial difference. Thus, victory would, ultimately, only come to pass by the death of the other—Jews or Germans. If the former, it would mark the end of the German people, and, thus, the

86 | Martyrdom, Sanctifying the Name of God

only solution was the forced removal of all Jews from Germany. Here, too, the embryonic seeds of Nazism are already in evidence.

Toward the end of his life, Marr attempted to rehabilitate himself, unsuccessfully, with a final essay entitled "Testament of an Antisemite," attributing the error of his ways to succumbing to the false belief in German Romanticism and arguing that he had, at least initially, been a philosemite. He also wrote that those who currently professed a much cruder expression of antisemitism were themselves seduced by mysticism and a false sense of nationalism, neither of which boded well for the German future. On this last point, Marr was, tragically, presciently correct, as the events of both World War II and the Holocaust have shown. However, his popularization of *Antisemitismus* into *antisemitism* has enjoyed a remarkable success as has the hatred that it labeled, the longest prejudice known to the human community.

Poverty-stricken and largely ignored, Marr died in 1904.

See also: Alt-Right; Barnes, Harry Elmer; Carto, Willis; Holocaust; National Socialism/Nazism; Nationalism; Social Darwinism

Further Reading

(*Note:* There are many articles addressing both Marr and his writings that are easily available on Google.org, e.g., Werner Bergmann. "Wilhelm Marr's A Mirror to the Jews," 2016. https://dx.doi.org/10.23691/jgo:article-107.en.v1.)

Marr, Wilhelm. Preface to "The Victory of Judaism over Germanism." 1879. www.ghdi.ghi-dc.org> sub_document
Zimmerman, Moshe. *Wilhelm Marr: The Patriarch of Anti-Semitism*. Oxford and New York: Oxford University Press, 1987.

Martyrdom, Sanctifying the Name of God

Introductory Terminology

Martyrdom in the Jewish religious and historical tradition is best expressed by the Hebrew term *al Kiddushat Ha-Shem*, those who die "for the Sanctification of the [Holy] Name of God" rather than subject themselves to forced conversions or violations of Judaic holidays, holy days, festivals, fast

Martyrdom, Sanctifying the Name of God | 87

days, or bodily desecrations (e.g., violations of sexual norms). This includes the disregarding of the dietary system or the moral-ethical value system of Jewish Law (in Hebrew, *Halakha*), all of which encompass the "Jewish way of life." Thus, its opposite, *Hillul Ha-Shem*, may be best translated as "Desecration of the [Holy] Name of God" and equates those acts with denigrating, or worse, both Judaism and the Jewish people and being practiced by rebellious Jews (e.g., turncoats, informers, self-haters). Although the terms do not appear in the Torah/Hebrew Bible/Old Testament, the concepts are there, at least in their initial configurations; they are increasingly apparent in postbiblical rabbinic literature and occupy even more centrality in the modern period with the murder of more than six million Jewish women, children, and men in the aftermath of the Holocaust/*Shoah*, when the label *Kedoshim* (Holy Ones, i.e., martyrs) was (and remains) applied to them. Derivatively, however, one may legitimately argue that, conceptually, Leviticus 22:32 ("Neither shall you profane My Holy Name, but I will be hallowed among the children of Israel. I am the Lord which hallows you.") locates this understanding positively as an obligation. Although initially applied to the priests of ancient Israel, it was quite quickly applied to the entire Israelite community. Postbiblically, however, the rabbis place enormous restrictions on mandating martyrdom so as not to encourage it, but, instead, continually affirm that the purpose of the laws of Judaism (in Hebrew, *halakhot*) is to "live by them," following Leviticus 18:5. Additionally, since the founding of the modern state of Israel in May 1948, and the subsequent wars of 1956, 1967, 1973, 1981, and 2001, and the regularity of terrorist incursions that have resulted in the deaths of innocent children, women, and men, there are those among the religiously devout Jews who would label *all* such victims as martyred holy ones. Also, there are those among the devout who would go so far as to label those Jews whose own violent responses to both Palestinians and Muslims that result in their deaths and who, in the process, lose their own lives are to be understood as martyrs, Baruch Goldstein (1956–1994) being a primary example.

In the Biblical Period and Initially Beyond

To be sure, there are rather dramatic stories in the Torah/Hebrew Bible/Old Testament and the additional literature of what we, today, understand as martyrdom: for example, the story of Hannah and her sons in 2 Maccabees, chapter 7. Then, too, one manner of possibly understanding Genesis 22 and the *Akedat Yitzhak* ("The Binding of Isaac" rather than "Sacrifice

88 | Martyrdom, Sanctifying the Name of God

of Isaac," as understood by Christian commentators as a prefiguration of the Christ event) was Isaac's silence and willingness to surrender his own life in obedience to the Divine command communicated to Abraham.

Subsequently, the story of the surviving zealots who took their last refuge to Masada, Herod's summer palace in the Judean desert, beginning in 67 CE, and chose suicide rather than enslavement to the Romans three years later, may be read as an example of collective martyrdom, despite its historical contestations by later scholars. The case of Hananiah, Mishael, and Azariah in Daniel, chapter 3, is but a further example. The rebellious example of Bar Kokhba and his revolt, also against the Romans, in 132–135 CE, which resulted in his own death rather than subjugation, adds to this history. (Rabbi Akiba, the acknowledged religious leader of Palestinian Jewry at the time and who labeled Bar Kokhba as the "messiah," also died at Roman hands.)

Rabbinic Restrictions

Over time, the rabbis became increasingly concerned that, due to the vulnerability of their Jewish communities, Jews would continue to opt for martyrdom, increasing their deaths and lessening the survival of their communities. Thus, we find increasing legislation that proscribed martyrdom except in cases of murder, incest, and other forms of gross sexual immorality and public idolatry; equally permitted accepting forced conversion (both to Christianity and Islam rather than death) but not sanctioning the deaths of oneself or one's children except when facing the immediacy of their own deaths; permitted the surrendering of one whose name is already known and requested by the authorities or even the mob outside rather than the deaths of the entire group; permitted misleading or deceiving non-Jews as to one's true identity to save one's life or the lives of others; and permitted seeking protection among willing non-Jews. (These latter two scenarios obviously became applicable in the case of the Holocaust/*Shoah*.) The process of this rabbinically restrictive legislation began in the second century in the town of Lydda in post-Roman Palestine, when leading rabbis met to discuss and legislate this and other issues of import to Jewish communal survival.

During the Middle Ages, when the Jewish communities of Europe found themselves increasingly vulnerable, Jews were frequently slaughtered, and thus the terminology of *Kedoshim* (Holy Ones) entered Jewish religious vocabulary, where it has remained ever since.

A Liturgical Sanctification

In addition to these somewhat obvious scenarios, the rabbis quite profoundly suggested that the repetition of two liturgical expressions were acts of holy commitment to honoring the Holy Name of God: (1) the *Kedusha* of Isaiah 6:3 ("Holy, holy, holy is the LORD of hosts; the whole earth is full of God's glory"), now a major affirmation in Jewish worship, and (2) the *Kaddish*, now more associated with the prayer said at funerals and memorials but which bears no mention of death and is a series of recognitions of God's holiness.

The Problematics of the Holocaust/*Shoah*

To be sure, Jews of all ages were murdered simply because they were Jews, falsely perceived by the Nazis and other antisemitic organizations hostile to Jews as being of a different racial and genetic structure with no possibilities whatsoever of changing their identity. Thus, conversion to Christianity, either in Germany or elsewhere within Nazi-controlled Europe, was not an option; Jews whose parents or grandparents had long ago converted—even with vetted documentation—and Jews who were thoroughly assimilated into larger European cultures or who had consciously rejected any identification with Jews communally or individually were still understood to be fully Jewish and subject to all the discriminations and brutalities of which their enemies were capable.

And yet, honest evaluation compels the observation that not all who were murdered proved themselves worthy of the label *Kedoshim* (Holy Ones), no matter that the intention remains to somehow ennoble their deaths by attributing to them saintly manners or Jewish commitments they may or may not have possessed. Their murders were not matters of their own choosing, even if some went unwillingly to their deaths refusing to debase themselves in the presence of their persecutors. And what of those who did everything they could to survive or attempt the survival of their own loved ones, even at the expense of others (family or friends), even in a minor key? It was easier for those who betrayed family or friends to the Nazis or their allies in exchange for momentary protection, initial financial gain, or to escape opportunities; such acts and others were most assuredly acts of *Hillul Ha-Shem*, desecration of the Holy Name of God. Forgers, bribers, and false identifiers (including those who donned Nazi uniforms) are to be judged on an individual basis rather than

90 | Martyrdom, Sanctifying the Name of God

blanket condemnations and thus, ultimately, impossible to assess from the outside.

Equally problematic in this context is to label those who survived, sometimes by their own devices, other times by the devices of others, as "heroes" and thus attribute to them a title less appropriate in all contexts. Some survivors were, indeed, heroes whose great acts of courage resulted in their own survival as well as that of others. Others survived simply because of luck or circumstance or being in the right location at the right time, not because of any direct or even indirect action on their own part, and they were certainly not heroic, no matter their good fortune.

Thus, again by way of summary, while honoring or desecrating the Holy Name of God is most definitely part of the historical and religious Jewish traditions, since the Holocaust/*Shoah*, the discussion of martyrdom has receded into the background of public Jewish discussion—despite the murders of innocent civilian Jewish children, women, and men in the State of Israel since 1948 (and before, for example, the slaughter of rabbinical students in Hebron in 1929) from terror attacks, suicide bombers, and the like. Among the less religiously devout, the use of such heavily laden theological vocabulary remains uncomfortable and difficult. While they, too, share the sense of tragedy and loss associated with this victimhood, they do not see these murderous acts of innocent victims as part of a larger divine-human context.

See also: *Adversus Judaeos*; Blood Libel; Crusades; Deicide; Luther, Martin; Oberammergau Passion Play

Further Reading

Droge, Arthur J., and James D. Tabor. *A Noble Death: Suicide and Martyrdom among Christians and Jews in Antiquity*. New York: HarperCollins, 1992.

Goldin, S. *The Ways of Jewish Martyrdom*. Turnhout, Belgium: Brepols Publishing, 2008.

N

National Socialism/Nazism

As a political-economic philosophy in the aftermath of Germany's defeat in World War I and the failing Weimar Republic and given public voice through its most articulate spokesperson in Adolf Hitler (1889–1945), National Socialism was already in existence prior to Hitler's leadership. Additionally, although the word *socialism* was part of its presentation and originally designed to attract left-wing radicals and revolutionaries, in reality, it was (and is) much more akin to the fascism of the right and built upon the ideas of Italian dictator Benito Mussolini (1883–1945) but initially fashioned by Russian leader Vladimir Lenin (1870–1924). Summarily, its ideas can be grouped around the following: populist nationalism, antisemitism, racism and racialism (the primacy of racial motivations), eugenics (improvement of the human species according to Aryan fantasy), anti-Communism, anti-liberalism, Social Darwinism (survival of the fittest of the species resulting from evolutionary "natural" selection), and a propensity for violence. Central to its ethos was the concept of the "people's community" (in German, *Volksgemeinschaft*) and its attempt at a pan-Germanism attempting to unite all Germanic peoples—Germans, Austrians, Sudeten Czechs—thus legitimating the necessity of a geographic takeover of other lands and nation-states and the removal/displacement/enslavement/extermination of all non-German peoples (*Lebensraum*).

Already in 1920, the fledging National Socialist German Workers Party (NSDAP, or Nazis, though ironically the word itself was already in use derogatorily for a backward, clumsy farmer or peasant) released its 25-point program, which included the following:

92 | National Socialism/Nazism

1. We demand the unification of all Germans in the Greater Germany based on the right of self-determination of peoples.

2. We demand equality of rights for the German people in respect to the other nations; *abrogation of the peace treaties of Versailles and St. Germain.*

3. We demand land and territory (colonies) for the sustenance of our people, and colonization for our surplus population.

4. Only a member of the race can be a citizen. A member of the race can only be one who is of German blood, without consideration of creed. *Consequently, no Jew can be a member of the race.*

5. Whoever has no citizenship is to be able to live in Germany only as a guest and must be under the authority of legislation for foreigners.

   . . .

6. (8) Any further immigration of non-citizens is to be prevented. We demand that all non-Germans who have immigrated to Germany since 2 August 1914 be forced immediately to leave the Reich.

   . . .

7. (18) We demand struggle without consideration against those whose activity is injurious to the general interest. Common national criminals, usurers, Schieber [black marketeer], and so forth are to be punished with death, without consideration of confession or race.

   . . .

8. (22) We demand abolition of the mercenary troops and formation of a national army.

   . . .

9. (24) We demand freedom of religion for all religious denominations with the state so long as they do not endanger its existence or oppose the moral senses of the Germanic race. The Party as such advocates the standpoint of a positive Christianity without binding itself confessionally to any one denomination. *It combats the Jewish-materialistic spirit within and around us* and is convinced that a lasting recovery of our nation can only succeed from within on the framework: common utility precedes individual utility. (Emphases added)

Economically, National Socialism opposed both capitalism and Communism, seeing both as constructed by Jews to dominate the world's nation-states, and further buttressed by the belief in the "truth" of the notorious antisemitic forgery the *Protocols of the Learned Elders of Zion.* Politically, the Nazis were also committed to a "classless society" and a traditional and largely conservative view of morality and family structures. Thus, men led society, women were responsible for home and children, and homosexuality was contrary to everything for which National Socialism stood. Central to both its economics and its politics was the commitment to a strong central government in the person of its unifying leader Adolf Hitler, who was understood to be the very incarnation of *der Führerprinzip* (the leadership principle) by which everything good came from Hitler and everything bad manifested itself in opposition to Hitler.

Historically speaking, each of the following thinkers contributed their own ideas to what would ultimately result in the National Socialist philosophy: Johann Gottlieb Fichte (1762–1814), the "father" of German nationalism and an antisemite; Georg Ritter von Schönerer (1842–1921), a proponent of pan-Germanism; Karl Lueger (1844–1910), the antisemitic mayor of Vienna; Arthur de Gobineau (1816–1882), a theorist of the "Aryan race"; Houston Stewart Chamberlain (1855–1927), a racist and antisemitic nationalist; Eugen Diederichs (1867–1930), a radical antisemite; Paul de Lagarde (1827–1891), a radical antisemite; Julius Langbehn (1851–1907), a radical antisemite; Wilhelm Stapel (1882–1954), an intellectual antisemite; Hans F. K. Günther (1891–1968), a racial theorist; and Alfred Rosenberg (1893–1946), Hitler's ideological thinkers. Even the theologian and founder of Lutheranism, Martin Luther (1483–1546), was exploited propagandistically, most especially for his notorious antisemitic tract *On the Jews and Their Lies*.

Post–World War II, with the defeat of the Nazis and their allies, one would have thought National Socialism as a philosophy would have fallen into thorough disrepute. However, this has not been the case, as the far-right neo-Nazi-like movement continues to manifest in Europe: for example, Golden Dawn in Greece, Fidesz in Hungary, Alternative für Deutschland (AfD) in Germany, and Front National in France.

In the United States, the most prominent example was the American Nazi Party founded in 1959 by the late George Lincoln Rockwell (1918–1967), a veteran of both World War II and the Korean War, who was assassinated by one of his own members in 1967. His successor, Matt Koehl (1935–2014), was ultimately unable to sustain Rockwell's vision, even changing its name to New Order in 1983. Today (2019), its heirs are now known as the National Socialist Movement (NSM) and under the leadership of Jeff Schoep (b. 1973). Committing itself to the so-called 14 Words—"We must secure the existence of our people and a future for white children"—authored by the late white supremacist David Lane

National Socialism/Nazism

(1938–2007), NSM has issued its own "25 Points of American National Socialism," which include the following:

1. We demand the union of all Whites on the basis of the right of national self-determination.
2. We demand equality of rights for the American people in its dealings with other nations, and the revocation of the United Nations, the North Atlantic Treaty Organization, the World Bank, the North American Free Trade Agreement, and the International Monetary Fund.
3. Only members of the nation may be citizens of the state. Only those of pure White blood, whatever their creed, may be members of the nation. Non-citizens may live in America only as guests and must be subject to laws for aliens. *Accordingly, no Jew or homosexual may be a member of the nation.*
   . . .
4. (7) All Non-White immigration must be prevented. We demand that all non-Whites currently residing in America illegally be required to leave the nation forthwith and return to their land of origin.
   . . .
5. (17) We demand the ruthless prosecution of those whose activities are injurious to the common interest. Murderers, rapists, pedophiles, drug dealers, usurers, profiteers, race traitors, etc. must be severely punished, whatever their creed or race by all legal means available.
   . . .
6. (24) We demand absolute religious freedom for all denominations in the State, provided they do not threaten its existence nor offend the moral feelings of the White race. *The Party combats the Jewish-materialistic spirit within and without us* and is convinced that our nation can achieve permanent health only from within on the basis of the principle: **The common good before self-interest.** (Bold in original; italic emphases added) (https://sourcebooks.fordham.edu/mod/25points.asp)

See also: Fascism; Holocaust; Nationalism; Social Darwinism; Yockey, Francis Parker

Further Reading

Bracher, Karl. *The German Dictatorship.* Translated by Jean Steinberg. New York: Penguin Books, 1970.

Evans, Richard J. *The Coming of the Third Reich.* New York: Penguin Books, 2003.

Evans, Richard J. *The Third Reich at War.* New York: Penguin Books, 2008.

Evans, Richard J. *The Third Reich in Power*. New York: Penguin Books, 2005.

Fordham University. "Modern History Sourcebook: The 25 Points 1920: An Early Nazi Program." https://sourcebooks.fordham.edu/mod/25points.asp

Kaplan, Jeffrey, ed. *Encyclopedia of White Power: A Sourcebook on the Radical Right*. Walnut Creek, CA: AltaMira Press, 2000.

Paxton, Robert. *The Anatomy of Fascism*. New York: Penguin Books, 2005.

Simonelli, Frederick J. *American Fuehrer: George Lincoln Rockwell and the American Nazi Party*. Urbana: University of Illinois Press, 1999.

Nationalism

In theory, at least, nationalism is the positive commitment on the part of the citizenry of a nation-state—both native-born and naturalized through a legal process—to commit themselves to supporting the established form of government and defending the nation-state as well. Although scholars will continue to debate its origins, the consensus is that this concept arose during the eighteenth century in Western Europe and possibly earlier in other locales. Thus, definitionally, there is nothing inherently negative about either the expectations of governmental leadership or the responsibilities of followership.

However, turning to the dark side, over the last several centuries, various nation-states have either chosen to exclude certain subgroups from citizenship (depriving those who are already citizens or inhibiting others from achieving it) or redefined it based on such nebulous categories as race, religion, or ethnicity (i.e., ethnic nationalism or ethnonationalism). An additional term worth mentioning in this context is that of "right-wing populism," in which a smaller cadre of often self-designated leaders, in vocal opposition to the established government, attack and critique those in power and supposedly speak for and represent "the will of the people." Here, too, there is a history of exclusionary rhetoric whereby some loosely defined "others" are not seen and understood as part of the majority and thus deprived of their own voices in the political process. Taken to not necessarily logical conclusions, such deprivations of citizenship have resulted in overwhelming violence up to and including genocide.

In modern times, the most dramatic example of the deprivation of citizenship is that of Nazi Germany vis-à-vis its Jewish citizens. Emblematic

96 | Nationalism

of a whole host of Nazi declarations under the general rubric of the Nuremberg Laws of September 15, 1935, encompassing both specific and general decrees, the following are reflective of excluding Jews from citizenship along the route from initial immigration to ultimate annihilation and extermination:

1. The Law for the Protection of German Blood and Honor begins, "Moved by the understanding that purity of German blood [in a literal not metaphorical sense] is the essential condition for the continued existence of the German people and inspired by the inflexible determination to ensure the existence of the German nation for all time, the Reichstag [German Parliament] unanimously adopted the following law, which is promulgated herewith." Its seven articles (1) forbade marriages between Jews and Germans; (2) forbade extramarital relations between Jews and Germans; (3) forbade Jews from employing German female help under age 45; (4) forbade Jews from displaying German flags and access to German courts; (5) punished violations with either prison terms or hard labor; (6) had specific regulation coordinated by the minister of the interior, deputy of the führer, and minister of justice; and (7) took effect on September 16, 1935, except for Article 3, which took effect on January 1, 1936.
2. The Reich Citizenship Law specifies that (1) Reich citizens have obligations under law, (2) Reich citizens are accorded full rights, and (3) its administration is the coordinated responsibility of the minister of the interior and the deputy of the führer.

It should also be noted that as the German war and political machines proved increasingly successful, other nation-states within the German orbit passed their own variations on these laws and thus deprived their own Jews of citizenship rights in those countries as well: Italy (1938), Hungary (1938, 1939, 1941), Romania (1940), Slovakia (1941), Bulgaria (1941), and Croatia (1941). Although not within that Nazi orbit, it must also be noted that, historically, both Britain and France also had a long history of discrimination against their Jewish citizens but proved continually reluctant to pass such transparently antisemitic laws, though Vichy France would do so in 1940 and 1941 and Britain would institute various legal obstacles throughout the war to forestall mass immigration of Jewish refugees to pre-state Israel (Palestine) as well.

Turning to the United States, it also engaged in various roadblocks through its State Department to curtail refugee immigration throughout World War II. American history as well finds the original thirteen colonies passing discriminatory laws against Jews, especially when it came to holding office (Jews were "non-Christians"), with Maryland becoming the last state to grant Jews full citizenship rights in 1826, fifty years after the American Revolution and founding of the country. While other subgroups have faced continuous legal discriminations—African Americans, Japanese Americans, Hispanic Americans—Jews have successfully integrated and assimilated themselves into the American fabric, and, at the present time, one would be hard put to find antisemitic laws still in force in the United States.

However, beginning in 2016, dissident voices within this country have become increasingly vocal in their strident opposition to immigrants from both Central and South America; some of them have turned violent and, in online rants, declarations, and manifestos, have seen Jews as the behind-the-scenes orchestrators and puppeteers of this immigration. In the latter half of the twentieth century, some politically far-to-the-right-of-center groups have even gone so far as to call for secession from the United States, which they fully believe is controlled by a Zionist occupation government (ZOG) in the grip of the Israelis. One such group, the Aryan Nations, attempted to segregate itself in the Hayden Lakes, Idaho, area and turned militantly violent, taking to robbing banks and murdering those with whom they did not agree, including Jews and blacks. Much of the rhetoric and publications of these groups was and remains rife with antisemitic pronouncements, conspiracy theories, Holocaust denialism, and hate-filled attacks on the State of Israel. Jews are also condemned by these groups as being "globalists" with an agenda of world takeover and reminiscent of the notorious antisemitism forgery the *Protocols of the Learned Elders of Zion.*

Finally, and ever so briefly, the various nation-states of the Middle East, many of which came into being in the aftermath of World War I, despite their own histories (Iran, Iraq, Jordan, Saudi Arabia), view their own historical Jewish constituencies as aliens to be subjugated or forced to flee, which many of them did after the creation of the reborn State of Israel in May 1948. Collectively, though it has never taken full hold, the concept of Pan-Arabism in the nineteenth and twentieth centuries and now in somewhat of a serious decline, encompassing *Dar al-Islam* (the world of Islam) in opposition to *Dar al-Harb* (the world of War), viewed and views Israel as an intrusion or, worse, a nation-state imposed upon its geography and region by an imperialist West as guilt payment for its collective failure to save its own Jews during the Holocaust.

98 | Nationalism

Thus, we may conclude that it is not nationalism per se that is at the root of this antisemitic turn, but, rather, it is antisemitism that causes some committed to nation-state loyalty to regard Jews as aliens or foreigners within their midst who can never be full citizens and thus must be excluded from any legal protections whatsoever.

See also: Christian Identity; Fascism; Holocaust; National Socialism/Nazism; Social Darwinism; Spanish Inquisition; White Supremacy

Further Reading

Burleigh, Michael, and Wolfgang Wipperman. *The Racial State: Germany 1933–1945*. Cambridge, UK, and New York: Cambridge University Press, 1991.

Gellately, Robert. *The Gestapo and German Society: Enforcing Racial Policy, 1933–1945*. Oxford: Clarendon Press, 1991.

Goldwag, Arthur. *The New Hate: A History of Fear and Loathing on the Populist Right*. New York: Pantheon, 2012.

Karsh, Efraim. *Islamic Imperialism: A History*. New Haven, CT, and London: Yale University Press, 2006.

Khalidi, Rashid. *The Rise of Arab Nationalism*. New York: Columbia University Press, 1993.

Majer, Diemut. *"Non-Germans" under the Third Reich*. Baltimore, MD, and London: Johns Hopkins University Press, 2003.

Schleunes, Karl. *The Twisted Road to Auschwitz: Nazi Policy towards German Jews, 1933–1939*. Urbana: University of Illinois Press, 1970.

Oberammergau Passion Play

Definitionally, passion plays are dramatic stage attempts to tell the story of the birth, death, and resurrection of the Christ (Jesus) as depicted in the various Gospel accounts of Matthew, Mark, Luke, and John and are oftentimes, but not necessarily, associated with the celebrations of both Easter, primarily, and Christmas, secondarily. Such plays have been and are today produced all over the world. The oldest of such depictions is that of the mountain village of Oberammergau, Bavaria, which began in 1634 and has been performed every decade since in years ending in zero. The play itself resulted from a collective commitment of the original villagers as a celebration of their faith in God after having been spared from the ravages of the bubonic plague in 1633. The play has only been cancelled twice: in 1770, at the order of the elector Maximillian Joseph (1770–1825), and in 1940, because of World War II. It was also postponed once, from 1920 to 1922, due to World War I.

The play is a quite lengthy outdoor production of several hours that involves almost the entire membership of the village. It is composed of a prelude and the following sixteen acts or tableaux scenes, replete with costuming and musical expressions:

- Jesus and the Money Changers
- Conspiracy of the High Council
- Parting at Bethany
- The Last Journey to Jerusalem
- The Last Supper
- The Betrayer
- Jesus at the Mount of Olives
- Jesus before Annas

Oberammergau Passion Play

- Condemned by the High Council
- Despair of Judas
- Christ before Pilate
- Christ before Herod
- Christ Sentenced to Death on the Cross
- The Way of the Cross
- Jesus on Calvary
- Resurrection and Apotheosis

From the outset until 2000, the play continued to depict the Jews as villainous and responsible for the death of the Christ; one of the highlights was the courtyard scene, where the Jews, following Matthew 27:25, respond to Pilate's "washing of his hands" regarding the fate of Jesus with the collective cry, "His blood be upon us and upon our children." During the Nazi era, Adolf Hitler (1889–1945) saw the production as being consistent with the Nazi ideology of the Jews as eternal enemies of Western civilization, though he had little use for Christianity itself.

With the end of World War II and the revelations of the Holocaust, the play—still mired in its historic antisemitism of Jewish perfidy and deicide—slowly began to undergo changes to its scripts. Since 2000 and again in 2010, among those incremental changes are the following:

- The priests' costuming no longer includes horn-shaped hats, thus likening them (and the Jews) with the Devil.
- Jesus, on several occasions, is addressed as "Rabbi."
- Fragments of prayers *in Hebrew* are inserted in several places.
- Pontius Pilate, the Roman procurator, is now portrayed as more villainous.
- The text of Matthew 27:25 (see above) has been removed.
- Jesus recites the wine blessing at the Last Supper in Hebrew.

The next production of the Oberammergau Passion Play is scheduled for 2020. Given its long history of antisemitic characterizations of Jews and having only twice attempted to ameliorate those depictions, whether its positive redirection in telling its story will continue remains an open question.

Finally, it should also be noted and addressed that Hollywood actor Mel Gibson's (b. 1956) 2004 movie *The Passion of the Christ* was seen, reviewed, and understood by many—clergy, laity, and scholars—as continuing the antisemitic portrayal of Jews long associated throughout history with such dramatic productions.

See also: *Adversus Judaeos*; Blood Libel; Crusades; Deicide; Luther, Martin; Martyrdom, Sanctifying the Name of God; Spanish Inquisition; Usury

Further Reading

Friedman, Saul S. *The Oberammergau Passion Play: A Lance against Civilization.* Carbondale: Southern Illinois University Press, 1984.

Shapiro, James. *Oberammergau: The Troubling Story of the World's Most Famous Passion Play.* New York: Pantheon, 2000.

Waddy, Helena. *Oberammergau in the Nazi Era: The Fate of a Catholic Village in Hitler's Germany.* New York and Oxford: Oxford University Press, 2010.

P

Pierce, William Luther

At the time of his death, William Luther Pierce (1933–2002) was the most "successful" white nationalist, racist, neo-Nazi (a term he rejected), and antisemite in the United States, largely as a result of his business acumen and organizational skills with a database of more than twenty-five hundred members regularly paying dues to the National Alliance; a publishing company, National Vanguard Books; and a record label, Resistance Records. All told, Pierce's combined revenues were more than $2,000,000 annually. After his death, however, his two primary successors, Eric Gliebe (b. 1963) and Kenneth Alfred Strom (b. 1956), were unable to keep his enterprise significantly afloat, and by the turn of the twenty-first century, it continues to be a relatively minor player on the hate scene. Pierce is also well known for his two novels, *The Turner Diaries* (1978) and *Hunter* (1989), both under the pseudonym Andrew MacDonald and published by National Vanguard Books; both books remain required reading in hate circles.

Pierce was born in Atlanta, Georgia, and he maintained that he was a direct descendant of Thomas H. Watts (1819–1892), the governor of Alabama (1863–1865) and the attorney general of the Confederate States of America, on his mother's side. He received his BA from Rice University and his MSc and PhD in physics from the University of Colorado at Boulder, and for three years (1962–1965), he was an assistant professor at Oregon State University. He left the university in 1965 and joined the aerospace firm of Pratt & Whitney in Connecticut and became increasingly involved with George Lincoln Rockwell (1918–1967) and his American Nazi Party, moving to Washington, DC, in 1966. By that time, Pierce was convinced that Jews were behind both the Vietnam War and the African American civil rights movement. (He had briefly joined the

Pierce, William Luther | 103

far-right John Birch Society but left because he felt that they were not addressing either "the Jewish question" or "the Black question" enough.)

In 1968, Pierce cofounded the National Youth Alliance (NYA)—originally called Youth for Wallace—with the antisemitic Holocaust denialist Willis Carto (1926–2015). The two split rather nastily while both were working on Alabama governor George Wallace's (1919–1998) unsuccessful presidential campaign. Pierce took the NYA's mailing list with him but began broadening its base, creating the adult organization National Alliance in 1974. On Pierce's board of directors was Professor Revilo P. Oliver (1908–1994), a professor at the University of Illinois at Urbana-Champaign, a far-right conservative and white nationalist who would remain an adviser and lifelong friend.

Under Pierce's guidance, the National Alliance advocated white supremacy, racial cleansing of inferior peoples, eugenics, overthrowing the federal government, Holocaust denialism, antisemitism, and anti-Zionism. In 1985, Pierced purchased a large farm outside of Mill Point/ Hillsboro, West Virginia, for $95,000 to center his growing organization and attempted to convince the Internal Revenue Service (IRS) that it was a religious organizational home for his created religion, "cosmotheism," a variation of the concept of panentheism, the belief that the divine pervades and interpenetrates every part of the universe and also extends beyond space and time, along with elements of German Romanticism and Darwin's theory of natural selection and the survival of the fittest. (For Pierce, that meant the white race.) The IRS rejected his full claim but granted him religious exemptions for 60 acres out of his compound of 346 acres for his "Cosmotheist Community Church."

Pierce's first novel, *The Turner Diaries*, which has been called the "bible of the racist right" by the Southern Poverty Law Center (SPLC), was, according to Pierce himself, a "blueprint and handbook for a white victory." The novel tells the story of a race war against blacks, Jews, and gays in consistently and graphically violent descriptions through the diary entries of Earl Turner, a member of "the Organization." The entries cover the period September 21, 1991–November 9, 1993, when Turner supposedly died. (According to its second edition, more than 350,000 copies were printed, and the book remains available in English, German, and Polish editions.)

Perversely, *The Turner Diaries* proved an inspiration for two rather dramatic and violent undertakings. In April 1995, Timothy McVeigh (1968–2001, executed), a former soldier, and Terry Nichols (b. 1955;

Pierce, William Luther

serving life imprisonment) bombed the Alfred P. Murrah Federal Building in Oklahoma City, Oklahoma, murdering 168 people, including children. Pages of *The Turner Diaries* were found in McVeigh's car, and he admitted sending copies to friends and selling them at various gun shows throughout the United States. Eerily, the bombing sounds remarkably like the one described in the book.

In the early 1980s, a group of radical revolutionaries led by Robert Jay Matthews (1953–1984), who later died in a shootout with the FBI, and David Lane (1938–2007) founded the white supremacist antisemitic terrorist group "the Order" and acknowledged their inspiration was the Organization modeled in *The Turner Diaries*. The Order engaged in armed robbery, racketeering, conspiracy, and murder, the most prominent example being that of the Denver, Colorado, talk show host Alan Berg, who was gunned down in 1984.

Following up on the supposed "success" of *The Turner Diaries*, in 1989, Pierce released *Hunter*, which tells the story of Oscar Yeager, a Vietnam veteran, who goes on a murder spree, killing interracial couples, liberals, journalists, politicians, and bureaucrats in the Washington, DC, area. *Hunter* was dedicated to white supremacist and serial killer Joseph Paul Franklin (1950–2013, executed).

Pierce died of cancer in his compound in 2002.

See also: Barnes, Harry Elmer; Carto, Willis; Christian Identity; Duke, David; Faurisson, Robert; Holocaust, Denial of; Icke, David; Irving, David; Ku Klux Klan; National Socialism/Nazism; Rassinier, Paul; Rockwell, George Lincoln; White Supremacy; World Church of the Creator; Yockey, Francis Parker

Further Reading

Connor, Claire. *Wrapped in the Flag: A Personal History of America's Radical Right*. Boston: Beacon Press, 2013.

Gardell, Mattias. *Gods of the Blood: The Pagan Revival and White Separatism*. Durham, NC: Duke University Press, 2003.

Hall, Davis, Tym Burkey, and Katherine Ramsland. *Into the Devil's Den*. New York: Ballantine Books, 2008.

Hilliard, Robert R., and Michael C. Keith. *Waves of Rancor: Turning to the Radical Right*. New York: M. E. Sharpe, 1999.

Morris, Travis. *Dark Ideas: How Neo-Nazi and Violent Jihad Ideologues Shaped Modern Terrorism*. Lanham, MD: Lexington Books, 2017.

Quarles, Chester A. *The Ku Klux Klan and Related American Racialist and Antisemitic Organizations*. Jefferson, NC: McFarland, 1999.

Swain, Carol M., and Russ Nieli. *Contemporary Voices of White Nationalism in America*. Cambridge, UK: Cambridge University Press, 2003.

Pius XII, Pope

Pope Pius XII (born Eugenio Pacelli, 1876–1958; pontificate 1939–1958) remains the most controversial pope in modern history, largely because of his philo-German orientation and his lack of publicly condemning the Nazi regime of Adolf Hitler (1889–1945) for its murderous treatment of Jews in the Holocaust. Born into a politically and religiously conservative Roman Catholic family, where both his father and grandfather played significant roles in the Curia, or Catholic bureaucracy, Pius saw his primary task as pope to save and preserve the institution of the church during World War II. Experiencing firsthand the excesses of Communist insurgents in Germany in the aftermath of World War I during his period of service there, he made the decision that, ultimately, National Socialism—despite its excesses, up to and including violence against its own citizens as well as those in conquered nation-states—was preferable to Communism. In addition, his conservative theological training and orientation, building upon two thousand years of contempt for Jews as a deicide people primarily responsible for the death of the Christ during the period of Roman oppression in Palestine in the first century, are factors in his silence that cannot be easily dismissed.

In 1917, in the aftermath of World War I, Pope Benedict XV (1854–1922) appointed Pacelli as the papal nuncio (ambassador) to the German state of Bavaria and three years later, in 1920, as the papal nuncio to the newly formed Weimar Republic. With both appointments, he was to secure a concordat, or agreement, that preserved the church's freedom to act and whatever privileges he had already secured. Although successful with the Bavarian government in 1924 and Prussia in 1929, he was unsuccessful with the Weimar government. He would, however, follow these up with Baden in 1932, Austria in 1933, and Nazi Germany that same year. This latter agreement would prove controversial, as it undermined and

106 | Pius XII, Pope

diminished whatever political influence the Catholic Center Party (*Deutsche Zentrumspartei*) could and would exercise under both the Weimar government and its successor Nazi government.

Between 1935 and 1937, Pacelli helped draft Pope Pius XI's (1857–1939; pontificate 1922–1939) encyclical *Mit brenender Sorge* ("With Burning Anxiety") in the aftermath of the infamous Nazi racial laws of that year. In his capacity as Vatican secretary of state, he did file protests with Nazi Germany over its actions more than fifty times. With the sudden death of his processor, Pius XI's encyclical *Humani generis unitas* ("The Unity of the Human Race"), which condemned both racism and antisemitism, was shelved and never saw the light of day during Pius XII's pontificate.

Pope Pius II's first encyclical, *Summi pontificatus* ("On the Limitations of the Authority of the State" and subtitled "On the Unity of Human Society"), in 1939, as the drums of war were sounding loudly one month after Germany invaded Poland on September 1, maintained that the church would place itself above the increasing conflicts, which some saw as indirectly supporting Germany's efforts. (Somewhat ironically, the Nazi government was the only one not to send a representative to his coronation on March 2, 1939.) However, in 1942, as the staggering plight of refugees increased, Pius XII established the Vatican Information Service to keep him informed of their plight, and he maintained a secret rescue conduit for many, though actual figures of those saved are in dispute, from several hundred to several thousand. Some have even gone so far as to argue that these efforts in this period of heightened antisemitism were too little too late.

Post–World War II, Pius did not hesitate to condemn Soviet Russia as opportunities presented themselves. However, in somewhat more complicated situations, he signed concordats with Spanish dictator Francisco Franco (1892–1975) in 1953 and the Dominican Republic's dictator Rafael Trujillo (1891–1961) in 1954, and he excommunicated Argentinean dictator Juan Peron (1805–1974) in 1955.

In 1960, Israel's consul in Italy, Pinchas Lapide (1922–1997), and her first and only woman prime minister, Golda Meir (1898–1978), both publicly praised Pius for his efforts during World War II. However, some have argued that they did so out of political necessity. In another still shocking event, the chief rabbi of Rome from 1940 to 1945, Israel Zolli (1881–1956), took refuge in the Vatican in 1942, and after the war, he converted to Catholicism and took the name Eugenio in honor of his benefactor.

Because of the controversy surrounding Pope Pius II, including the failure of the Vatican to fully open his and its archives during this war period—though Pope Francis (b. 1936; pontificate 2013–present) has said they will be fully opened in 2020—the church's commitment to having him canonized for sainthood remains on hold. A preliminary 1999 report by a Jewish-Catholic scholarly consortium entitled "The Vatican and the Holocaust" refuted the claim that Pius and the Vatican knew far too little about what was happening to the Jews; that his and its commitment to neutrality was not always observed; and that, during the war itself, as a supposed life-saving measure, he had Jewish babies baptized as Roman Catholics—and that they were not to be returned to their surviving parents. Those who continue to advocate on his behalf argue that difficult though his evident silence was in condemning Nazi antisemitism, he did so for the following reasons: (1) a genuine fear that public condemnation would only make the plight of the Jews worse and a better course of action was working behind the scenes with private and quiet diplomacy, (2) concern that such condemnation would provoke a schism on the part of Germany's Roman Catholics, (3) a commitment to political neutrality as a necessity, and (4) his and his church's position as a bulwark against Communism after World War II.

See also: *Adversus Judaeos*; Blood Libel; Crusades; Deicide; Fascism; Holocaust; National Socialism/Nazism; Nationalism; Oberammergau Passion Play; Spanish Inquisition; Usury

Further Reading

Cornwell, John. *Hitler's Pope: The Secret History of Pius XII*. New York: Penguin Books, 1999.

Dalin, David. *The Myth of Hitler's Pope: Pope Pius XII and His Secret War against Nazi Germany*. Washington, DC: Regnery, 2005.

Falconi, Carlo. *The Silence of Pius XII*. New York: Little Brown and Company, 1970.

Friedlander, Saul. *Pius XII and the Third Reich: A Documentation*. New York: Alfred A. Knopf, 1966.

Goldhagen, Daniel Jonah. *A Moral Reckoning: The Role of the Church in the Holocaust and Its Unfulfilled Duty of Repair*. New York: Alfred A. Knopf, 2002.

Kertzer, David I. *Unholy War: The Vatican's Role in the Rise of Modern Antisemitism*. New York: Macmillan, 2002.

Lewy, Guenter. *The Catholic Church and Nazi Germany*. New York: McGraw-Hill, 1964.

108 | *Protocols of the Learned Elders of Zion*

Passelecq, Georges, and Bernard Suchecky. *The Hidden Encyclical of Pius XI*. New York: Harcourt Brace Jovanovich, 1998.

Phayer, Michael. *The Catholic Church and the Holocaust, 1930–1945*. Bloomington: Indiana University Press, 2000.

Phayer, Michael. *Pius XII, the Holocaust, and the Cold War*. Bloomington: Indiana University Press, 2008.

Sanchez, Jose M. *Pius XII and the Holocaust: Understanding the Controversy*. Washington, DC: Catholic University of America Press, 2002.

Zuccotti, Susan. *Under His Very Windows: The Vatican and the Holocaust in Italy*. New Haven, CT, and London: Yale University Press, 2000.

*Protocols of the Learned Elders of Zion**

As perhaps the world's most "successful" and notorious forgery, the *Protocols of the Learned Elders of Zion* supposedly describes a secret midnight cabal in an undisclosed Jewish cemetery somewhere in Europe, likely Prague, Czechoslovakia. In this alleged gathering, the chief rabbi informs his fellow rabbis of the "master plan" to subjugate the Gentile world under Jewish monarchical hegemony and the twenty-four protocols that will enable them to do so (e.g., subverting the morals of Gentiles, exercising economic and journalistic controls, destroying the religious basis of civilization, destroying the political and constitutional foundations of the various nation-states, and the like, which all leads to the eventual coronation of a king in Jerusalem, a descendant of the Davidic line, to rule the world).

In the main, scholars have concluded that the original text upon which the *Protocols* was based was French lawyer Maurice Joly's (1829–1878) 1864 satiric book, *Dialogue aux enfers entre Machiavel et Montesquieu ou la politique de Machiavel au XIXe siècle* (*Dialogue in Hell between Machiavelli and Montesquieu*), about the French government under Louis-Napoleon Bonaparte (1808–1873), of whom Joly was a staunch opponent and severe critic. Additionally, a chapter of the 1868 novel *Der Schmuggler von Biarritz* (*The Smuggler of Biarritz*) by German novelist Hermann Goedsche (1815–1878), writing under the pseudonym Sir John Retcliffe,

---

* This entry appears in a somewhat different form in Michael Jerryson, ed., *Religious Violence Today: Faith in Conflict in the Modern World* (Santa Barbara, CA: ABC-CLIO, 2020).

Protocols of the Learned Elders of Zion | 109

is also said to have contributed by providing the geographic locale for this supposed meeting and the actual "speech" of the rabbi. Both texts, not surprisingly given the climate in Europe at the end of the nineteenth century, with conspirators and agents provocateur everywhere, found their way to the attention of the Okrana, the Russian secret police, and later became publicly available in *The Great within the Small: The Coming of the Anti-Christ and the Rule of Satan on Earth* by the dissident and later disgraced Russian Orthodox priest Sergei Nilus (1862–1929) in 1905. From these strange and perverse beginnings, the text as a stand-alone document has traveled the world.

Translated into any number of languages, including English and Arabic, the *Protocols* were already discredited in 1921 by reporter Phillip Graves in the *Times of London* in three lengthy articles (August 16, 17, and 18) and later republished in booklet form under the title "The Truth about 'The Protocols': A Literary Forgery." The document itself would also be put on trial as a hate text in Berne, Switzerland, in 1934–1935, where the chief presiding judge termed the *Protocols* "ridiculous nonsense" and also found them to be a forgery. Its most notorious English-language publication, however, appeared in the Henry Ford–owned newspaper the *Dearborn Independent*, originally serialized in 1920–1922, and later published separately as *The International Jew: The World's Foremost Problem* with a press run of five hundred thousand copies, which were distributed to Ford automobile dealerships throughout the United States (for which Ford, under coercion, later apologized and withdrew its publication).

Adolf Hitler (1889–1945) also included a reference to the authenticity of the *Protocols* in his political autobiography/testament *Mein Kampf*:

> To what extent the whole existence of this people is based on continuous lies is shown incomparably by the *Protocols of the Wise Men of Zion*, so infinitely hated by the Jews. They are based on a forgery, the *Franfurter Zeitung* moans and screams once every week: the best proof that they are authentic. What many Jews may do unconsciously is here consciously exposed. . . . Anyone who examines the historical development of the last hundred years from the standpoint of this book will at once understand the screaming of the Jewish press. For once this book becomes the common property of a people, the Jewish menace may be considered as broken. (de Michelis 2004)

Despite its obvious forgery, the *Protocols* remains a staple of the modern antisemitic world and is still available in a variety of languages and on

110 | *Protocols of the Learned Elders of Zion*

the Internet as well. Most perniciously, it is still easily available in bookstores throughout the Arab world and is sometimes referenced; for example, in the 1988 Hamas Charter, it is called "the Zionist blueprint for a world takeover." Also, it is well known that the late king Faisal of Saudi Arabia (1906–1975) used to present visiting dignitaries with leather-bound copies of the *Protocols* during their audiences with him.

See also: Barnes, Harry Elmer; Carto, Willis; Coughlin, Charles E.; Duke, David; Farrakhan, Louis; Faurisson, Robert; Holocaust, Denial of; Irving, David; Pierce, William Luther; Rassinier, Paul; Rockwell, George Lincoln; Social Darwinism

Further Reading

Ben-Itto, Hadassa. *The Lie That Wouldn't Die: One Hundred Years of* The Protocols of the Elders of Zion. London and Portland, OR: Vallentine Mitchell, 2005.

Bernstein, Herman. *The Truth about "The Protocols of Zion."* Hoboken, NJ: KTAV Publishing House, 1971. [Reprint]

Bronner, Stephen Eric. *A Rumor about the Jews: Reflections on Antisemitism and the Protocols of the Learned Elders of Zion.* Oxford and New York: Oxford University Press, 2003.

Cohn, Norman. *Warrant for Genocide: The Myth of the Jewish World Conspiracy and the* Protocols of the Elders of Zion. London: Eyre & Spottiswoode, 1967.

Curtiss, John Shelton. *Appraisal of the Protocols of Zion.* New York: Columbia University Press, 1942.

de Michelis, Ceasare G. *The Non-Existent Manuscript: A Study of the Protocols of the Sages of Zion.* Lincoln and London: University of Nebraska Press, 2004.

Eisner, Will. *The Plot: The Secret Story of the Protocols of the Elders of Zion.* New York: W. W. Norton & Company, 2005.

Gwyer, John. *Portraits of Mean Men: A Short History of the Protocols of the Elders of Zion.* London: Cobden-Sanderson, 1938.

Hitler, Adolf. *Mein Kampf.* New York: Houghton Mifflin, 1969, pp. 293–294.

Jacobs, Steven L., and Mark Weitzman. *Dismantling the Big Lie: The Protocols of the Elders of Zion.* Jersey City, NJ: KTAV Publishing House, 2003.

Joly, Maurice. *The Dialogue in Hell between Machiavelli and Montesquieu: Humanitarian Despotism and the Condition of Modern Tyranny.* Translated by John S. Waggoner. Lanham, MD: Lexington Books, 2003.

Landes, Richard, and Steven Katz, eds. *Paranoid Apocalypse: A Hundred-Year Retrospective on "The Protocols of the Elders of Zion."* New York: New York University Press, 2012.

Larsson, Goran. *Fact or Fraud?* The Protocols of the Elders of Zion. Jerusalem: AMI-Jerusalem Center for Biblical Studies and Research, 1995.

Segal, Benjamin W. *A Lie and a Libel: The History of the Protocols of the Elders of Zion.* Translated by Richard S. Levy. Lincoln and London: University of Nebraska Press, 1996.

Wolf, Lucien. *The Myth of the Jewish Menace in World Affairs: The Protocols of the Learned Elders of Zion.* Calgary, AB: Theophania Publishing, 2011. [Reprint]

Proud Boys

The Proud Boys—whose name was taken from a song in the 1992 Disney film *Aladdin* that was cut before the final release but brought back in the stage adaptation in 2011 and since become something of an anthem—is, as of this writing (2019), perhaps the newest iteration of a hate group that is racist, misogynistic, and antisemitic and that advocates both political and physical violence against leftists as the solution to the problems affecting society. It is also a far-right group, rather than alt-right, and most assuredly neo-Nazi. Its founder has suggested that the Proud Boys can best be described as "new right."

Proud Boys was founded in the United States in 2016 by Canadian ex-patriate Gavin McInnes (b. 1970), who was born in England and is the cofounder of both Vice Media and *Vice Magazine* in 1994 and a regular contributor to racist right-wing hate sites. Although he has presently taken great pains to distance himself from the organization's day-to-day affairs and leadership, McInnes remains its mentoring figurehead. Its present leader is Enrique Tarrio.

McInnes's views, and thus those of the Proud Boys, may be summarized as follows: (1) the superiority of Western culture; (2) advocating violence; (3) white supremacy, white nationalism, and racism, arguing that blacks, Palestinians, Asians—all nonwhites—as well as Jews are inferior beings intent on white genocide; (4) antisemitism, Holocaust denialism, and anti-Zionism; (5) Islamophobia; (6) anti-immigrant; and (7) anti-feminism, the inherent inferiority of women as lazy and less ambitious and the superiority of men. Perversely, it has a women's

112 | Proud Boys

auxiliary called Proud Boys' Girls that shares its ideology. At present, there are small chapters of the Proud Boys in Canada, Australia, and Great Britain, and the overall U.S. membership is estimated at fewer than six thousand males.

In 2018, McInnes was banned from Twitter, Facebook, and Instagram for his racist and violent views. In 2019, he filed a lawsuit against the Southern Poverty Law Center (SPLC), challenging its depiction of Proud Boys as a hate group and the damage to his personal reputation. In turn, the SPLC has filed a motion asking that the lawsuit be dismissed by the court as frivolous. Both McInnes and the SPLC are still awaiting a judge's ruling as of the fall of 2019.

The initiation process into the Proud Boys is fourfold: (1) taking a loyalty oath: "I'm a proud Western chauvinist, and I refuse to apologize for creating the modern world"; (2) getting punched while espousing its views and yelling out the names of five breakfast cereals to demonstrate physical control; (3) getting a Proud Boys tattoo and agreeing not to masturbate (indicating a lack of self-control and overinterest in women and sex); and (4) getting into a major physical confrontation or altercation and possibly getting arrested. In some of their gatherings, members shout the world "Uhuru," which is Swahili for "freedom."

In 2017 and 2018, Proud Boys was involved in major confrontations in Berkeley, California; Chicago, Illinois; Islamberg, New York; Portland, Oregon; and Halifax, Nova Scotia. Members also participated in the August 2017 Unite the Right rally in Charlottesville, Virginia, which turned violent and resulted in the death of Heather Heyer (1985–2017); nineteen anti-right protestors were also wounded. Roger Stone (b. 1952), an American Republican political consultant, lobbyist, strategist, and unofficial adviser to President Donald J. Trump (b. 1946), who is presently under arrest and indictment for witness tampering, obstruction of justice, and lying to federal officials, has regularly used members of the Proud Boys as his personal bodyguards, though he has repeatedly denied membership in the organization. In 2017, Kyle Chapman, who has an extensive criminal history, formed a paramilitary subset of the Proud Boys that he has called the Fraternal Order of the Alt-Knights (FOAK) with attorney, neo-Nazi, and white nationalist Augustus Sol Invictus (b. Austin Gillespie, 1983) as his second-in-command, though they parted company shortly thereafter.

The ten points of the Proud Boys politics are (1) abolish prisons, (2) give everyone a gun, (3) legalize drugs, (4) end welfare, (5) close the borders, (6) outlaw censorship, (7) venerate the housewife, (8) glorify the entrepreneur, (9) recognize that the West is best, and (10) shut down the government.

Finally, specifically in regard to the issue and concern of antisemitism, McInnes has posted a video of himself giving the infamous Nazi salute and uttering the words "Heil Hitler" and another one entitled "Ten Things I Hate about Jews," which he later retitled "Ten Things I Hate about Israel." He has also referenced books by the academic psychologist, racist, and antisemite Kevin MacDonald (b. 1944) of California State University Long Beach and of white supremacist and white nationalist David Duke of KKK infamy (b. 1950) of Louisiana. As noted above, McInnes continues to be regarded as the inspirational figurehead of Proud Boys, and thus its espousal of antisemitism, like his own racism and misogynism, remains central to its members' overall orientation to society, the ills that must be corrected by violence as they understand them, and their own self-perceptions.

See also: Duke, David; Holocaust, Denial of; Pierce, William Luther; *Protocols of the Learned Elders of Zion*; Rockwell, George Lincoln; Social Darwinism; White Supremacy

Further Reading

(*Note:* Because of the relative newness of Proud Boys, there is yet no serious book-length academic or other study of the organization or its founder Gavin McInnes. Most of the material found about the organization and its activities, as well as those of McInnes and others, including Roger Stone, are confined to newspaper reporting of specific events, interviews, etc. No serious journal articles or analyses have yet to appear. See, however, the annotated bibliography regarding other similar organizations—e.g., the American Nazi Party, Christian Identity, the KKK, and the National Alliance (William Luther Pierce), all of which share the propensity for violence.)

Skocpol, Theda, and Vanessa Williamson. *The Tea Party and the Remaking of Republican Conservatism*. Oxford and New York: Oxford University Press, 2012.

Q

Qutb, Sayyid

Sayyid Qutb (1906–1966) may rightfully be regarded as the ideological father of both Arab antisemitism and anti-Zionism in the modern era that has been framed by a narrow fundamentalist view of Islam (what some scholars have now labeled *Islamism*). As a consequence, his extensive writings have provided a foundational intellectual pillar to the violent work of the Muslim Brotherhood in Egypt and, later, both Hezbollah in the Arab/Palestinian-Israeli conflict and al-Qaeda in its attacks in various countries, including the United States and Israel.

Qutb was born in a small village in Upper Egypt, where his father was a landowner, political activist, and someone in whose home the Qur'an was regularly recited and discussed. Fascinated by literature, especially poetry, and somewhat a precocious child, Qutb is said to have memorized the entire Qur'an by age ten. As he grew into his teenage years and his literary interests broadened to include both secular and Western authors, he increasingly became a critic of traditional religious education.

Moving to Cairo, he became a teacher in the Ministry of Education after a British-style schooling, and he later became a member of the Ministry itself and an inspector of its schools. He also began his literary career publishing both poetry and literary criticism. However, even in his new role as a government official, his critiques ultimately got him in trouble. As a response, Qutb was sent to the United States in 1948 (the same year Israel became a nation-state) to study its educational methods, and he lived for two years in Greely, Colorado, and attended the Colorado State College of Education (now the University of Northern Colorado), where he acquired a master's degree in education. It was at this point that he turned toward a narrower view of Islam, partially in response to what he perceived as the gross and offensive materialism of Americans; their racism, superficiality, and sports mania; and the freedom of young girls and women, even in the early 1950s, despite his seeming love of Western classical music, Western literature, and Hollywood films.

Upon his return to Egypt in 1950, he wrote critically of the United States in "The America I Have Seen" and joined the Muslim Brotherhood, which had been under the leadership of its founder and fellow teacher Hassan al-Bana (1906–1949), who was assassinated one year earlier. Rather quickly, he became the editor of its weekly newspaper/letter *Al-Ikhwan al-Muslimin* and fast became the chief propagandist, all the while continuing his literary output.

In 1952, the government of Egypt was overthrown by the Free Officers Movement headed by Gamal Abdel Nasser (1918–1970), whom the Muslim Brotherhood had supported despite its secularist affirmations. Prior to the takeover, Nasser met with Qutb in his home, where they discussed political ideas and Islamic understandings. There is reason to believe that Qutb fully expected a position in the new government, possibly as its minister of education. However, Nasser's secularism won out, and he soon concluded that the Muslim Brotherhood and its adherents were a threat to his power. In 1954, the Brotherhood plotted to assassinate Nasser. The plot was discovered, and Qutb and others were jailed. After ten years, Qutb was released from prison, where he had written his two most important works: *In the Shade of the Qur'an*, a multivolume commentary on the Qur'an, and *Milestones*, a manifesto of political Islam.

One year later, in 1965, Qutb was again arrested on charges of plotting to overthrow the government of Nasser and to assassinate him along with several members of the Muslim Brotherhood. On August 29, 1966, Qutb was executed by hanging.

Qutb's views may best be summarized as follows: (1) theologically, all understandings of reality and all authority ultimately come from God through his divine word in the Qur'an, given to the seal of the Prophet Muhammad (571–632); (2) secularism is the very antithesis of faith and commitment and must be destroyed as evil; (3) Islam is a complete way of life, and thus the political structures established by human beings are best constructed through the legal system of government known as Sharia; and, most importantly, (5) the true enemies of Arabs and Islam, including the Prophet Muhammad, historically and as the ultimate evil, are the Jews and the State of Israel (and its primary supporter, the United States, itself guilty of "Crusaderism") in their planned conspiracy to rule the world, as is made clear in his text *Our Struggle against the Jews*, what Professor Emeritus

116 | Qutb, Sayyid

Bassam Tibi (b. 1944) of Germany has termed "the Islamization of Antisemitism"; (6) this struggle/battle against the Jews, the State of Israel, and their allies will ultimately result in a genocidal "cosmic" war of annihilation with Islam victorious and Jews and Judaism thoroughly defeated and vanquished. (Like many before and after Qutb, he draws no distinctions whatsoever between Jews and Zionists, equating them totally as one enemy.)

Because of his many writings, Qutb was both an inspirational source and ideological father to later Islamist movements, noticeably both Hamas and al-Qaeda. In the aftermath of the 9/11 terrorist attack in the United States, which saw the murders of 2,996 people in 2001, the 2004 *9/11 Commission Report*, in chapter 2, "The Foundation of the New Terrorism," states the following:

> Three basic themes emerge from Qutb's writings. First, he claimed that the world was beset with barbarism, licentiousness, and unbelief (a condition he called *jahiliyya,* the religious term for the period of ignorance prior to the revelations given to the Prophet Mohammed). . . . Second, he warned that more people, including Muslims, were attracted to *jahiliyya* and its material comforts than to his view of Islam; *jahiliyya* could therefore triumph over Islam. Third, no middle ground exists in what Qutb conceived as a struggle between God and Satan. (50, 466n12) (National Commission on Terrorist Attacks 2004)

See also: al-Banna, Hassan; al-Husseini, Amin; Martyrdom, Sanctifying the Name of God

Further Reading

Badmas, Lanre Yusuf. *Sayyid Qutb: A Study of His Tafsir*. New York: Other Press, 2009.

Calvert, John. *Islamism: A Documentary and Reference Guide*. Westport, CT: Greenwood Publishing Group, 2007.

Calvert, John. *Sayyid Qutb and the Origins of Radical Islamism*. New York and Oxford: Oxford University Press, 2009.

Herff, Jeffrey. *Nazi Propaganda for the Arab World*. New Haven, CT, and London: Yale University Press, 2010.

Moussali, Ahmad S. *Radical Islamic Fundamentalism: The Ideological and Political Discourse of Sayyid Qutb*. Beirut, Lebanon: American University of Beirut, 1992.

Musallam, Adnan. *From Secularism to Jihad: Sayyid Qutb and the Foundations of Radical Islamism*. Westport, CT: Greenwood Publishing Group, 2005.

National Commission on Terrorist Attacks. *The 9/11 Commission Report Final Report of the National Commission on Terrorist Attacks Upon the United States* (Authorized Edition). New York: W. W. Norton & Co., 2004.

Nettler, Ronald L. *Past Trials & Present Tribulations: A Muslim Fundamentalist's View of the Jews*. New York and London: Pergamon Press, 1987.

Shepard, William. *Sayyid Qutb and Islamic Activism: A Translation and Critical Analysis of Social Justice*. Leiden, Netherlands: E. J. Brill, 1996.

Springer, Devin R., James L. Regens, and David N. Edger. *Islamic Radicalism and Global Jihad*. Washington, DC: Georgetown University Press, 2009.

Toth, James. *Sayyid Qutb: The Life and Legacy of a Radical Islamic Intellectual*. New York and Oxford: Oxford University Press, 2013.

R

Rassinier, Paul

Paul Rassinier (1906–1967), an ardent pacifist and political activist, has rightly been labeled the "father of Holocaust denial"—in French, *négationnisme*—though his path to that title is somewhat convoluted to be sure. Rassinier was a "graduate" of both the Buchenwald and Mittelbau-Dora concentration camps during World War II, resulting from his membership in the French Resistance; therefore, one would think that his evolution to denialism would have been the opposite: upholding the reality of what the Nazis and their allies had done, primarily to the Jews. However, such was not the case. His father, the son of a farmer and a veteran of World War I, was a pacifist, which led to his imprisonment, a lesson his son never forgot.

Early on, Rassinier, already a pacifist as well, turned to Communism in his early teens, and after initially becoming a teacher, he became a professor of history and geography in Belmont, his hometown. In 1927, he served in the French Army in Morocco, where he saw its colonialist brutalities firsthand, reinforcing his commitments both to Communist political activism and pacifism. Five year later, in 1932, he was expelled from the Communist Party for his efforts to entice the French middle class into socialism and Communism. All the while, Rassinier continued his journalistic efforts as war with Germany neared, opposing both the Fascism of Italy and the Nazism of Germany. Once war was declared, he joined the French Resistance and engaged in printing false identity cards and leading efforts to establish an underground network to smuggle resisters, including Allied pilots *and Jews*, to safety in Switzerland. He also cofounded the Resistance newspaper the *Fourth Republic*, condemning both Italy and Germany for starting World War II and the crimes of the Nazis (but also recognizing the damage done to Germany in the aftermath of World War I by the Versailles Treaty of 1919).

In 1943, Rassinier was arrested by the German SD (Security Service) along with his wife and son, who were later released. He, however, was first transported to Germany and then on to Buchenwald and finally Mittelbau-Dora. By that time, he had developed serious kidney ailments as a result of his initial beatings and interrogations, which would remain with him even after his escape in 1945 and return to France in 1946.

After the war, he returned to his teaching but became more and more disturbed by what he regarded as the false and sensationalist accounts of what had transpired in the concentration camps and deportations—neither of which he had personally experienced—as well as the total and single condemnation of Germany alone. His first book, *Crossing the Line: The Human Truth* (1949), recounted his time in Buchenwald and was applauded as a literary success throughout France. His second book, *The Lie of Ulysses: A Glance at the Literature of Concentration Camps* (1950), proved highly controversial, as he attacked any number of published accounts of others' camp experiences. His third book, *Ulysses Betrayed by His Own* (1961), furthered that same theme and was a collection of the speeches he gave after a lecture tour in Germany sponsored by former SS office Karl-Heinz Priester (1913–1960). In those speeches, he also attacked Raul Hilberg's 1961 magisterial *The Destruction of European Jews*, long regarded as a landmark synthesis based on his masterful reading of German documents. His next book, *The True Eichmann Trial or the Incorrigible Victors* (1962; 1965), condemned not only the Israelis for their capture, trial, and execution of Adolf Eichmann (1906–1962) but also the Nuremberg Trials of the International Military Court (1945–1946) and the Frankfurt Auschwitz Trials (1963–1965). At that time, his condemnations blamed the "Zionists" and the Communists as enemies of Europe.

By the time of his 1964 text, *The Drama of European Jews*, Rassinier had convinced himself and had tried publicly to convince others that Nazi Germany had no fixed plan to exterminate much less gas Jews, even at Auschwitz-Birkenau, having "assessed" their deaths at fewer than 1,600,000, writing "never at any moment did the responsible authorities of the Third Reich intend to order, or in fact order, the extermination of the Jews in this or any other manner" (270). One year later, in 1965, he published a defense of Pope Pius XII (1876–1958) entitled *Operation Vicar: The Role of Pius XII before History*, his response to Rolf Hochhuth's (b. 1931) highly controversial play *The Deputy* (in German, *Der Stellvertreter. Ein christliches Trauerspiel*) for its overt condemnation of Pope Pius XII's seeming silence (and complicity?) in the face of

Rockwell, George Lincoln

the Nazi onslaught. In 1967, he also published *Those Responsible for the Second World War*.

In 1977, through the efforts of American Holocaust denier Harry Elmer Barnes (1889–1968), Noontide Press, in California, translated and published four of Rassinier's books under the title *Debunking the Genocide Myth: A Study of the Nazi Concentration Camps and the Alleged Extermination of European Jewry* (unfortunately, it is easily available online today). He also wrote and published *The Speech of the Last Chance: An Introductory Essay to the Doctrines of Peace* (1953); his autobiography, *Candasse, or the Eighth Capital Sin: A History over Time* (1955); *Parliament in the Hands of the Banks* (1955); *The Equivocal Revolutionary* (1961); and *Those Responsible for the Second World War* (1967).

Rassinier died in 1967 while working on his book *The History of the State of Israel*, having been an invalid for the prior two decades of his life, the result of his physical sufferings from his incarceration and the beatings, torture, and imprisonment.

See also: Barnes, Harry Elmer; Carto, Willis; Duke, David; Faurisson, Robert; Holocaust, Denial of; Irving, David; Pierce, William Luther; Rockwell, George Lincoln; White Supremacy; Yockey, Francis Parker

Further Reading

Dawidowicz, Lucy S. *The Holocaust and the Historians*. Cambridge, MA: Harvard University Press, 1983.

Lipstadt, Deborah. *Denying the Holocaust: The Growing Assault on Truth and Memory*. New York: Free Press, 1993.

Moyn, Samuel. *A Holocaust Controversy: The Treblinka Affair in France*. Waltham, MA: Brandeis University Press, 2005.

Vidal-Naquet, Pierre. *Assassins of Memory: Essays on the Denial of the Holocaust*. New York: Columbia University Press, 1993.

Rockwell, George Lincoln

Eerily echoing his hero Adolf Hitler's (1889–1945) string of failures, George Lincoln Rockwell's (1918–1967) legacy of racism and antisemitism continues to this day. Frederick J. Simonelli, the author of *American*

Rockwell, George Lincoln | 121

Fuehrer, referred to him as the "martyred prophet of racial survival," and author Alex Haley, in his quasi-famous interview of Rockwell in *Playboy* magazine in 1966, called him the "self-styled messiah of white supremacy and intransigent anti-Semitism" and "the most universally detested public figure in America today." After that interview, Rockwell went on the lecture circuit and spoke at several colleges and universities. He was also the founder of the American Nazi Party (ANP) and the author and promoter of the phrase "White Power."

Rockwell's parents, who would divorce after his sixth birthday, were both vaudeville comedians who, ironically, counted among their friends many Jewish notables in the entertainment industry. Shuttling between his parents' homes in New Jersey and Maine, Rockwell enrolled at Brown University, in Providence, Rhode Island, but he dropped out and enlisted in the Navy in 1940, becoming a fighter pilot in World War II and serving in both the Atlantic and Pacific theaters. He married his college sweetheart during the war, and at its end, he moved his family to New York, where he studied art at the Pratt Institute and won a $1,000 prize for a poster for the American Cancer Society. After dropping out again, he relocated to Maine and briefly and unsuccessfully opened his own advertising agency.

Rockwell was recalled to active duty during the Korean War and assigned to train both navy and marine pilots in San Diego, California. It was during this period that he divorced his wife and remarried, honeymooning in Berchtesgaden, Germany, where Hitler owned his infamous Berghof retreat in the Bavarian Alps. He then turned to the writings of Adolf Hitler and became a staunch advocate of Senator Joseph McCarthy's (1908–1957) anti-Communism campaign. Rockwell and his Icelandic-born wife had three children, but she divorced him because of his racist and antisemitic activities and returned to her home country.

In 1958, under the patronage of wealthy extremist Harold Noel Arrowsmith Jr. of Baltimore, Maryland, they cofounded the National Committee to Free America from Jewish Domination. Arrowsmith also gifted Rockwell with both a house and a printing press, but he later reclaimed both after a nasty break. One year later, Rockwell founded the World Union of Free Enterprise National Socialists (WUFENS, possibly a wordplay on the Nazi Waffen SS), later changing its name to the American Nazi Party and relocating its headquarters to Arlington, Virginia.

Flamboyant in the extreme and a manipulator of the press media, Rockwell and his small entourage of Stormtroopers staged publicity stunts such as demonstrating in front of the White House and accusing then

122 | Rockwell, George Lincoln

president Dwight D. Eisenhower (1890–1969) of being in the pay of and manipulated by Jews; planning a rally in full Nazi regalia on the National Mall in April, around the time of Hitler's birthday, April 20; having his cronies drive a "hate bus" decorated with racist and antisemitic slogans; and picketing in various locales at the showing of the 1960 movie *Exodus*, which tells the story of the founding of the modern State of Israel in 1948.

While claiming to be an agnostic, Rockwell foresaw the value in linking his racism, antisemitism, and Holocaust denialism to the Christianity Identity Movement, and he deluded himself into thinking that, during the turbulent days of the 1960s, the American people would find him an attractive presidential candidate as "a man who stands unequivocally for the white Christian majority," as he told Alex Haley in the *Playboy* interview.

In 1967, Rockwell was assassinated by his former follower John Patler (b. 1938 as Yanaki Patsalos, a Greek American), whom he had thrown out of the ANP and accused of trying to inject "Marxist ideas" into the American Nazi Party. (Patler would serve eight years of his twenty-year sentence for the murder.) One of Rockwell's lieutenants, Matthias/ Matthew Koehl (1935–2014) succeeded him and moved the organization to Wisconsin. Another more notorious associate, William Luther Pierce (1933–2002), would found the National Alliance. In high school at the time, the racist, antisemite, and Holocaust denialist David Duke (b. 1950), upon learning of Rockwell's death, was reported to have said, "The greatest American who ever lived has been shot down and killed."

Rockwell's body was cremated, and his ashes are believed to be held by the New Order, the successor to the ANP, in New Berlin, Wisconsin. Neither Koehl's group nor the New Order have acquired a significant following and remain relatively moribund organizations.

Throughout the years of its existence under Rockwell's leadership, the ANP remained small and ready to commit to violence with, at most, one hundred members, and it was always in financially dire straits. Rockwell claimed to have more than five hundred supporters nationwide and more than fifteen hundred supporters on his mailing list. Internationally, his dream of linking up with other neo-Nazi movements globally, with himself as fuehrer, never materialized. Yet, the 2017 Unite the Right rally in Charlottesville, Virginia, which saw predominantly young white males marching and carrying Nazi flags while shouting, "Jews will not replace us" and "Blood and Soil" (a translation of the Nazi slogan *Blut und Boden*), is graphic evidence of George Lincoln Rockwell's perverse legacy in this twenty-first century.

Rockwell also self-published several volumes, including his autobiography *This Time the World* (1961) and *White Power* (1966).

See also: Barnes, Harry Elmer; Carto, Willis; Duke, David; Holocaust, Denial of; Ku Klux Klan; National Socialism/Nazism; Pierce, William Luther; White Supremacy; Yockey, Francis Parker

Further Reading

Bell, Leland V. *In Hitler's Shadow: The Anatomy of American Nazism.* Port Washington, WI, and London: Kennikat Press, 1975.

Downs, Donald Alexander. *Nazis in Skokie: Freedom, Community, and the First Amendment.* Notre Dame, IN: University of Notre Dame Press, 1985.

Obermayer, Herman J. *American Nazi Party in Arlington, Virginia, 1958–1984.* Scotts Valley, CA: CreateSpace Independent Publishing Platform, 2012.

Schmaltz, William H. *Hate: George Lincoln Rockwell and the American Nazi Party.* Chapel Hill: University of North Carolina Press, 1999.

Simonelli, Frederick J. *American Fuehrer: George Lincoln Rockwell and the American Nazi Party.* Champaign and Urbana: University of Illinois Press, 1999.

S

Social Darwinism

Social Darwinism is something of a misnomer, attempting to apply the evolutionary theories of the Englishman Charles Darwin (1809–1882) vis-à-vis plants and animals to human societies in his 1859 magnum opus *On the Origin of Species by Means of Natural Selection, or the Preservation of Favoured Races in the Struggle for Life*, something that he definitely did not initially do. However, persuaded by both supporters and critics, he did address these concerns somewhat in his second volume, *The Descent of Man, and Selection in Relation to Sex*, published in 1871. It would fall to others in Great Britain, France, the United States, and most especially in Germany, up to and including the Nazi period (1933–1945), to make adaptational use of his work to rather pernicious ends in the categorization of various people groups (superior vs. inferior) and spawn the "science" of eugenics (improving the human species by weeding out lesser "others"). The term *Social Darwinism* first appeared in 1877, but that reference was to landholding practices in Ireland.

For Darwin, from the results of both his observations and his travels, what intrigued him the most was the various manifestations of both plants and animals in the same species as he explored different geographic locales. He, therefore, concluded that such was the result of "the survival of the fittest"—though the term itself was not his—in various competitive environments, with the hardiest always winning out. One important influence on Darwin's thinking was fellow Englishman Thomas Malthus (1776–1834), whose 1798 book, *An Essay on the Principle of Population*, warned against unbridled population growth, as various groups would end up struggling for existence as resources diminished. Philosopher and biologist Herbert Spencer (1820–1903) developed an all-embracing conception of evolution as the progressive development of the physical world, biological organisms, the human mind, and human culture and societies, and he coined the term *survival of the fittest* in his 1864 *Principles of Biology* after having read Darwin's work. Darwin's half-cousin Francis Galton (1822–1911) coined the term *eugenics* and was its leading advocate.

However, it would fall to Ernst Haeckel MD (1834–1919), a philosopher and naturalist, to adapt Darwin's (and others') works more to human societies, and he provided the bases upon which the Nazis were able to draw for their eliminationist agendas against Jews, Sinti-Roma, homosexuals, the mentally and physically infirm, "asocials," and others who did not accord with their so-called Aryan ideal of physical and mental perfection, that is, the supposed "superior" or "master race." Thus, seen from this perspective, German/Nazi Social Darwinism, from Adolf Hitler (1889–1945) on down, embraced racism, antisemitism, nationalism, imperialism, colonialism, militarism, eugenics, euthanasia, sterilization, and a strident and dark notion of the inequality of peoples. Put into practice, the launch of World War II found the Nazis attempting to exterminate others through both war and incarceration and engaging in highly dubious medical experiments to improve their own population, all in accord with their political agenda of making the world *Judenrein* (Jew-free).

Finally, it must also be stated that although Nazi Social Darwinism assumed its most vitriolic and violent expression, the United States also has a long history of flirtation with eugenics, genocidal treatment of Native Americans, and racism in regard to both African Americans and Hispanic Americans, not to mention its treatment of Japanese Americans during World War II. The ongoing controversy in the United States regarding the immigration of nonwhite persons and families in the nineteenth century (i.e., the Chinese), which according to its opponents would result in the inferiorization of the white race by interbreeding with others, is likewise a manifestation of the eugenic argument about maintaining the racial status quo.

See also: Alt-Right; Intersectionality; National Socialism/Nazism; White Supremacy; Yockey, Francis Parker

Further Reading

Bashford, Alison, and Philippa Levine, eds. *The Oxford Handbook of the History of Eugenics*. Oxford and New York: Oxford University Press, 2010.

126 | Social Darwinism

Black, Edwin. *War against the Weak: Eugenics and America's Campaign to Create a Master Race*. New York: Four Walls Eight Windows, 2003.

Carlson, Elof Axel. *The Unfit: A History of a Bad Idea*. Cold Spring Harbor, NY: Cold Spring Harbor Laboratory Press, 2001.

Deichmann, Uwe. *Biologists under Hitler*. Cambridge, MA: Harvard University Press, 1996.

Engs, Ruth C. *The Eugenics Movement: An Encyclopedia*. Westport, CT: Greenwood Publishing, 2005.

Galton, David. *Eugenics: The Future of Human Life in the 21st Century*. London: Abacus, 2002.

Gasman, Daniel. *Haeckel's Monism and the Birth of Fascist Ideology*. New York: Lang, 1998.

Gasman, Daniel. *The Scientific Origins of National Socialism: Social Darwinism in Ernst Haeckel and the German Monist League*. London: Macdonald, 1971.

Glad, John. *Future Human Evolution: Eugenics in the Twenty-First Century*. Schuylkill Haven, PA: Hermitage Publishers, 2006.

Hawkins, Mike. *Social Darwinism in European and American Thought*. Cambridge, UK: Cambridge University Press, 1997.

Kelly, Alfred. *The Descent of Darwin: The Popularization of Darwinism in Germany, 1860–1914*. Chapel Hill: University of North Carolina Press, 1981.

Kerr, Anne, and Tom Shakespeare. *Genetic Politics: From Eugenics to Genome*. Cheltenham, UK: New Clarion, 2002.

Kevles, Daniel J. *In the Name of Eugenics: Genetics and the Use of Human Heredity*. Berkeley: University of California Press, 1985.

Largent, Mark. *Breeding Contempt: The History of Coerced Sterilization in the United States*. New Brunswick, NJ: Rutgers University Press, 2008.

Lynn, Richard. *Eugenics: A Reassessment*. Westport, CT: Greenwood Publishing, 2001.

McGovern, William M. *From Luther to Hitler: The History of Fascist Nazi Political Philosophy*. Boston: Houghton Mifflin, 1941.

Ordover, Nancy. *American Eugenics: Race, Queer Anatomy, and the Science of Nationalism*. Minneapolis: University of Minnesota Press, 2003.

Pine, Lisa. *Nazi Family Policy: 1933–1945*. New York: Berg, 1997.

Richards, Robert W. *The Tragic Sense of Life: Ernst Haeckel and the Struggle over Evolutionary Thought*. Chicago: University of Chicago Press, 2008.

Silver, Lee M. *Remaking Eden: Cloning and Beyond in a Brave New World*. New York: Harper Perennial, 1998.

Weikart, Richard. *From Darwin to Hitler*. New York: Palgrave Macmillan, 2004.

Spanish Inquisition

The Spanish Inquisition (*Tribunal del Santo Officio de la Inquisición*), established in 1478, was not initially and originally intended as an antisemitic persecution of Jews within the realm. Rather, it was an attempt to ferret out insincere Catholic Christians—both born and *conversos* (converts) or *marranos* (forced converts), the so-called New Christians (originally Jews and Muslims)—who had either lapsed in their practice of the faith or, in the case of the latter, who secretly practiced their Judaism or Islam. Additionally, with the political control of the inquisitional courts and their overseers, especially Tomas de Torquemada (1420–1498), confessor to Queen Isabella I of Castile (1451–1504), and the opportunities to enrich the royal coffers and wrest power away from papal authority, King Ferdinand II of Aragon (1452–1516) saw the potential to further solidify his hold over his kingdom and further unify both Aragon and Castile. Portugal, like its neighbor, also engaged in these activities and only ceased doing so in 1821. Italy, too, fell under the power of the Inquisition, but it remained under papal control. It should also be noted that Moors (Muslim converts from Islam, though now labeled as *moriscos*), too, came in for inquisitional terrors but to a somewhat lesser extent than converts or later Jews, though one of the fears on the part of the Inquisition was that the Muslims were secretly attempting to regain power and control for the Ottoman Empire. For both Jews and Muslims, their alternatives were, initially, either further conversion or expulsion, and a significant number of both chose the latter.

According to the 1906 *Jewish Encyclopedia* article "Inquisition (called *Sanctum Officium* or (Tribunal of the) Holy Office"), the following acts merited the attention of the Inquisition in the case of converts:

Celebrate the (Saturday) Sabbath by engaging in practices associated with Judaism:

- Wear a clean shirt or better garments on Saturday
- Spread a clean tablecloth
- Light no fire
- Eat the food which had been cooked overnight in the oven
- Perform no work on that day
- Eat meat during Lent
- Take neither meat nor drink on the Day of Atonement [Yom Kippur]

128 | Spanish Inquisition

- Go barefoot or ask forgiveness of another on that day
- Celebrate the Passover with unleavened bread or eat bitter herbs
- Celebrate the Feast of Tabernacles [Sukkot] using green branches or send fruits as gifts to friends
- Marry according to Jewish customs or take Jewish names
- Circumcise their sons
- Throw a piece of dough in the stove before baking
- Wash their hands before praying
- Bless a cup of wine before meals and pass it around among the people at the table
- Pronounce blessings while slaughtering poultry
- Separate the veins from the meat
- Soak the flesh in water before cooking, and cleanse it from blood
- Eat no pork, hare, rabbits, or eels
- Give Old Testament names to their children, or bless the children by laying on of hands
- Women not attending Church within forty days after confinement [childbirth]
- Turning the dying toward the wall [i.e., eastward toward Jerusalem]
- Warm a corpse with warm water
- Recite psalms without concluding "Glory to the Trinity"

Those brought up on such charges were typically thrown into prisons under hellish conditions, where food was meager and poor and punishments included various forms of torture, including hanging by the wrists, "waterboarding," the rack, and, ultimately, death.

Less well known, however, is the fact that the Inquisition spread its tentacles to the New World of the Americas under Spanish control, especially Mexico, and between 1581 and 1776, 129 acts of public penance and condemnation (*auto da fé*) took place, including fifty-nine persons being burned alive and eighteen in effigy.

British Jewish scholar and historian Cecil Roth (1899–1970), writing in the *Encyclopedia Judaica* (2007, 2nd edition), summarizes the Inquisition:

Whatever the true reasons for the establishment of the Inquisition were, it cannot be denied that social, economic, racial and political reasons nourished the trials of the Inquisition and the anti-Converso attitude that existed in Christian society. According to many Old and New Christian sources the hatred of the Conversos was due to the envy their economic and social achievements aroused in society in general. Many of them were able to translate their economic and social strength into political power which added to the antagonism they aroused among many Old Christians.

In that same article, Roth suggests that the number of deaths, public humiliations, and other indignities resulting from the Inquisition in Spain amounted to more than 340,000 persons of all ages and more than 30,000 individuals in Portugal.

On July 15, 1834, the Spanish Inquisition was finally abolished. The Polish-Israeli scholar Benzion Netanyahu (1910–2012)—the father of the current Israeli prime minister Benjamin Netanyahu (b. 1949) and the late Jonathan Netanyahu (1946–1976), a hero of the raid on the Entebbe Airport in Uganda to rescue hostages held by the Palestine Liberation Organization (PLO)—in his magnum opus *The Origins of the Inquisition in Fifteenth Century Spain* argues that what transpired in Spain laid the foundation for the racialist antisemitism of Nazism that ultimately resulted in the Holocaust.

See also: *Adversus Judaeos*; Blood Libel; Crusades; Deicide; Martyrdom, Sanctifying the Name of God; Oberammergau Passion Play; Usury

Further Reading

Aguinis, Marcos. *Against the Inquisition*. Translated by Caroline de Roberts. Seattle: AmazonCrossing, 2018. [Novel]

Catlos, Brian A. *Kingdoms of Faith: A New History of Islamic Spain*. New York: Basic Books, 2018.

Gottheil, Richard, and Meyer Kayserling. "Inquisition," *Jewish Encyclopedia*, 1906. www.jewishencyclopedia.com

Kamen, Henry. *The Spanish Inquisition: A Historical Revision*. 4th edition. New Haven, CT, and London: Yale University Press, 2014.

Netanyahu, Benzion. *The Origins of the Inquisition in Fifteenth Century Spain*. New York: Random House, 1995.

Roth, Cecil, and Yom Tov Assis. "Inquisition." *Encyclopaedia Judaica*, edited by Michael Berenbaum and Fred Skolnik, 2nd ed., vol. 9, Macmillan Reference USA, 2007, pp. 790–804. *Gale eBooks*. https://link-gale-com.libdata.lib. ua.edu/apps/doc/CX2587509541/GVRL?u=tusc49521&sid=GVRL&xid=bfa cb31b. Accessed March 1, 2020.

Usury

Negatively, and largely antisemitically, usury has largely been understood as the charging of exorbitantly high interest rates on loans *by Jews*, though, historically, it was simply the practice of charging interest on any loan. The Hebrew Bible/Old Testament already references such a practice in Deuteronomy 23:19–20:

> You shall not lend upon interest to any brother [Israelite]: interest of money, interest of foodstuffs, interest of anything that is lent upon interest. Unto a foreigner, you may lend upon interest; but unto your brother [Israelite], you shall not lend upon interest; that the Lord your God may bless you in all that you put your hand to where you go into to possess it.

Other relevant biblical passages include Exodus 22:25 ("If you lend money to one of my people among you who is needy, do not treat it like a business deal; charge no interest."); Leviticus 25:35–37 ("If any of your fellow Israelites become poor and are unable to support themselves among you, help them as you would a foreigner and stranger, so they can continue to live among you. Do not take interest or any profit from them, but fear your God, so that they may continue to live among you. You must not lend them money at interest or sell them food at a profit."); and Psalm 15:5 ([He] who lends money to the poor without interest; who does not accept a bribe against the innocent, whoever does these things, never be shaken.").

Later Jewish law permitted but strictly regulated the charging of interest to both non-Jews and Jews, and some rabbinic authorities stipulated that such could not be charged to either Christians or Muslims. Within the last two hundred years, possibly also in response to biblical precedent, Jewish communities both in Europe and the United States have established

Hebrew Free Loan Societies (HFLS) to lend money to needy Jews without interest or with minimal interest and with favorable repayment schedules.

Commensurately and paralleling the increasing split between original Judaism and later Christianity, primarily Roman Catholicism, by the fourth century, the church had declared such a practice sinful. Somewhat ironically, however, like the various kingdoms of the realm, the church, too, needed regular infusions of funds to support its growing institutional network, and it turned to Jewish moneylenders, who were already excluded from owning land and from various occupations, guilds, and professions and so found themselves gravitating to this choice of vocation, oftentimes to the dismay and enmity of the larger population. (This antipathy was like that of the tax collectors and rent collectors, who were also often Jews who had no other sources of income, having agreements with their lords, bishops, and kings that certain percentages of those monies collected would be allowed to remain with them and thus provide for their own families and communities.)

Over time, especially in Western Europe, the hated figure of the moneylender came to be more and more identified with the Jews, most notoriously with William Shakespeare's (1564–1616) somewhat reprehensible character Shylock in his 1596 play *The Merchant of Venice*, who promised to exact "a pound of flesh" from Antonio for his failure to pay back a loan. His name has now become the generic noun *shylock* and equates, at least in English, with *loan shark*. At about the same time, playwright Christopher Marlowe (1564–1593) produced his *The Jew of Malta*, which is about a vengeful merchant by the name of Barabbas. An equally reprehensible character in British literature is Fagin or "Fagin the Jew"—who is identified as such more than two hundred times in Charles Dickens's (1812–1870) 1837 novel *Oliver Twist*—a receiver of stolen goods who entices young boys into his trade. And although Dickens attempted to disavow any antisemitic intentions on his part, stating that his character only reflected the reality of criminal life in East London, and later edited out such designations in later editions, he remained unsuccessful in doing so during his lifetime.

Over time, we see an expansion of this antisemitic stereotyping of Jews with an economic cast; that is, Jews are wealthy, stingy, greedy, business oriented, obsessed by profits and materialism, cheaters, and parasites benefiting from the productivity of others. In the nineteenth- and twentieth-century forgery, the *Protocols of the Learned Elders of Zion*, several of the so-called protocols (2, 3, 4, 21, and 22) present the Jewish cabal of world takeover as having a decided economic agenda to subvert the

132 | Usury

world's economy and monetary systems. In 1807, under the supposed guise of integrating/assimilating the Jewish community of France, Emperor Napoleon Bonaparte (1769–1821) convened a "Great Sanhedrin" of rabbis and lay leaders and asked them twelve questions regarding their status as citizens; two of twelve dealt with Jewish-Gentile loan transactions. In the United States, antisemites in the twentieth century have accused Jews of controlling the Federal Reserve System.

Already in 1906, the *Jewish Encyclopedia* concluded its article on usury with this comment: "The reputation of usurers has clung to the Jews even to modern times, though there is little evidence of their being more addicted to it than other persons who trade in money" (www.jewishencyclopedia.com).

See also: *Adversus Judaeos*; Blood Libel; Crusades; Deicide; Luther, Martin; Martyrdom, Sanctifying the Name of God; Oberammergau Passion Play

Further Reading

Baron, Salo W., and Arcadius Kahan. *The Economic History of the Jews*. New York: Schocken Books, 1975. [Reprint]

Dembitz, Lewis N., and Joseph Jacobs. "Usury," *Jewish Encyclopedia*, 1906. www.jewishcyclopedia.com

Eisner, Will. *Fagin the Jew*. New York: Random House 2003. [Graphic novel]

Foxman, Abraham H. *Jews & Money: The Story of a Stereotype*. New York: St. Martin's Press, 2010.

Gross, John. *Shylock: A Legend and Its Legacy*. New York: Simon and Schuster, 1994.

Gross, Nachum. *The Economic History of the Jews*. 2nd edition. New York: Schocken Books, 1975.

Jacobs, Steven Leonard, and Mark Weitzman. *Dismantling the Big Lie: The Protocols of the Elders of Zion*. Hoboken, NJ: KTAV Publishing House, 2003.

Krefetz, Gerald. *Jewish and Money: The Myths and the Reality*. New York: Book Sales, 1984.

Muller, Jerry Z. *Capitalism and the Jews*. Princeton, NJ, and London: Princeton University Press, 2010.

Penslar, Derek J. *Shylock's Children: Economics and Jewish Identity in Modern Europe*. Berkeley: University of California Press, 2001.

Sombart, Werner. *The Jews and Modern Capitalism*. Translated by Mordecai Epstein. New York: Martino Fine Books, 2015/1913. [Reprint]

Wagner, Richard

Richard Wagner (1813–1883) remains a towering figure in the world of operatic music and productions, but he is tainted by controversy because of his overt antisemitism and the easy adaptability of that legacy by the Nazis, specifically Adolf Hitler, for whom he remained a musical muse and inspiration. Although his musical scores continued to be played around the world—including in Israel—and his productions less so, his antisemitism remains a part of his legacy.

Wagner was a prodigious author who wrote about music, culture, and politics, and his ignominy rests primarily on his 1850 essay *Das Judenthum in der Musik* ("Jewishness in Music"), originally published anonymously under the pen name K. Freigedank (K. Freethought) and later republished under his own name in 1859, in which he castigates Jewish contributions to both music and culture as inferior copies and inauthentic expressions of true German greatness and creativity. His solution to these derivative presentations was for Jews to give up their Judaism and convert to Christianity. Two specific objects of his attack were the Jewish composers Felix Mendelssohn (1809–1847) and Giacomo Meyerbeer (1791–1864), both of whom he believed thwarted his journey to recognition and greatness. This happened even though, all his life, he had Jewish friends, and early on, after a period of exile, they had enabled the production of his first opera, *Parsifal*. In his later years, as has been recorded and noted by scholars, Wagner developed an appreciation of the writings of the French racialist Count Arthur de Gobineau (1816–1882), who was said to have given expression to a "scientific" theory of racism in his 1848 book *Essai sur l'inégalité des races humaines* (*An Essay on the Inequality of the Human Races*). Furthermore, his own son-law, Houston Stewart Chamberlain (1855–1927), published his own book, *Die Grundlagen des neunzehnten*

134 | Wagner, Richard

Jahrhunderts (*The Foundations of the Nineteenth Century*), that went on to become an essential Nazi ideological text.

In the city of Bayreuth, Bavaria, Wagner built his *Festspielhaus* opera house, which opened its doors in 1876 to stage his theatrical productions. After his death in 1883, his widow, Cosima (1887–1930), whose own anti-semitism was self-evident, attracted increasing circles of right-wing German nationalists, though it had attracted them even prior to Wagner's death. After her death and that of her brother-in-law Siegfried (1869–1930), the reins of leadership fell to his English-born widow, Winnifred (1887–1980), herself an antisemite and also a friend of Hitler. According to her grandson Gottfried (b. 1947), Winnifred had turned down a marriage proposal from Hitler, and all her life, she maintained that the Holocaust was a lie and a fiction foisted on Germany by "the Jews."

The Winnifred-Hitler connection was further cemented by the fact that Hitler openly acknowledged the influence of Wagner's music on his own thinking as a true presentation of German national genius, and he had attended several productions of Wagner's operas in Bayreuth. His appreciation of Wagner was understood by all within the Nazi leadership circle and never challenged. Several academic and scholarly articles on Wagner's contribution to German Nazi culture appeared during the years of Hitler's governance, for example, Paul Bülow's "Adolf Hitler and the Bayreuth Ideological Circle" in 1933 in the journal *Zeitschrift fur Musik*. That same year, the Nazis established the German-Nordic Richard Wagner Society for Germanic Art and Culture.

In Israel today, concerts containing Wagner's music continue to stir up their own controversies in a country that initially housed the largest number of Holocaust survivors. The first public concert took place in 2000 in Rishon LeTzion and was conducted by Mendi Rodan (1929–2009), himself a Holocaust survivor. The conductor and pianist Daniel Barenboin (b. 1942) included an excerpt of Wagner's music in his concert in Tel Aviv in 2001. Barenboin has also stated in "Wagner, Israel, and the Palestinians" on his website (www.danielbarenboim.com), "When one continues to uphold the Wagner taboo today in Israel, it means in a certain sense that we are giving Hitler the last word, that we are acknowledging that Wagner was indeed a prophet and predecessor of Nazi anti-Semitism, and that he can be held accountable, even if only indirectly, for the final solution [*sic*]." Somewhat ironically, even during World War II, Wagner's music was still played by Jews in the Palestine Symphony Orchestra, the precursor to the Israeli Philharmonic Orchestra of today.

Wagner, Richard | 135

Two highly critical early works about Wagner the man and his music are by the German philosopher Friedrich Nietzsche (1844–1900), *The Case of Wagner: A Musician's Problem,* detailing his break with his friend, published in 1889, six years after his mental collapse, and Theodor Adorno's (1903–1969) *In Search of Wagner,* written in 1952, when he was already living in the United States.

See also: Fascism; Holocaust; National Socialism/Nazism; Nationalism; Oberammergau Passion Play; Social Darwinism

Further Reading

Conway, David. *Jewry in Music: Entry into the Profession from the Enlightenment to Richard Wagner.* Cambridge, UK: Cambridge University Press, 2012.

Deathridge, John. *Wagner: Beyond Good and Evil. Berkeley*: University of California Press, 2008.

Harrowitz, Nancy, ed. *Tainted Greatness: Antisemitism and Cultural Heroes.* Philadelphia: Temple University Press, 1994.

Hilmes, Oliver, and Stewart Spencer. *Cosima Wagner: The Lady of Bayreuth.* New Haven, CT, and London: Yale University Press, 2010.

Kater, Michael H. *The Twisted Muse: Musicians and Their Music in the Third Reich.* Oxford: Oxford University Press, 1997.

Katz, Jacob. *The Darker Side of Genius: Richard Wagner's Anti-Semitism.* Hanover, MA, and London: Brandeis University Press, 1986.

Owen, Lee M. *Wagner: The Terrible Man and His Truthful Art.* Toronto, ON: University of Toronto Press, 1998.

Rose, Paul Lawrence. *Wagner, Race and Revolution.* London: Faber, 1996.

Sheffi, Na'ama. *The Ring of Myths: The Israelis, Wagner, and the Nazis.* Translated by M. Grenzeback and M. Talisman. Eastbourne, UK: Sheffield Academic Press, 2013.

Wagner, Gottfried. *He Who Does Not Howl with the Wolf: The Wagner Legacy.* London: Sanctuary Publishers Ltd., 1998.

Wagner, Gottfried. *Twilight of the Wagners: The Unveiling of a Family's Legacy.* New York: Picador, 1999.

Wagner, Gottfried, and Abraham Peck. *Unwanted Legacies: Sharing the Burden of Post-Genocide Generations.* Lubbock: Texas Tech University Press, 2014.

Weiner, Mark A. *Richard Wagner and His Anti-Semitic Imagination.* Lincoln and London: University of Nebraska Press, 1997.

White Supremacy

White supremacy is the belief that white persons, Caucasians, of European ancestry and history are superior in intelligence, creativity, spirituality, physical capabilities, and the like to all other supposed "inferior" races (e.g., black, Asian, Latino/a), especially Jews, and are under threat for their very survival due to the encroachment of these others. Its intellectual origins may be said to have arisen during the European Age of Enlightenment (1740–1770), which emphasized individualism, rational and secular reasoning, skepticism, and, most importantly, a "scientific" approach to human reality. As it has evolved, it has more and more become associated with the far-right politically both in Europe, where anti-Islamic and anti-Muslim prejudices against peoples emigrating from the Middle East have seen dramatic increases in violence, and the United States, which has its own long history of antiblack racism and antisemitism. On both continents, white supremacist movements remain threateningly active.

To be sure, the ultimate expression of white supremacy in Europe was that of Nazism and its presentation of its own Nordic ideal "Aryan": tall, well-muscled, blond-haired, blue-eyed, virile males and fertile females. Thus, in reverse, the notoriously antisemitic Nazi newspaper *Der Stürmer* (*The Stormer*), founded and published by the gauleiter (party leader/governing official) of Franconia, Julius Streicher (1885–1946), in 1923, regularly presented its readers with graphic portrayals of Jews as short, fat, kinky-haired, thick-lipped, and swarthy. Written texts also added the element of predatory sexuality toward young German girls and married German women. (Many of these same physical traits and sexual perversities in the United States were also attributed to African Americans.) Further legitimating Nazi white supremacy were the works of French racial theorist Arthur de Gobineau (1816–1882) in his text *An Essay on the Inequality of the Human Races* (in French, *Essai sur l'inégalité des races humaines*, 1848) and the British-born German philosopher Houston Stewart Chamberlain (1855–1927), the son-in-law of the antisemitic composer and theater director Richard Wagner (1813–1883), in his (1899) *Foundations of the Nineteenth Century* (in German, *Die Grundlagen des neunzehnten Jahrhunderts*). The former strenuously argued that "race mixing" was destroying the "purity" of the Nordic or Germanic race, and the latter argued that the Teutonic (German) peoples were the very apex of historical Western civilization and their very opposite were "the Jews" intent on destroying the West through wars and interbreeding while remaining "pure-blooded" themselves. Their writings and ideas later found themselves in the work of chief Nazi ideologist Alfred Rosenberg (1893–1946) in his (1930) *The Myth of the Twentieth Century* (in German, *Mythus des XX. Jahrhunderts*), which, again, argued that the Nordic peoples were in danger of biological corruption by Semitic peoples (i.e., the Jews).

In the United States, prior to the twentieth century, white supremacism was primarily manifested in the distinction between blacks and Native Americans (the "Indians," a term said to have originated with Christopher Columbus (1451–1506) labeling those he first encountered in the Caribbean as related to the peoples of the Indian continent) and whites. As the last group held the reins of political/governmental, social, economic, religious, and military power, it continued to enforce its practices of discrimination against what it, too, regarded as inferior peoples. Jews, having already arrived in 1654 in the Dutch colony of New Amsterdam, settled throughout the colonies and later the new nation-state, but they regularly found themselves discriminated against, with the most virulent antisemites articulating racial-biological differences as well. An important additional factor threatening white/Christian supremacy is that of immigration, for example, the Chinese between 1870 and 1900, approximately twelve million persons, but, more importantly, the large number of Jews from Western Europe already by the middle of the 1800s, from Eastern Europe early in the twentieth century, and both groups in the aftermath of World War II and the Holocaust, and now, in the twenty-first century, Hispanic persons primarily from Latin America.

Between 1790 and 2012, the U.S. Congress passed more than forty acts of legislation addressing immigration, among which are the following:

- Naturalization Act of 1790, establishing rules for naturalized citizenship
- Naturalization Act of 1795, lengthening the residency requirement for naturalization
- Alien Friends Act & Alien Enemies Act of 1798, granting the president the power to deport those deemed enemies of the United States
- Page Act of 1875, restricting entry to those deemed "undesirable"
- Chinese Exclusion Act of 1882, prohibiting naturalization and restricting numbers to be admitted
- Immigration Act of 1903, prohibiting entry to anarchists, epileptics, beggars, and pimps
- Immigration Act of 1907, restricting immigration of certain classes of disabled and diseased persons

138 | White Supremacy

- Immigration Act of 1917, restricting Asian immigrants
- Emergency Quota Act of 1921, restricting immigration to those populations already 3 percent of the American people
- Immigration Act of 1924/Johnson-Reed Act, setting numerical limits on immigration and establishing a national-origin quota system, with a total number of 150,000 immigrants
- Chinese Exclusion Repeal Act of 1943/Magnuson Act, repealing the Chinese Exclusion Act of 1882
- Immigration Action of 1990, increasing legal immigration ceilings in all categories
- Illegal Immigration Reform and Immigrant Responsibility Act of 1996, increasing border security
- Homeland Security Act of 2002, moving all immigration responsibilities to the Department of Homeland Security and outlining specific requirements for handling the immigration of children
- Deferred Action for Childhood Arrivals of 2012 (DACA), setting a two-year hiatus for action concerning immigrant children already in the United States

The issue of nonwhite immigration to the United States remains central to the white supremacist movement, and its supporters actively and publicly support any and all legislative attempts to restrict nonwhites from coming to the United States. Invariably, they are also antisemitic: in the current twenty-first century, white supremacists have also accused Jews of leading the movement for open borders across the United States and funding and encouraging nonwhites, regardless of circumstance (poverty or oppression), to come to the United States.

Early in the twentieth century in the United States, figures such as the eugenicist Madison Grant (1865–1937) argued that "race-mixing" was akin to racial suicide. That, in turn, became something of a battle cry for the Ku Klux Klan (KKK), which initially formed in the aftermath of the Civil War to address Southern losses, freed blacks, and Northern carpetbaggers but reinvigorated itself, becoming even more racist, antisemitic, and anti-immigrant. In the latter half of the twentieth century, Christian Identity added a quasi-religious component to the mix, arguing that they were, in fact and biblically, the "true Israel" and the Jews liars and thieves of that identity.

A not-so-subtle variation of white supremacy is the (global) "White Genocide Conspiracy Theory" said to be the work of neo-Nazi David Lane (1938–2007) and author of the "Fourteen Words": "We must secure the

White Supremacy | 139

existence of our people and a future for white children." In his 1995 "White Genocide Manifesto," he included the following:

. . .

12. That Judeo-Christianity is dedicated to the concept of racial leveling the oneness of mankind, and, therefore, genocide.

13. That the Zionist occupation governments of America and other Western nations promote the unnatural act of homosexuality, knowing full well the power of the male instinct for sexual union must be directed toward procreation with females of the same race to ensure racial survival.

14. That the Zionist occupation governments of America and other Western nations promote and protect infanticide of healthy, White babies, now called abortion, immensely to the detriment of the race.

Current supporters of this conspiracy theory in the United States include Fox News commentator Tucker Carlson (b. 1969), alt-right media personality Mike Cernovich (b. 1977), author Ann Coulter (b. 1961), white supremacist David Duke (b. 1950), media personality Alex Jones (b. 1974), Charlottesville white nationalist Jason Kessler (b. 1983), radio host Michael Savage (1942), and Pittsburgh shooter Robert Bowers (b. 1972). A European version of this thinking is found in the work of minor French writer Renaud Camus (b. 1946), whose "Great Replacement Conspiracy Theory" argues that white Christian European civilization is being attacked and replaced by non-European peoples, especially those from the Middle East (i.e., Muslims and Arabs).

Lastly, it should also be noted that the novels *The Turner Diaries* (1978) and *Hunter* (1989) by the late William Luther Pierce (1933–2002), the founder of the National Alliance, which were also written under the pseudonym Andrew Macdonald, and the Christian Identity movement were and are foundational supporters of white supremacy and the fear of white genocide. Pierce's books fictionally presented a coming race war, and at the heart of Christian Identity are the beliefs of "white Aryans" as the true descendants of biblical Israel, Jews as spawn of the Devil, and the final apocalypse as a battle between good and evil, translated to mean between whites and Jews.

See also: Barnes, Harry Elmer; Carto, Willis; Christian Identity; Duke, David; Fascism; Holocaust, Denial of; Pierce, William Luther; Proud Boys; Rockwell, George Lincoln; Social Darwinism; World Church of the Creator; Yockey, Francis Parker

140 | World Church of the Creator

Further Reading

Barkun, Michael. *Religion and the Racist Right*. Chapel Hill: University of North Carolina Press, 1997.

Belew, Katherine. *Bring the War Home: The White Power Movement and Paramilitary America*. Cambridge, MA: Harvard University Press, 2018.

Bridges, Tyler. *The Rise of David Duke*. Jackson: University Press of Mississippi, 1994.

Daniels, Jessie. *White Lies: Race, Class, Gender, and Sexuality in White Supremacist Discourse*. London and New York: Routledge, 1997.

Dobratz, Betty A., and Stephanie Shanks-Meile. *The White Separatist Movement in the United States*. Baltimore, MD, and London: Johns Hopkins University Press, 2000.

Ferber, Abby. *White Man Falling: Race, Gender, and White Supremacy*. Lanham, MD: Rowman & Littlefield, 1999.

Flint, Colin. *Spaces of Hate: Geographies of Discrimination and Intolerance in the USA*. London and New York: Routledge, 2004.

Frederickson, George. *White Supremacy*. Oxford: Oxford University Press, 1981.

Kaplan, Jeffrey. *Encyclopedia of White Power: A Sourcebook on the Radical Right*. Lanham, MD: AltaMira Press, 2000.

King, Richard, and David Leonard. *Beyond Hate: White Power and Popular Culture*. London and New York: Ashgate Publishing.

MacCann, Donnaree. *White Supremacy in Children's Literature*. London and New York: Routledge, 2000.

Novick, Michael. *White Lies, White Power: The Fight against White Supremacy and Reactionary Violence*. Monroe, ME: Common Courage Press, 1995.

Whitman, James. *Hitler's American Model: The United States and the Making of Nazi Race Law*. Princeton, NJ, and London: Princeton University Press, 2017.

World Church of the Creator

The World Church of the Creator, also previously known as the Church of the Creator but presently as either Creativity or the Creativity Movement, the result of a lawsuit forcing the change of name, was the creation of Ukrainian American and former Florida legislator Ben (Bernhardt) Klassen (1918–1993), who would ultimately commit suicide after seeing

World Church of the Creator | 141

his wife die of cancer and his small white separatist and antisemitic movement convolutedly apparently unable to sustain itself. However, it was
never able to draw in large numbers, and its legacy belies that failure. Its
attempt to link white separatism and white purity with a certain understanding of fundamentalist Christianity has proven a linkage that continues to attract other similar hate organizations, writers, and websites,
though Klassen himself rejected Christianity as a Jewish plot to weaken
the white race (paralleling Adolf Hitler's similar argument that Christianity was invented by Jews to weaken the German/Aryan race). In its
attempt to validate and legitimate itself, the "church" never disavowed
violence as either a tactic or method in its drive to preserve what its
founder and members truly believed to be the genius of Western
civilization—whiteness.

Klassen was also the creator of the abbreviation RaHoWa, which
stands for "racial holy war," and it remains something of a battle cry
among contemporary haters. Those engaged in this war see and understand Jews as being at the forefront of their enemies and black persons and
other "mud peoples" as the armies of evil who must be defeated by whatever means necessary. As Klassen himself said in 1987, "We gird for total
war against the Jews and the rest of the g— mud races of the world—
politically, militantly, financially, morally, and religiously."

The church was founded by Klassen in 1973 in Florida with the pub-
lication of his book *Nature's Eternal Religion*. After Klassen's death and
its revival by Illinois neo-Nazi, white supremacist, and convicted felon
Matthew "Matt" Hale (b. 1972)—presently serving forty years for plotting
to assassinate a district court judge—it has two present iterations: Creativity
Alliance (CA), or the Church of Creativity, and the Creativity Movement
(TCM). However, both groups remain small and relatively ineffectual.
Hale was also associated with Benjamin Nathaniel Smith (1978–1999),
whose suicidal shooting rampage left two dead and nine wounded, supposedly in response to the failure of the Illinois Bar to certify Hale to
practice law because of his "character and fitness" after he successfully
passed the exam.

The use of the word *creator* does not refer to God but, rather, to white
persons who created everything worthwhile in culture and civilization.
Accordingly, in the publication of the *Little White Book* by Victor Wolf
(?–?) in 1991, "A CREATOR, therefore, makes a careful distinction
between his loved ones, and his enemies. He loves, aids, and abets those
of his own race and his own kind, and hates his enemies, namely Jews,

142 | World Church of the Creator

n——, and the mud races." Thus, at its heart are the "Sixteen Commandments," among which are the following:

- It is the avowed duty and holy responsibility of each generation to assure and secure for all time the existence of the White Race upon the face of this planet.
- Remember that the inferior colored races are our deadly enemies, and the most dangerous of all is the Jewish race [*sic*]. It is our immediate objective to relentlessly expand the White Race and keep shrinking our enemies.
- Your first loyalty belongs to the White Race.
- Destroy and banish all Jewish thought and influence from society. Work hard to bring about a White World as soon as possible.
- Uphold the honor of your race at all time[s].
- Throughout your life you shall faithfully stand upon our pivotal creed of Blood, Soil, and Honor.

In addition, there are the "Five Fundamental Beliefs" that its adherents are expected to recite daily:

- WE BELIEVE that our Race is our Religion.
- WE BELIEVE that the White Race is Nature's Finest.
- WE BELIEVE that racial loyalty is the greatest of all honors, and racial treason is the worst of all crimes.
- WE BELIEVE that what is good for the White Race is the highest virtue, and what is bad for the White Race is the ultimate sin.
- WE BELIEVE that the one and only, true and revolutionary White Racial Religion—Creativity—is the only salvation for the White Race.

Creators also believe that the Jews were responsible for World War II; the Holocaust never happened; Jews control the U.S. Government, which they label JOG, for Jewish occupational government; and Jews also control the United Nations.

To the degree that Klassen and his followers agreed, including Matthew Hale, who took the title of *Pontifex Maximus* (high priest) after this appointment by its Guardians of Faith Committee, the group has male clergy who can only by ordained by other ministers of the church. It has a holiday calendar that includes Klassen Day (January 26), in honor of his birth; Founder's Day (February 20), when *Nature's Eternal Religion* was published; Kozel Day/Martyr's Day (September 15), in memory of one Kozel, a so-called martyr to the faith and a minister of the church as well;

and Festum Album (December 26–January 1), a weeklong celebration of white racial pride. It has also developed ritual ceremonies for its four "sacraments": marriage, pledging for children, confirmation, and eulogizing the dead. Its sacred text was also written by Klassen and is entitled *The White Man's Bible*; it was published in 1981.

The symbol associated with the group consists of three images on a white background: a halo symbolizing the purity of the white race, a red and black crown symbolizing the elite status of the white race, and a large black W standing for the white race itself.

See also: Christian Identity; Coughlin, Charles E.; Holocaust, Denial of; Nationalism; Social Darwinism; Yockey, Francis Parker

Further Reading

Aho, James. *Far-Right Fantasy: A Sociology of American Religion and Politics.* New York and London: Routledge, 2015.

Altman, Linda Jacobs. *Hate and Racist Groups: A Hot Issue.* Berkeley Heights, NJ: Enslow Publishers, 2001.

Bjorgo, Tore, ed. *Terror from the Extreme Right.* London: Frank Cass, 1995.

Dobratz, Betty A., and Stephanie L. Shanks-Meile. *White Power/White Pride: The White Separatist Movement in the United States.* New York: Twayne Publishers, 1997.

Dobratz, Betty A., and Stephanie L. Shanks-Meile. *The White Separatist Movement in the United States.* Baltimore, MD: Johns Hopkins University Press, 1997.

Gardell, Mattias. *Gods of the Blood: The Pagan Revival and White Separatism.* Durham, NC: Duke University Press, 2003.

Goodrick-Clark, Nicholas. *Black Sun: Aryan Cults, Esoteric Nazism, and the Politics of Identity.* New York: New York University Press, 2003.

Kaplan, Jeffrey, ed. *Encyclopedia of White Power: A Sourcebook on the Radical Right.* Lanham, MD: Rowman & Littlefield, 2000.

Kaplan, Jeffrey. *Radical Religion in America: Millenarian Movements from the Far Right to the Children of Noah.* Syracuse, NY: Syracuse University Press, 1997.

Kaplan, Jeffrey, and Tore Bjango, eds. *Nation and Race: The Developing Euro-American Racist Subculture.* Boston: Northeastern University Press, 2004.

Kaplan, Jeffrey, and Leonard Weinberg. *The Emergence of a Euro-American Radical Right.* New Brunswick, NJ: Rutgers University Press, 1998.

Marks, Kathy. *Faces of Right-Wing Extremism.* Boston: Brandon Publishing, 1996.

Michael, George. *Confronting Right-Wing Extremism and Terrorism in the USA.* New York: Routledge, 2003.

144 | World Church of the Creator

Michael, George. *Theology of Hate: A History of the World Church of the Creator.* Gainesville: University Press of Florida, 2009.

Morris, Travis. *Dark Ideas: How Neo-Nazi and Violent Jihadist Ideologies Shaped Modern Terrorism.* Lanham, MD: Lexington Books, 2016.

Perry, Barbara. *Hate Crimes.* Westport, CT: Praeger Publishers, 2009.

Quarles, Chester L. *The Ku Klux Klan and Related American Racialist and Antisemitic Organizations: A History and Analysis.* Jefferson, NC: McFarland Publishers, 1999.

Ryan, Nick. *Into a World of Hate: Among the Extreme Right.* New York and London: Routledge, 2003.

Swain, Carol M., and Russ Nieli. *Contemporary Voices of White Nationalism.* Cambridge, UK: Cambridge University Press, 2003.

Warren, Kinsella. *Web of Hate: Inside Canada's Far Right Network.* Toronto, ON: Harper Perennial, 1995.

Yockey, Francis Parker

Francis Parker Yockey (1917–1960) remains, perhaps, the most enigmatic American figure, historically and contemporarily, among white nationalists, racists, and antisemites. He is far less known today, but he is still an icon among those pseudo-intellectuals associated with its various movements. His so-called magnum opus, *Imperium: The Philosophy of History and Politics*, hurriedly written on an offshore Irish island in 1948 without notes or references and under the pseudonym Ulick Varange, was said by its supporters to be a "sequel" to German historian and philosopher Oswald Spengler's (1880–1936) *The Decline of the West* (1918, revised 1922); it argues for a culturally based overall remaking of Western civilization into a totalitarian unity. *Imperium* is a massive rambling volume of more than six hundred pages. The text is divided into the following sections: "The 20th Century Historical Outlook," "The 20th Century Political Outlook," "Cultural Vitalism (A) Culture Health," "Cultural Vitalism (B) Culture Pathology," "America" and "The World Situation." Jews, viewed by Yockey and others as the primary evildoers responsible for all the ills of civilization, would have no role in that future rebirth as evidenced in this and other writings (e.g., "What Is behind the Hanging of the Eleven Jews in Prague" (1952); "The Proclamation of London of the European Liberation Front" (1949); and "The World in Flames: An Estimate of the World Situation" (1961)). Thus, it is no surprise that Yockey was a strong early advocate of both German National Socialism (Nazism) and Italian Fascism and remained so even after the horrific revelations of World War II.

Whatever biographical knowledge there is on Yockey has primarily been culled from FBI intelligence and surveillance files, some of which are conjectural. This much is known, however:

146 | Yockey, Francis Parker

Yockey was born in Chicago, Illinois, and he was something of a child piano prodigy and elitist. He received his BA from the University of Arizona and his law degree from Notre Dame Law School cum laude (with distinction) in 1941. He later maintained that his racism was the result of an automobile accident and being assaulted by several African Americans. While a student, he had his first essay published in the magazine *Social Justice* by the isolationist and antisemitic Father Charles E. Coughlin (1891–1979) of Oak Park, Michigan. During the period of World War II and immediately prior (late 1930s to mid-1940s), Yockey identified himself with far-right organizations in both the United States, such as Fritz Kuhn's (1896–1951) German American Bund, and Great Britain, such as the British Union of Fascists led by Sir Oswald Mosely (1896–1980), and he continued to do so after 1945. In 1946, he secured a position with the War Department reviewing posttrial war crimes documents, where he concluded that the Allied occupation of Germany was "illegal" and the procedures of the various war crimes trials biased. In November of that year, he was fired.

Three years later, he published *Imperium* and dedicated it "To the Hero of the Second World War," which he later confirmed was, in fact, Adolf Hitler (1889–1945). That same year, he joined with European colleagues and founded the European Liberation Front (ELF), and he wrote many of the antisemitic anti-American, anti-Communist articles for its newsletter *Frontfighter*. ELF also published the aforementioned "The Proclamation of London." In that document, he brands "the Jews" as "cultural distorters" and "bearers of cultural disease" and sees the United States as the locale where Jews were actualizing their hatred of the West. In 1952, he traveled to Prague, Czechoslovakia, to witness firsthand the trial of eleven Jews for conspiring against Soviet Russia. He applauded the Soviets for purging their leadership of Jews and "Jewish influences." One year later, in 1953, he met Gamal Abdel Nasser 1918–1970), the president of Egypt, and worked briefly for Egypt's Information Ministry, writing both antisemitic and anti-Zionist propaganda opposing the newly founded State of Israel (1948) and "Jewish-American power."

Already on the radar of the Federal Bureau of Investigation (FBI), Yockey was arrested in California in 1960 and found to have in his possession several false passports and false birth certificates. While in prison, he was visited by Willis Carto (1926–2015), the founder of the Liberty Lobby, who later became his publishing advocate and wrote a lengthy introduction to *Imperium*. Shortly thereafter, Yockey was found dead in his San

Francisco jail cell, having committed suicide by ingesting a cyanide capsule. Suspicion has long remained about whether he brought it with him or it was given to him by an outside visitor or in-house guard or that he was intentionally murdered and the evidence planted to make it look like a suicide.

Be that as it may, Yockey's corrosive influence on the far right remains, largely due to his thinking and writing that the U.S. alliance with Zionism was the seed of its future downfall and far more deadly than Communism. Today, largely unknown, his legacy may be more influential on the various so-called New Right movements in Europe rather than the United States, though his text remains available both in print and online. New Zealand white nationalist and fascist Kerry Bolton (b. 1956)—himself a figure of controversy in his own country—continues to praise Yockey's work to this day in many of his publications. A follow-up collection of Yockey's thoughts were published by Liberty Bell Publications in 1981 under the title *The Enemy of Europe: The Enemy of Our Enemies*; it was edited by the right-wing white supremacist academic Revilo P. Oliver (1908–1994).

See also: Barnes, Harry Elmer; Carto, Willis; Duke, David; Fascism; National Socialism/Nazism; Nationalism; Pierce, William Luther; Rockwell, George Lincoln; Social Darwinism; White Supremacy

Further Reading

Coogan, Kevin. *Dreamer of the Day: Francis Parker Yockey and the Postwar Fascist International*. Brooklyn, NY: Autonomedia, 1998.

Kaplan, Jeffrey, and Leonard Weinberg. *The Emergence of a Euro-America Radical Right*. New Brunswick, NJ: Rutgers University Press, 1998.

Lee, Martin A. *The Beast Reawakens*. Boston: Little, Brown, and Company, 1997.

Mintz, Frank P. *The Liberty Lobby and the American Right: Race, Conspiracy and Culture*. Westport, CT: Greenwood Press, 1985.

Annotated Bibliography

Included here are books, multivolume series, journals, DVDs, websites, and institutions and organizations.

Books

Aizenberg, Salo. *Hatemail: Anti-Semitism in Picture Postcards*. Philadelphia: Jewish Publication Society, 2013.
This graphic collection of postcards, beginning in the 1890s through the Holocaust and beyond, is a reminder that antisemitism did not begin with World War II and Adolf Hitler; it was used even earlier by politicians, journalists, and rabble-rousers to defame the Jewish people and Judaism.

Almog, Shmuel, ed. *Antisemitism through the Ages*. Oxford and New York: Pergamon Press, 1988.
This book presents a collection of essays that address the question of antisemitism throughout Jewish history: in antiquity, in the Middle Ages, in the Christian world, in Muslim countries, and in the twentieth century. It examines and assesses not only the various forms and manifestations of antisemitism in history but also the diverse interpretations that have been placed on it by scholars and others.

Battini, Michele. *Socialism of Fools: Capitalism and Modern Anti-Semitism*. Translated by Noor Mazhar and Isabella Vergnano. New York: Columbia University Press, 2016.
This volume focuses on the critical moment during the Enlightenment in which anti-Jewish stereotypes morphed into a sophisticated, modern social antisemitism. It examines the anti-Jewish anti-capitalist propaganda that cemented the idea of a Jewish conspiracy in the European mind and connects it to the atrocities that characterized the Jewish experience in the nineteenth and twentieth centuries.

150 | Annotated Bibliography

Baum, Steven K. *Antisemitism Explained*. Lanham, MD: University Press of America, 2012.
Baum guides the reader through the social mind and explains how the formation of social beliefs can be used as a narrative to determine reality. He offers a new perspective regarding how antisemitic legends and folk beliefs form the basis of our ongoing social narrative.

Baum, Steven K., Keil J. Kressel, Florette Cohn-Abady, and Steven Leonard Jacobs, eds. *Antisemitism in North America: New World, Old Hate*. Leiden, Netherlands, and Boston: Brill, 2016.
The editors have brought together an array of scholars from diverse disciplines and political orientations to assess the condition of the Jews in the United States, Canada, Mexico, and the Caribbean. They offer perspectives of why the Jewish experience in North America has neither been free from antisemitism nor ever so unwelcoming and dangerous as the countries from which they came.

Beck, Norman A. *Mature Christianity in the 21st Century: The Recognition and Repudiation of the Anti-Jewish Polemic in the New Testament*. Expanded and revised edition. New York: Crossroad, 1994.
The author identifies the anti-Jewish polemic within the New Testament, discusses reasons for the development of that polemic, places the anti-Jewish polemic of the New Testament into a specific context, and suggests ways in which a mature Christianity can repudiate the defamatory anti-Jewish polemic of the New Testament without doing damage to the theology of Christianity.

Beller, Steven. *Antisemitism: A Very Short Introduction*. Oxford and New York: Oxford University Press, 2015.
This *Very Short Introduction* untangles the history of the phenomenon of antisemitism from ancient religious conflicts to the "new antisemitism" in the twenty-first century. The author reveals how antisemitism grew as a political and ideological movement in the nineteenth century, how it reached its peak in the Holocaust, and how antisemitism still persists around the world today.

Berenbaum, Michael, ed. *Not Your Father's Antisemitism: Hatred of the Jews in the 21st Century*. St. Paul, MN: Paragon House, 2008.
This collection of essays argues that contemporary hatred of the Jews is not a throwback to the 1930s but a unique manifestation of

twenty-first-century humanity and the postmodernist crises. It examines antisemitism in contemporary Europe and in classical and contemporary Islam; argues for American exceptionalism, maintaining that antisemitism is less acute in the United States; and further examines the impact of Israel both in quelling the flames and fueling the fires of contemporary antisemitism.

Bieringer, Reimund, Didier Pollefeyt, Frederique Vandercasteele-Vanneuville, eds. *Anti-Judaism in the Fourth Gospel.* **Louisville, KY: Westminster John Knox Press, 2001.**
The papers in this volume were presented at a special international colloquium held in January 2000, in Leuven, Belgium, which was convened to assemble acknowledged experts on the Gospel of John and issues of anti-Judaism in that text.

Bostom, Andrew G., ed. *The Legacy of Islamic Antisemitism: From Sacred Texts to Solemn History.* **Amherst, MA: Prometheus Books, 2008.**
This documented collection of scholarly articles presents evidence that a readily discernible and uniquely Islamic antisemitism has been continuously expressed since the beginning of Islam, and it further suggests that the Qur'an itself is a source of that hostility toward Jews along with other texts of the Islamic tradition.

Brustein, William I. *Roots of Hate: Anti-Semitism in Europe before the Holocaust.* **Cambridge, UK: Cambridge University Press, 2013.**
The author provides a systematic comparative and empirical examination of antisemitism in Europe before the Holocaust and addresses the four principal roots of antisemitism:—religious, racial, economic, and political. He thus explains the epidemic rise of modern antisemitism, societal differences in antisemitism, and how antisemitism varies from other forms of prejudice.

Carr, Steven Alan. *Hollywood and Anti-Semitism: A Cultural History up to World War II.* **Cambridge, UK: Cambridge University Press, 2001.**
The author looks at the "Hollywood Question" of the 1920s, 1930s, and 1940s and how Jews and others fretted over their participation within the entertainment industry.

152 | Annotated Bibliography

Chanes, Jerome A. *Antisemitism: A Reference Handbook*. Santa Barbara, CA: ABC-CLIO, 2004.
This text includes a survey of the historical, political, and sociological contexts of antisemitism in more than fifty countries; a detailed worldwide survey of antisemitism covering every major country, from Austria to Yemen; and biographical sketches of influential antisemitic figures.

Cohen, Jeremy. *Christ Killers: The Jews and the Passion from the Bible to the Big Screen*. Oxford and New York: Oxford University Press, 2007.
The author traces the Christ-killer myth from ancient times to the present day, the Gospels, and Mel Gibson's 2004 movie *The Passion of the Christ*. He further argues that the Christ-killer myth remains a dominant factor in the way Christians and Jews perceive each other.

Crim, Brian E. *Antisemitism in the German Military Community and the Jewish Response, 1914–1938*. Lanham, MD: Lexington Books, 2014.
Crim explores how German World War I veterans from different social and political backgrounds contributed to antisemitic politics during the Weimar Republic. He also looks at how the military, right-wing veterans, and Jewish veterans chose to remember their war experiences and translated these memories into a political reality that led to both World War II and the Holocaust.

Crossan, Dominic. *Who Killed Jesus? Exposing the Roots of Anti-Semitism in the Gospel Story of the Death of Jesus*. New York: Harper & Row, 1995.
The author shows that the traditional understanding of the Gospels as historical fact is not only wrong but dangerous. His radical reexamination shows that the belief that the Jews killed Jesus was an early Christian myth directed against rival Jewish groups that must be eradicated from authentic Christian faith to thus move forward.

Curtis, Michael. *Jews, Antisemitism, and the Middle East*. New Brunswick, NJ, and London: Transaction Publishers, 2013.
This book challenges the misrepresentations, propaganda, obsessions, and falsifications widely disseminated in the media and public discourse and explains the motivations behind them. Curtis divides his arguments into

five key areas: political correctness and the obsessive attacks on Israel, the rise of antisemitism, the Arab world and the Islamist threat, the Palestinian narrative, and the Israeli-Palestinian conflict.

Dinnerstein, Leonard. *Anti-Semitism in America.* **Oxford and New York: Oxford University Press, 1994.**
Long considered a classic work in the study of antisemitism, Dinnerstein provides an early comprehensive history of prejudice against Jews in the United States from colonial times to the end of the twentieth century. He traces American antisemitism from its roots in the dawn of the Christian era and the arrival of the first European settlers to its peak during World War II and contemporary permutations. He examines antisemitism in the South and among African Americans and shows that prejudice among both whites and blacks flowed from the same stream of Southern evangelical Christianity.

Dundes, Alan, ed. *The Blood Libel Legend: A Casebook in Anti-Semitic Folklore.* **Madison: University of Wisconsin Press, 1991.**
The editor has gathered the works of several scholars who examine the varied sources and elaborations of the blood libel legend (that Jews murdered Christian infants to obtain blood to make the Passover matzah).

Fine, Robert, and Philip Spencer. *Antisemitism and the Left: On the Return of the Jewish Question.* **Manchester, UK: Manchester University Press, 2017.**
The authors argue that the Jewish experience offers a test case that addresses the question of universal humanity. They claim universalism has stimulated the struggle for Jewish emancipation, but it has also helped to develop the idea that there is something peculiarly harmful to humanity about Jews—that there is a "Jewish Question" that needs to be "solved." This original book traces struggles within the Enlightenment, Marxism, critical theory, and the contemporary left, seeking to rescue universalism from its repressive, antisemitic undertones.

Fineberg, Michael, Shimon Samuels, and Mark Weitzman, eds. *Antisemitism: The Generic Hatred: Essays in Honor of Simon Wiesenthal.* **London and Portland, OR: Vallentine Mitchell, 2007.**
Dedicated to the memory of Simon Wiesenthal (1908–2005), this book brings together essays by a wide variety of authors on antisemitism and related forms of intolerance, racism, and xenophobia. Starting from the

154 | Annotated Bibliography

idea that antisemitism constitutes a paradigmatic case of collective and individual hatred, the contributors examine some of the reasons why it has prospered over the ages and persists in our time, even after the well-nigh universal condemnation of the Holocaust.

Flannery, Edward H. *The Anguish of the Jews: A Catholic Priest Writes of 23 Centuries of Anti-Semitism.* **New York: Macmillan, 1964.**
In this classic text in the study and history of antisemitism, Edward Flannery (1912–1998), a Catholic priest, provides a thorough account of the history of the world's persecution of the Jews without dwelling on the lurid details of the atrocities. He covers pagan antisemitism in the Greek and Roman Empires, the struggles between Judaism and the early church, Christian antisemitism in the Middle Ages in the various countries of Europe, the age of the ghetto, the rise of scapegoat antisemitism in the modern postreligious world—particularly in Russia—leading to Hitler's "new paganism" and the Holocaust as well as economic, racial, and social antisemitism in the United States.

Freudmann, Lillian C. *Antisemitism in the New Testament.* **Lanham, MD: University Press of America, 1994.**
Freudmann studies the anti-Jewish contents of the New Testament in a thorough, systematic, verse-by-verse manner. The author identifies every misquotation and mistranslation from the Hebrew Bible and attempts to refute every antisemitic assertion in the Christian Scriptures. She further examines the historical background in which the Gospels and Epistles were written and how contemporary conditions affected their contents before concluding with the impact of the New Testament on Jews and Christians since its canonization and the possibilities of negating a past negative history through alternative interpretations.

Gerdmar, Anders. *Roots of Theological Anti-Semitism: German Biblical Interpretation and the Jews, from Herder and Semler to Kittel and Bultmann.* **Leiden, Netherlands, and Boston: Brill, 2009.**
Gerdmar looks at the roots of theological antisemitism and how Jews and Judaism were positively and negatively constructed in German Protestant theology. He examines the leading exegetes from the 1750s to the 1950s and explores how theology legitimizes or delegitimizes the oppression of Jews, which is still a current issue in various Protestant circles today.

Annotated Bibliography | 155

Gerstenfeld, Manfred. *Europe's Crumbling Myths: The Post-Holocaust Origins of Today's Anti-Semitism.* **Jerusalem, Israel: Jerusalem Center for Public Affairs, 2003.**
This text explores how developments in post-Holocaust Europe prefigured the adversities that Israel and the Jews face there today. It explains how the "new antisemitism" is more of a continuation and development of historical and traditional antisemitism than an innovation.

Gerstenfeld, Manfred. *The War of a Million Cuts: The Struggle against the Delegitimization of Israel and the Jews, and the Growth of the New Anti-Semitism.* **Jerusalem, Israel: Jerusalem Center for Public Affairs, 2015.**
This book attempts to explain how the delegitimization of Israel and antisemitism overall can be fought. It describes the hateful messages of those who defame Israel and the Jews, details why antisemitism and anti-Israelism have the same core motifs, and discusses the main groups of inciters, including Muslim states, Muslims in the Western world, politicians, media, NGOs, church leaders, those on the extreme left and the extreme right, Jewish self-haters, academics, social democrats, and many others. It explains how the hate messages are effectively transmitted to the public at large and discusses what impact the delegitimization has already made on Israel and the Jews.

Gilman, Sander L., and Steven T. Katz, eds. *Anti-Semitism in Times of Crisis.* **New York and London: University of New York Press, 1991.**
Gilman traces the image of the Jew and the attitudes toward the Jew over the past two thousand years, from the Roman Empire to the reunification of Germany, showing the consistent pattern of antisemitism in Western societies.

Goldhagen, Daniel Jonah. *The Devil That Never Dies: The Rise and Threat of Global Antisemitism.* **New York and London: Little, Brown and Company, 2013.**
Goldhagen examines the widespread resurgence of antisemitism in the twenty-first century. In doing so, he shows the unprecedented global form of this age-old hatred, its strategic use by states, its powerful appeal to individuals and groups, and how technology has furthered the antisemitic agenda.

156 | Annotated Bibliography

Goldstein, Phyllis. *A Convenient Hatred: The History of Antisemitism.* **Brookline, MA: Facing History and Ourselves, 2011.**
Goldstein chronicles the history of antisemitism through powerful stories that allow her readers to see themselves in this tarnished mirror of history. She raises important questions about the consequences of our assumptions and beliefs and the ways in which we as individuals and as members of a society make distinctions between us and them, right and wrong, and good and evil. The questions raised are both universal and particular and, by necessity, force uncomfortable answers.

Goldwag, Arthur. *The New Hate: A History of Fear and Loathing on the Populist Right.* **New York: Vantage Books, 2012.**
Goldwag takes his readers on a surprising, shocking, and bizarrely amusing tour through the swamps of nativism, racism, antisemitism, and paranoid speculations about money that have long thrived on the American fringe. He shows the parallels between the hysteria about how the Illuminati historically supposedly ruined the American republic in the 1790s through the McCarthyism that roiled the United States in the 1950s. He also discusses the similarities between the anti–New Deal forces in the 1930s and the Tea Party movement today. He traces Henry Ford's (1863–1947) antisemitism and the John Birch Society's "insiders" back to the notorious *Protocols of the Elders of Zion*, and he relates white supremacist nightmares about racial pollution to nineteenth-century fears of papal plots and their continuation today.

Griech-Polelle, Beth. *Anti-Semitism and the Holocaust: Language, Rhetoric and the Traditions of Hatred.* **New York and London: Bloomsbury Academic, 2017.**
This book examines varieties of antisemitism that have existed throughout history, from religious antisemitism in the ancient Roman Empire to the racial antisemitism of political antisemites in Germany and Austria in the late nineteenth century. The author analyzes the tropes, imagery, legends, myths, and stereotypes about Jews that have surfaced at these various points in time. She considers how this language helped to engender an innate distrust, dislike, and even hatred of the Jews in twentieth-century Europe and further explores the shattering impact of World War I and the rise of Weimar Germany, Hitler's rhetoric, and the first phase of Nazi antisemitism before illustrating how ghettos, SS *Einsatzgruppen* killing squads, death camps, and death marches were used

Annotated Bibliography | 157

to drive this antisemitic agenda toward what would ultimately become the Holocaust.

Harrison, Bernard. *The Resurgence of Anti-Semitism: Jews, Israel, and Liberal Opinion.* **Lanham, MD: Rowman & Littlefield, 2006.**
This book by a non-Jewish analytic philosopher assesses the relative merits of these opposite views—moral concerns about Israel versus anti-Zionism not being an expression of antisemitism—and offers a detailed examination of the moral and intellectual credentials of the widespread current of opinion that seemingly undergirds both.

Harrowitz, Nancy A. *Tainted Greatness: Antisemitism and Cultural Heroes.* **Philadelphia: Temple University Press, 1994.**
The authors in this edited volume ask whether the revelation of prejudice devalues the work of those regarded as intellectual heroes? What does it mean to continue to revere intellectual greatness despite the presence of antisemitism? Is antisemitism an inextricable part of such persons' work as much as a part of their lives and thus a significant part of their overall contribution? Is it the concept of heroism or greatness itself that invites or even generates the notion of taintedness that needs to be examined?

Heni, Clemens. *Antisemitism: A Specific Phenomenon: Holocaust Trivialization—Islamism—Post-Colonial and Cosmopolitan Anti-Zionism.* **Berlin: Edition Critic, 2013.**
Heni, a German scholar, analyzes the specifics of antisemitism and Jew-hatred in the twenty-first century. He includes an assessment of the political leanings of many prominent scholars in the field. According to the author, today's antisemitism extends far beyond right-wing circles and can be found among liberals, leftists, anti-racist communities, Islamists, and postcolonial scholars in the Western world. Using English and German sources, he demonstrates the need to oppose Holocaust trivialization as well as other so-called modern forms of antisemitism, such as anti-Zionism and the defamation of the Jewish state of Israel.

Herf, Jeffrey, ed. *Anti-Semitism and Anti-Zionism in Historical Perspective: Convergence and Divergence.* **New York and London: Routledge, 2015.**
This book presents the reflections of historians from Israel, Europe, Canada, and the United States concerning the similarities and differences

158 | Annotated Bibliography

between anti-Zionism and antisemitism, primarily in Europe and the Middle East, at the end of the twentieth century and the beginning of the twenty-first century.

Hirsch, David. *Contemporary Left Antisemitism*. London and New York: Routledge, 2017.
This book looks at the kind of antisemitism that appears to be tolerated or that goes unacknowledged in such democratic places as trade unions, churches, left-wing and liberal politics, social gatherings, seminaries, and journals of radical intellectuals. It analyzes how criticism of Israel can mushroom into antisemitism, and it looks at the struggles over how antisemitism is defined. It further focuses on ways in which those who raise the issue of antisemitism are often accused of doing so in bad faith to silence opponents or smear them.

Idinopulos, Thomas A. *Betrayal of the Spirit: Jew-Hatred, the Holocaust, and Christianity*. Aurora, CO: Davies Group, 2007.
The author draws on a combination of personal experiences and theological reflections to examine how antisemitism invaded, occupied, and dominated the human mind throughout history. His theological interpretations of the history of Jew-hatred in Christendom provides a way of understanding how anti-Judaism differs from antisemitism and created the possibility of, but was not a direct cause of, the Holocaust. He addresses questions such as the following: In what ways does the history of antisemitism explain the Holocaust? In what ways does it not explain the Holocaust? How do we explain the unexplainable? What was the role of religion in Nazi thinking? What should we make of the intentionalist versus functionalist debates among historians? Responses to these questions reveal the interplay between the rational and the nonrational as well as the religious and racial components that combined to make the Holocaust a dreadful reality.

Isser, Natalie. *Antisemitism during the French Second Empire*. New York and Berlin: Peter Lang, 1991.
This book analyzes the development of antisemitism in France from 1850 to 1870. Based on archival material and contemporary press accounts and journals, the author traces the experience of antisemitism through World War II to the present and reveals the antecedents of prejudice that poisoned French life during the Dreyfus Affair (1884–1906).

Annotated Bibliography | 159

Jacobs, Jack. *The Frankfurt School, Jewish Lives, and Antisemitism.* **Cambridge, UK: Cambridge University Press, 2016.**
The author argues that the history of the Frankfurt School cannot be fully told without examining the relationship of critical theorists to their Jewish family backgrounds. Jewish matters had significant effects on such key figures in the Frankfurt School as Max Horkheimer (1895–1973), Theodor W. Adorno (1903–1969), Erich Fromm (1900–1980), Leo Lowenthal (1900–1993), and Herbert Marcuse (1898–1979).

Jacobs, Jack, ed. *Jews and Leftist Politics: Judaism, Israel, Antisemitism, and Gender.* **Cambridge, UK: Cambridge University Press, 2017.**
This edited volume contains new and insightful chapters that consider such matters as the political implications of Judaism; the relationship of leftists and Jews; the history of Jews on the left in Europe, the United States, and Israel; contemporary anti-Zionism; the associations between specific Jews and Communist parties; and the importance of gendered perspectives. It also contains fresh studies of canonical figures, including Gershom Scholem (1897–1982), Gustav Landauer (1870–1919), and Martin Buber (1878–1965), and examines the affiliations of Jews to prominent institutions, calling into question previously widely held assumptions.

Jaher, Frederic Cople. *A Scapegoat in the New Wilderness: The Origins and Rise of Anti-Semitism in America.* **Cambridge, MA, and London: Harvard University Press, 1994.**
Jaher raises the questions of how antisemitism became a presence in the United States and how the country's beginnings and history affected the course of this bigotry? Comprehensive in its approach, this book combines psychological, sociological, economic, cultural, anthropological, and historical interpretations to reveal the nature of antisemitism in the United States.

Julius, Anthony. *Trials of the Diaspora: A History of Anti-Semitism in England.* **Oxford and New York: Oxford University Press, 2010.**
This text reveals the full history of antisemitism in England by focusing on four distinct versions of English antisemitism: (1) the medieval persecution of Jews, which included defamation, expropriation, and murder and culminated in 1290 when King Edward I (1239–1307) expelled all Jews from England; (2) literary antisemitism, which revealed the negative portrayals of Jews that have been continuously present in English literature, from the anonymous ballad "Sir Hugh, or the Jew's Daughter" (eighteenth

160 | Annotated Bibliography

century) to Shakespeare's *Merchant of Venice* (sixteenth century) to T. S. Elliot (1888–1965) and beyond; (3) modern antisemitism during the Jews' "readmission" to England in the mid-seventeenth century through the late twentieth century; and (4) contemporary antisemitism, which emerged in the late 1960s and the 1970s and continues to be present today.

Katz, Jacob. *From Prejudice to Destruction: Anti-Semitism, 1700–1933*. Cambridge, MA: Harvard University Press, 1982.
Katz argues for a revision of the prevalent thesis that medieval and modern animosities against Jews were fundamentally different. He also rejects the scapegoat theory, according to which the Jews were merely a lightning rod for underlying economic and social tensions. He further argues that there were very real tensions between Jews and non-Jews because the Jews were a highly visible and cohesive group and came into conflict with non-Jews in competing for social and economic rewards.

Klein, Charlotte. *Anti-Judaism in Christian Theology*. Translated by Edward Quinn. Philadelphia: Fortress Press, 1975.
Klein, a Jewish convert to Christianity, traces anti-Judaism in the history of Christian theology from its beginning to the present day. She further shows that anti-Judaism is more deeply rooted in Christianity than might at first be supposed.

Küntzel, Matthias. *Jihad and Jew-Hatred: Islamism, Nazism, and the Roots of 9/11*. Translated by Colin Meade. New York: Telos Publishing, 2007.
The author traces the impact of European fascism and Nazism on Arab and Islamic activists and investigates the shift of global antisemitism from Nazi Germany to parts of the Arab world during and after World War II. He argues that antisemitism is not merely a supplementary feature of modern jihadism but instead lies at its ideological core.

Laqueur, Walter. *The Changing Face of Anti-Semitism: From Ancient Times to the Present Day*. Oxford, and New York: Oxford University Press, 2008.
The author begins with a historical account overview of antisemitism, tracing its evolution from a predominantly religious antisemitism to a racial antisemitism that developed in the late nineteenth and early twentieth centuries. Laqueur shows that what was historically a preoccupation of

Christian and right-wing movements has become even more frequent among Muslims and left-wing groups today.

Lazare, Bernard. *Antisemitism: Its History and Causes.* **Translated from the French. Lincoln and London: University of Nebraska Press, 1995/1894.**
Bernard Lazare's (1865–1903) controversial magnum opus, originally published in France in 1894, asks why the Jews have aroused such hatred for three thousand years. Though severed from his Jewish upbringing, Lazare was fiercely committed to social justice and could not ignore a shocking antisemitism in the fin-de-siècle circles he knew. Lazare began his "impartial study" by considering what in the Jewish character might be to blame for antisemitism. He then looked outward to those nations among which the Israelites dispersed, examining the different faces of antisemitism from Greco-Roman antiquity to the end of the nineteenth century.

Levenson, Alan T. *Between Philosemitism and Antisemitism: Defenses of Jews and Judaism in Germany, 1871–1932.* **Lincoln and London: University of Nebraska Press, 2004.**
This book offers an assessment of the non-Jewish defense of Jews, Judaism, and Jewishness from the foundation of the German Reich in 1871 until the ascent of the Nazis in 1932, when befriending Jews became a crime. It shows the dynamic process by which a generally despised minority attracted defenders and supporters. It also demonstrates that there was sympathy for Jews and Judaism in Imperial and Weimar Germany.

Levy, René H. *Baseless Hatred: What It Is and What You Can Do about It.* **Jerusalem, Israel, and New York: Gefen Books, 2011.**
According to Levy, baseless hatred is understood within Jewish tradition to have been the cause of the longest exile of the Jewish people from the Land of Israel. He further shows how the cement that has kept the Jewish people united as a nation, known as *arevut*—"mutual responsibility"—continues to provide the remedy for the devastating problem of baseless hatred.

Levy, Richard S., ed. *Antisemitism: A Historical Encyclopedia of Prejudice and Persecution.* **2 vols. Santa Barbara, CA: ABC-CLIO, 2005.**
This encyclopedia offers coverage of the origins, forms, practitioners, and effects of antisemitism that led to the Holocaust and survive to the present day. It includes 650 A–Z entries by over two hundred scholars from

162 | Annotated Bibliography

twenty-one countries; illustrations, such as caricatures, political cartoons, maps, and pictures of famous antisemites and historical episodes; citations of recent literature that follow each entry; a detailed index listing people, places, concepts, and events that enables users to find information about subjects not treated in dedicated articles; and directions at the end of each entry to other articles with special relevance to the topic.

Lindemann, Albert A. *The Jew Accused: Three Anti-Semitic Affairs (Dreyfus, Beilis, Frank)*. Cambridge, UK: Cambridge University Press, 1992.
This text explores the nature of modern antisemitism and the ways that politicians in the generation before World War I attempted to use hatred of Jews as a political device to mobilize the masses in the specific cases of three Jews accused of "disloyalty": Alfred Dreyfus (1859–1935), Mendel Beilis (1874–1934), and Leo Frank (1884–1915).

Lindemann, Albert S. *Esau's Tears: Modern Anti-Semitism and the Rise of the Jews*. Cambridge, UK: Cambridge University Press, 2000.
This text explores the rise of modern racial-political antisemitism in Europe and the United States. It suggests that antisemitism was more ambiguous than usually presented, less pervasive and central to the lives of both Jews and non-Jews, and by no means clearly pointed to a rising hatred of Jews everywhere and even less to the likelihood of mass murder.

Lipstadt, Deborah E. *Antisemitism Here and Now*. New York: Schocken Books, 2019.
This text is an analysis of the hate that will not die, focusing on its current virulent incarnations on both the political right and left. Where is all this hatred coming from? Is there any significant difference between left-wing and right-wing antisemitism? What role has the anti-Zionist movement played? And what can be done to combat the latest manifestations of an ancient hatred? In a series of letters to an imagined college student and imagined colleague, both of whom are perplexed by this resurgence, the author gives us her own responses to these troubling questions.

Maccoby, Hyam. *Judas Iscariot and the Myth of Jewish Evil*. New York: Free Press, 1992.
Maccoby studies the roots of antisemitism and examines how the myth describing Judas as the malevolent betrayer of the Christ has been

exaggerated and used throughout history to justify genocidal persecution of Jews both individually and collectively.

Marcus, Kenneth. *The Definition of Anti-Semitism.* **Oxford and New York: Oxford University Press, 2015.**
This book-length study explores the central question of definition in the context of the new antisemitism. The author explores the various ways in which antisemitism has historically been defined, demonstrates the weaknesses in prior efforts, and develops a new definition of antisemitism, especially in the context of the "new antisemitism" in American higher education.

McElligott, Anthony, and Jeffrey Herf. *Antisemitism before and since the Holocaust: Altered Contexts and Recent Perspectives.* **New York: Palgrave Macmillan, 2017.**
This book examines the issue of Holocaust denial, and in some cases "Holocaust inversion" in North America, Europe, and the Middle East and its relationship to the history of antisemitism before and since the Holocaust, and offers both a historical and contemporary perspective. It provides a discussion on the relationship between Christianity and Islam as well as the historical and contemporary issues of antisemitism in the United States, Europe, and the Middle East.

Michael, Robert, and Philip Rosen. *Dictionary of Antisemitism.* **Lanham, MD: Scarecrow Press, 2007.**
This dictionary is solely dedicated to the subject of antisemitism. Spanning three thousand years of antagonism to Jews, the dictionary details not only this longest hatred but also its most widespread manifestations, covering the five major continents. It contains twenty-five hundred entries, ranging from "Aaron of Lincoln" to "Zyklon." Entries can be found on all forms of antisemitism, such as ancient, medieval, and modern antisemitism; pagan, Christian, and Muslim antisemitism; and religious, economic, psychosocial, racial, cultural, and political antisemitism.

Nirenberg, David. *Anti-Judaism: The Western Tradition.* **New York and London: W. W. Norton and Company, 2013.**
This history argues that anti-Judaism is a central way of thinking in the Western tradition, both historically and contemporarily, but also in behaviors, from the birth of Christianity two thousand years ago to the present.

164 | Annotated Bibliography

Perry, Marvin, and Frederick M. Schweitzer, eds. *Antisemitic Myths: A Historical and Contemporary Anthology.* **Bloomington: Indiana University Press, 2008.**
This anthology presents ninety documents that focus on the nature, evolution, and meaning of the principal myths that have made antisemitism such a lethal force in history: Jews as deicides, ritual murderers, agents of Satan, international conspirators, and conniving, unscrupulous Shylocks. Documents that illustrate the recent revival of classical myths about Jews among black nationalists, Holocaust deniers, and Islamic fundamentalists are also included.

Perry, Marvin, and Frederick M. Schweitzer. *Antisemitism: Myth and Hate from Antiquity to the Present.* **New York: Palgrave Macmillan, 2002.**
This book analyzes the lies, misperceptions, and myths about Jews and Judaism that antisemites have propagated throughout the centuries. Beginning with antiquity and continuing into the present, the authors explore the irrational fabrications that have led to numerous acts of violence and hatred against Jews and the ancient and medieval myths central to the history of antisemitism, such as Jews as "Christ-killers," instruments of Satan, and ritual murderers of Christian children. It also explores the scapegoating of Jews in the modern world as conspirators bent on world domination, extortionists who manufactured the Holocaust as a hoax designed to gain reparation payments from Germany for the State of Israel, and the leaders of the slave trade that put Africans in chains.

Pollack, Eunice G., ed. *From Antisemitism to Anti-Zionism: The Past & Present of a Lethal Ideology.* **Brighton, MA: Academic Studies Press, 2017.**
The authors in this edited collection document and trace the numerous parallels and continuities between the tropes attached for centuries to the Jewish people and the more recent vilifications of the Jewish state. They evaluate—and discredit—many of the central claims anti-Zionists have promoted in their relentless efforts to delegitimize the Jewish state. They show how mainstream anti-racist communities, courses, and texts have ignored—or denied—the antisemitic hatred that pervades much of the Muslim world.

Prager, Dennis, and Joseph Telushkin. *Why the Jews? The Reasons for Antisemitism.* **New York and London: Simon & Schuster, 2003.**
Why have Jews been the object of the most enduring and universal hatred in history? Why is the Jewish state the most hated country in the world today? Drawing on extensive historical research, the authors argue that

Judaism's distinctive conceptions of God, law, and peoplehood have rendered the Jews and the Jewish state outsiders and labeled them as threatening to the many societies and nation-states where they have lived.

Rensmann, Lars. *The Politics of Unreason: The Frankfurt School and the Origins of Modern Antisemitism.* **Albany: State University of New York Press, 2017.**
This book is a systematic study of the Frankfurt School's philosophical, psychological, political, and social research and theorizing on the problem of antisemitism. Examining the full range of these critical theorists' contributions, from major studies and prominent essays to seemingly marginal pieces and aphorisms, the author reconstructs how the Frankfurt School, faced with the catastrophe of the genocide against the European Jews, explains forms and causes of anti-Jewish politics of hate. The book also pays special attention to research on coded and "secondary" antisemitism after the Holocaust and how resentments are politically mobilized under conditions of democracy

Renton, James, and Ben Gidley, eds. *Antisemitism and Islamophobia: A Shared Story?* **New York: Palgrave Macmillan, 2017.**
This book examines the relationship between European antisemitism and Islamophobia, from the Crusades until the twenty-first century, in the principal flashpoints of the two racisms. With case studies that range from the Balkans to the United Kingdom, the contributors take the debate away from politicized polemics about whether Muslims are the new Jews and interrogate how the dynamic relationship between antisemitism and Islamophobia has evolved over time and space. The result is the uncovering of a previously unknown story in which European ideas about Jews and Muslims were indeed connected but were also ripped apart. Religion, empire, nation-building, and war all played their part in the complex evolution of this relationship. In addition to being a study of prejudice, this book also opens a new area of inquiry: how Muslims, Jews, and others have responded to these historically connected racisms. The authors show how a Europe in which Jews and Arabs were once called Semites are widely thought to be on two different sides of the war on terrorism today.

Rosenfeld, Alvin H., ed. *Deciphering the New Antisemitism.* **Bloomington: Indiana University Press, 2015.**
This book addresses the increasing prevalence of antisemitism on a global scale. The essays in this wide-ranging volume deal with many issues of

166 | Annotated Bibliography

importance: European antisemitism, antisemitism and Islamophobia, antisemitism and anti-Zionism, and efforts to demonize and delegitimize Israel.

Rosenfeld, Alvin H., ed. *Resurgent Antisemitism: Global Perspectives.* **Bloomington: Indiana University Press, 2013.**
This book presents original research that elucidates the social, intellectual, and ideological roots of the "new" antisemitism and the place it has come to occupy in the public sphere. By exploring the sources, goals, and consequences of today's antisemitism and its relationship to the past, this book contributes to an understanding of this phenomenon that may help diminish its appeal and mitigate its more harmful effects.

Schoenfeld, Gabriel. *The Return of Anti-Semitism.* **San Francisco: Encounter Books, 2004.**
This book traces the confluence of several lethal currents marking today's antisemitism: the infusion of Judeophobia into Islamic fundamentalism; the rise of terrorist movements (including al-Qaeda) that are motivated in large measure by a pathological hatred of Jews; the deliberate and well-financed export of antisemitism from the Muslim world into Europe and from there into the United States; and the rebirth of older antisemitic traditions in the West that were thought to have ended along with Nazism.

Schwarz-Friesel, Monika, and Jehuda Reinarz. *Inside the Antisemitic Mind: The Language of Jew-Hatred in Contemporary Germany.* **Waltham, MA: Brandeis University Press, 2017.**
This empirical study examines written examples of antisemitism in contemporary Germany. It concretely demonstrates that hostility against Jews is not just a right-wing phenomenon or a phenomenon among the uneducated; it is manifested among all social classes,

Shainkman, Mikael, ed. *Antisemitism Today and Tomorrow: Global Perspectives on the Many Faces of Contemporary Antisemitism.* **Brighton, MA: Academic Studies Press, 2018.**
This book illustrates the two clear trends in antisemitism today: "old" antisemitism, based in religious and racist prejudices, which has largely disappeared from public discourse in the West after the defeat of Nazi Germany but has resurfaced in the last quarter century in the face of right-wing frustration of weakening nation-states in a globalized world, and "new"

antisemitism, or the antisemitic hatred of Israel, which is most commonly found on the left, in the Muslim world, and in the postcolonial discourse. This collection of essays analyzes both the old and new antisemitisms to understand their place in the world of today and tomorrow.

Sharan, Shlomo, and David Bukay. *Crossovers: Anti-Zionism & Anti-Semitism.* **New Brunswick, NJ, and London: Transaction Publishers, 2010.**
This book compares Jewish anti-Zionism and Palestinian antisemitism from political and philosophical points of view. The authors' goal is to expose what is unique about these phenomena and what they share so that both ideologies and their practical impacts can be better understood. The authors identify a symbiotic relationship between antisemitic Palestinian doctrines and those Jews who are anti-Zionists.

Stav, Arieh. *Peace: The Arabian Caricature of Anti-Semitic Imagery.* **New York and Jerusalem, Israel: Gefen Books, 1999.**
In this book, the author examines the antisemitic caricatures and illustrations of the medieval Christian Church, the Nazis, and especially the modern Arab world's graphic anti-Jewish and anti-Israel depictions. Though the images do not tell the whole story, they do paint a grisly picture of Arab attitudes toward peace with Israel.

Steinweis, Alan E. *Studying the Jews: Scholarly Antisemitism in Nazi Germany.* **Cambridge, MA, and London: Harvard University Press, 2006.**
This book investigates the careers of a few dozen German scholars who forged an interdisciplinary field, drawing upon studies in anthropology, biology, religion, history, and the social sciences to create a comprehensive portrait of the Jew—one with devastating consequences. Working within the universities and research institutions of the Third Reich, these men fabricated an elaborate empirical basis for Nazi antisemitic policies. They supported the Nazi campaign against Jews by defining them as racially alien, morally corrupt, and inherently criminal. In a chilling story of academics who perverted their talents and distorted their research in support of persecution and genocide, the author explores the intersection of ideology and scholarship, the state and the university, and the intellectual and his motivations to provide a new appreciation of the use and abuse of learning and the horrors perpetrated in the name of reason.

168 | Annotated Bibliography

Stern, Frank. *The Whitewashing of the Yellow Badge: Antisemitism and Philosemitism in Postwar Germany.* **Translated by William Templer. Oxford and New York: Pergamon Press, 1992.**
The central themes of this book are the attitudes, behaviors, and actions of non-Jews toward Jews in postwar Germany. The analysis focuses on antisemitism and developing philosemitism in all aspects of life in the Federal Republic. Topics include Jews caught in between Germans and occupiers; American military government and German antisemitism; antisemitic and philosemitic stereotypes among blue-collar and white-collar workers; and the political role of antisemitism and philosemitism in the formative period of the Federal Republic of Germany.

Sternberg, Robert J., ed. *The Psychology of Hate.* **Washington, DC: American Psychological Association, 2005.**
This book brings together experts on the psychology of hate to present their diverse viewpoints in a single volume. The contributors address a set of questions that include the following: How do you conceptualize hate, and what evidence is there for this conceptualization? What do you see as the role of hate in terrorism, massacres, and genocides? How can hate be assessed? It also provides concrete suggestions for how to combat hate and attempts to understand the minds of both those who hate and those who are hated.

Taguieff, Pierre-André. *Rising from the Muck: The New Anti-Semitism in Europe.* **Chicago: Ivan R. Dee, 2004.**
In this book, the author surveys the landscape of contemporary antisemitism in Europe, describing its leading figures, the role of the conflict between Israelis and Palestinians, the Islamic influence in promoting anti-Zionism, and the blindness, complacency, or connivance of various institutions, groups, and individuals. The author shows that the new wave of antisemitism spreading around the world is based on a polemical and fanciful amalgam of Jews, Israelis, and "Zionists" as representatives of an evil power. The old European antisemitism, the author notes, was a kind of racism directed against Jews. The new worldwide antisemitism seeks to turn the charge of racism against the Jews.

Weiss, John. *The Politics of Hate: Anti-Semitism, History, and the Holocaust in Modern Europe.* **Chicago: Ivan R. Dee, 2003.**
In this book, the author shows how antisemitism and racism developed as major elements in the European political processes of Germany, Austria, France, and Poland from the late nineteenth century to the Holocaust. In a

Annotated Bibliography | 169

separate chapter on Italy, he explains why antisemitism never took hold there and why even during World War II, under Nazi control, Jews in Italy were relatively protected.

Williamson, Clark J. *Has God Rejected His People? Anti-Judaism in the Christian Church*. Nashville, TN: Abingdon, 1982.
The point of this book is simple: to make Christians aware of a story that they have not been told—the story of relations between Christians and Jews. This involves tracing the church's anti-Judaism to its source in the Gospels of Matthew, Mark, Luke, and John and the Book of Acts and describing the development of the church's displacement-replacement theology according to which Gentiles—spiritual, universal, and inclusive Christians—replace the old, carnal, ethnocentric legalist, and works-righteous Jews in the favor of God. The book also details the actions of the churches, specifically a long chain of canons (laws) governing relations between Jews and Christians that ranged from banning Christians from socializing or dining with Jews, marrying Jews, and asking rabbis for blessings to requiring all Jews to live in ghettos. This history of actions comes down to the present and its consequences in the Holocaust, in which all the killers were Christians, and in the Nazi laws governing Jewish behavior. The point of making people aware of anti-Judaism is to prompt them not to shrug it off when scripture readings regularly teach contempt for Jews with the rhetoric of vilification.

Williamson, Clark M., and Ronald H. Allen. *Interpreting Difficult Texts: Anti-Judaism and Christian Preaching*. Philadelphia and London: Trinity Press International and SCM Press, 2012.
This volume shows how to identify anti-Judaism in the Bible, in worship, and in preaching and how to avoid it. The authors begin with a description of how anti-Judaism is present throughout the church's history. Then a study of specific New Testament texts follows, resulting in a demonstration of where anti-Judaism has crept in and why. Concluding chapters focus on what can be done with these difficult texts and on what preaching and worship services without anti-Judaism will look like.

Wistrich, Robert S., ed. *Demonizing the Other: Antisemitism, Racism and Xenophobia*. Amsterdam, Netherlands: Harwood Academic Publishers, 1999.
This book is an interdisciplinary, cross-cultural approach to antisemitism that brings together an array of historians, anthropologists, psychologists,

170 | Annotated Bibliography

literary critics, and feminists. The historical sweep covers Greco-Roman antiquity, the Middle Ages, and the modern era. Antisemitism is analyzed within the much broader framework of racism and xenophobia.

Wistrich, Robert S. *A Lethal Obsession: Anti-Semitism from Antiquity to the Global Jihad.* **New York: Random House, 2010.**
The author examines the long and ugly history of antisemitism, from the first recorded pogrom in 38 BCE to its shocking and widespread resurgence in the present day. This comprehensive text reveals the causes behind this shameful and persistent form of hatred and offers a sobering look at how it may shape and reshape the world in years to come. In the concluding chapters, the author warns of a possible nuclear "Final Solution" at the hands of Iran, a land in which a formerly prosperous Jewish community has declined in both fortunes and freedoms.

Zimmerman, Moshe. *Wilhelm Marr: The Patriarch of Antisemitism.* **Oxford and New York: Oxford University Press, 1986.**
This book is the biography of radical writer and politician Wilhelm Marr (1819–1904), the man who introduced the term *antisemitism* into politics and founded the League of Antisemites. Drawing on Marr's published and unpublished works as well as on previously unexamined journals and voluminous correspondence, the author sets out to discover why an intellectual radical like Marr would become a virulent antisemite. He reveals the diverse ways that antisemitism came to permeate German thought and illuminates critical moments in the emergence of the German Reich.

Zipes, Jack, trans. *The Operated Jew: Two Tales of Anti-Semitism.* **New York and London: Routledge, 1991.**
A turn-of-the-century Jew undergoes a series of disfiguring operations that transform him into a "European." Oskar Panizza's (1853–1921) chilling story "The Operated Jew" (1893) mingles loathing with compassion for its title character. Thirty years later, Panizza's tale was answered by "Mynona," a pseudonym for Salomo Friedlaender (1871–1946), an urban German Jew who turned the story's tale into "The Operated Goy" (1922). The author translates these two stories into English and provides an extensive introduction as well as bibliographic essays that recover these two writers, placing their often bizarre tales within the history of modern antisemitism. Panizza and Mynona were both haunted and persecuted by religious and racist fanaticism in Germany. Taken together, these writers form a

dialectical image, the operated Jew/German, a figure that in turn casts its shadow on our present, illustrating why we devastate our bodies in a quest for purity and perfection.

Zuckerman, Nathan. *Wine of Violence: An Anthology on Anti-Semitism.* **New York: Association Press, 1947.**
This anthology of antisemitism—compiled more than seven decades ago—is a sizeable compilation of much that has been written about the Jewish problem by both Jews and non-Jews. The material here has been broken down into sections on the nature of antisemitism, its techniques, and its alleged causes (racial, political, psychological, economic, etc.). The author also includes countermeasures and their defendants, both individuals and organizations; proposed solutions to the problem of antisemitism; and a special supplement on the then current "Jewish-Black problem."

Multivolume

Cohen, Susan Sarah, ed. *Antisemitism: An Annotated Bibliography.* **22 vols. Berlin: De Gruyter, 1984–2006.**
This series includes international secondary literature on antisemitism published throughout the world, from the earliest times to 2006. It lists books, dissertations, and articles from periodicals and collections from many disciplines (history, political science, psychology, religion, sociology, and the arts). An abstract in English is provided for each entry, and Hebrew titles are transliterated and accompanied by English translations.

Journals

Antisemitism Studies
As a double-blind, peer-reviewed academic journal, *Antisemitism Studies* is a venue for scholarship on antisemitism, both past and present. Multidisciplinary and international in scope, *Antisemitism Studies* publishes a variety of perspectives on, and interpretations of, the problem of antisemitism and its impact on society. It is published semiannually.

Journal for the Study of Antisemitism
The *Journal for the Study of Antisemitism* (*JSA*) was a biannual peer-reviewed academic journal that covered anthropological, sociological,

172 | Annotated Bibliography

psychological, legal, historical, philosophical, and political aspects of contemporary antisemitism. It is no longer published.

Journal of Contemporary Antisemitism
The Journal of Contemporary Antisemitism covers all forms of antisemitism found in the contemporary world with a particular focus and emphasis on the post-Holocaust era, including Islamist antisemitism in Europe, the West, and the Arab and Muslim worlds; Holocaust distortion in postcolonial and Eastern European scholarship and activism; and conspiracy-driven, or "old-style," Christian and secular characteristics of antisemitism.

Journal of Hate Studies
The *Journal of Hate Studies* is an international scholarly journal that promotes the sharing of interdisciplinary ideas and research related to the study of what hate is, where it comes from, and how to combat it. It aims to provide a deeper understanding of the processes by which hate is encouraged and promoted.

Moreshet, the Journal for the Study of the Holocaust and Antisemitism
Moreshet is published annually through the Mordecai Anielevich Memorial Holocaust Study and Research Center in conjunction with the Stephen Roth Institute for the Study of Antisemitism and Racism at Tel Aviv University. The Hebrew version of *Moreshet* has been published since 1963, with the English version now over ten years old.

Patterns of Prejudice
Patterns of Prejudice is a journal about historical and contemporary social exclusion published by Taylor & Francis. It is a double-blind peer-reviewed journal that has been published five times a year since 1967 to study "racial and religious prejudice" throughout the world and to report on contemporary political events as well.

DVDs

Crossfire (90 minutes, 1947)
Crossfire is an early fictional story about antisemitism. A police detective finds no usual motive when investigating the beating death of a man killed because he was a Jew. "Hate," he says, "is like a gun."

Annotated Bibliography | 173

Defamation: Anti-Semitism the Movie (91 minutes, 2009)
Intent on shaking up the ultimate "sacred cow" for Jews, Israeli director Yoav Shamir embarks on a quest to answer the question, What is antisemitism today? Does it remain a dangerous and immediate threat? Or is it a scare tactic used by right-wing Zionists to discredit their critics?

Ever Again (74 minutes, 2006)
Ever Again examines the resurgence of violent antisemitism in Europe and its connection to the international terrorism currently threatening the world. It exposes the dangerous Islamic extremism and culture of death being preached from mosques in Europe's major cities and the new neo-Nazism spreading from Germany across the continent. It documents the roots of recent terrorist attacks in Madrid and London that left hundreds dead and thousands wounded. It examines the shift from the traditional antisemitism of the right to the new antisemitism of the extreme left.

Gentleman's Agreement (90 minutes, 1947)
Gentleman's Agreement is a classic fictional story with a serious message. A journalist is assigned to write a series of articles on antisemitism. Searching for an angle, he decides to pose as a Jew, and he soon discovers what it is to be a victim of antisemitism.

Longest Hatred: A Revealing History of Anti-Semitism (150 minutes, 2004)
Segment one, "From the Cross to the Swastika," traces an image that begins with the earliest writings of Christianity, which leveled the charge that Jews were responsible for Jesus's death. Historians show how this demonizing dogma has affected Jews throughout the centuries in Italy, Spain, England, and Germany, culminating in the development of Nazi ideology.

Segment two, "Enemies of the People," takes a humanistic look at relations between Arabs and Israelis, once linked by pseudoscience under the degrading label "Semite" and now enmeshed in one of the world's most violent conflicts. Experts on both sides tell how Arabs and Jews, who for centuries lived in relative peace and harmony, have been drastically alienated by political turmoil and how the anti-Jewish propaganda now disseminated in the Arab world eerily parallels that seen in Europe before, during, and immediately after World War II.

Segment three, "From Moses to Mohammad," shows how antisemitic sentiments have accompanied a growing nationalism in Europe in recent

174 | Annotated Bibliography

decades, causing a mass exodus of Jews from Russia, and even resurfaced in Poland and Austria, where few Jews remain. In Germany, the remarkable collapse of the Berlin Wall has been followed by the rise of neo-Nazism among German youth.

Monster among Us (57 minutes, 2008)
Sixty-five years after the Holocaust, a new brand of antisemitism has reared its ugly head again in Europe. It has the same purpose but a different face. Antisemitism has surfaced on university campuses, in the media, on the streets, at political demonstrations, on the Internet, and in innocent social situations, and this DVD explores all of these different locales.

Protocols of Zion (95 minutes, 2006)
Despite all the evidence, millions around the world continue to blame the Jews for 9/11. This belief is a modern-day incarnation of the infamous *Protocols of the Elders of Zion*, the century-old forgery that some people still claim to be the Jews' master plan to rule the world.

Unmasked Judeophobia: The Threat to Civilization (88 minutes, 2011)
Unmasked Judeophobia exposes the current political assault against the State of Israel as fundamentally being a war against the Jewish people and their right to self-determination. Jews are forced to confront the possible destruction of the idea that there should even be a nation-state of the Jewish people as well as the genocide of the Jewish people themselves.

Websites

Anti-Defamation League (ADL), www.adl.org
The Anti-Defamation League (ADL) is an international Jewish non-governmental organization based in the United States. Describing itself as "the nation's premier civil rights/human relations agency," the ADL states that it "fights anti-Semitism and all forms of bigotry, defends democratic ideals, and protects civil rights for all," and it does so through its educational programs, informational materials, and advocacy.

Felix Posen Bibliographic Project on Antisemitism: A Computerized Bibliography on Antisemitism and the Holocaust, http://sicsa.huji.ac.il
The Felix Posen Bibliographic Project on Antisemitism is a project of the Vidal Sassoon International Center for the Study of Anti-Semitism

(SICSA) at the Hebrew University in Jerusalem, Israel. The SICSA was established in 1982 as an interdisciplinary research center dedicated to an independent, nonpolitical, and critical approach to understanding the phenomenon of antisemitism.

H-Antisemitism Network, networks.h-net.org
H-Antisemitism's purpose is to facilitate the exchange of scholarly information about antisemitism. It seeks to enable scholars to communicate their own research and teaching interests, discuss methodology, comment on current historiography, and share information about new data, sources of funding, and publishing. It explores with its subscribers new ways of making electronic communications a useful tool for serious studies of antisemitism.

Institute for the Study of Contemporary Antisemitism (ISCA), http://isca.indiana.edu
The Institute for the Study of Contemporary Antisemitism (ISCA) at Indiana University, in Bloomington, Indiana, offers courses and pursues high-level scholarly research into present-day manifestations of antisemitism. ISCA examines both aggressive acts and words and the relationships between them, especially the intellectual and ideological roots of the "new" antisemitism. In doing so, it seeks to examine the social, cultural, religious, and political forces that nurture antisemitism.

Southern Poverty Law Center (SPLC), www.splcenter.org
The Southern Poverty Law Center (SPLC) is an American nonprofit legal advocacy organization that specializes in civil rights and public interest litigation. Based in Montgomery, Alabama, the SPLC is noted for its successful legal cases against white supremacist groups, its classification of hate groups and other extremist organizations, and its promotion of tolerance through educational programs.

Institutions and Organizations

Alfred Weiner Library for the Study of the Holocaust and Genocide, London, England
The rationale of this library is to have a library, archive, and information service for Great Britain and the international community that supports research, learning, teaching, and advocacy about the Holocaust and genocide and their causes and consequences.

176 | Annotated Bibliography

American Jewish Committee (AJC), New York, NY
The American Jewish Committee (AJC) is among the leading global Jewish advocacy organizations. It addresses such issues as rising antisemitism and extremism, defending Israel's place in the world, and safeguarding the rights and freedoms of all people.

Anti-Defamation League (ADL), New York, NY
According to its own mandate, the purpose of the Anti-Defamation League (ADL) is "to stop the defamation of the Jewish people, and to secure justice and fair treatment to all." It remains at the forefront of educational programs directed toward young people and various adult groups, including police, politicians, and others interested in combating antisemitism.

Canadian Institute for the Study of Antisemitism (CISA), Winnipeg, MB, Canada
The Canadian Institute for the Study of Antisemitism (CISA) promotes scholarship and facilitates public education about antisemitism in its classic and contemporary forms. CISA sponsors an academic journal on the subject, *Antisemitism Studies*, which is published by the Indiana University Press, in Bloomington, Indiana, and edited by the institute's director, Dr. Catherine Chatterley, at the University of Manitoba, Canada.

Center for Research on Anti-Semitism (ZfA), Berlin, Germany
The Center for Research on Antisemitism (ZfA) at Technische Universitat in Berlin, Germany, focuses its efforts on researching and teaching about such prejudices as antisemitism, antigypsyism, xenophobia, and racism while also addressing such related topics as German-Jewish history, the Holocaust, and right-wing extremism in Germany and elsewhere.

Institute for Jewish Policy Research (JPR), World Jewish Congress (WJC), London, England
The Institute for Jewish Policy Research (JPR) is committed to Jewish community planning and development, providing empirical data for policy debates, and discussions about the future of Jewish life in Great Britain, Europe, and across the Jewish world.

Institute for the Study of Contemporary Antisemitism (ISCA), Bloomington, IN
The Institute for the Study of Contemporary Antisemitism (ISCA) at Indiana University, in Bloomington, Indiana, offers courses and pursues high-level scholarly research into present-day manifestations of antisemitism.

The ISCA examines the relationships between words and actions, especially the intellectual and ideological roots of the "new" antisemitism, and attempts to elucidate the social, cultural, religious, and political forces that nurture anti-Jewish hostility.

Institute for the Study of Global Antisemitism and Policy (ISGAP), New York, NY

The mission of the Institute for the Study of Global Antisemitism an Policy (ISGAP), founded in 2004, is to develop the study of critical contemporary antisemitism studies and ensure that it becomes an accepted component of university education and curricula, thus allowing the exploration of anti-semitism within a comprehensive, interdisciplinary framework from an array of approaches and perspectives as well as global, national, and regional contexts. In keeping with that mission, ISGAP's work encompasses the study of such subjects as changing historical phases of antisemitism, how antisemitism relates to other forms of hatred, to what extent antisemitism is unique, how some societies can resist antisemitism, and how policies could be developed and utilized to combat it. It has also developed the ISGAP-Oxford Summer Institute for Curriculum Development on Critical Antisemitism Studies, an international seminar series, research projects that address pertinent contemporary subject matter, and policies to map, decode, and confront contemporary antisemitism effectively. Scholars and researchers are regularly invited to present seminar papers and engage in research projects at both the conceptual and empirical levels and to publish those papers as well as making them available online.

Kantor Center for the Study of Contemporary Jewry, Tel Aviv, Israel

The Kantor Center for the Study of Contemporary European Jewry, founded in 2010 at Tel Aviv University, Israel, provides an academic framework for the interdisciplinary research of European Jewry from the end of World War II until the present day. The Center initiates, encourages, and coordinates research projects, conferences, seminars, and publications in the following areas:

- Worldwide legislation and enforcement in the promotion of minority rights and nondiscrimination and against racism, hate crimes, hate speech, antisemitism, and Holocaust denial
- Expansion of the Moshe Kantor Database for the Study of Antisemitism and Racism (in cooperation with the Stephen Roth Institute for the Study of Contemporary Antisemitism and Racism) and an annual press conference that presents the situation of antisemitism worldwide

178 | Annotated Bibliography

Pears Institute for the Study of Antisemitism, London, England
The Pears Institute for the Study of Antisemitism is based at Birkbeck, University of London. It is one of just two institutes in Europe whose mission is to promote understanding of antisemitism. Its founding principle is that the study of antisemitism is vital to understanding other forms of racialization, racism, religious intolerance, and xenophobia.

Stephen Roth Institute for the Study of Contemporary Antisemitism and Racism, Tel Aviv University, Tel Aviv, Israel
The Stephen Roth Institute for the Study of Contemporary Antisemitism and Racism at Tel Aviv University (TAU), Israel, undertakes academic research and provides a forum for discussion of issues related to antisemitism and racism, their history, and their social, institutional, and cultural settings following the end of World War II. It undertakes research projects on antisemitism and racism, publishes an annual survey of antisemitic trends throughout the world in cooperation with TAU's Kantor Center for the Study of European Jewry, and provides support for graduate students from a variety of faculties and departments at TAU whose research projects focus on various aspects of antisemitism or racism.

United States Holocaust Memorial Museum, Washington, DC
The purpose of the United States Holocaust Memorial Museum in Washington, DC, is to inspire citizens and leaders worldwide to confront hatred and antisemitism, prevent genocide, and promote human dignity. Each year, the museum teaches millions of people about the dangers of unchecked hatred and the need to prevent genocide. Through the William Levine Family Institute for Holocaust Education, the museum works closely with professionals from the fields of law enforcement, the judiciary, and the military, as well as diplomacy, medicine, education, and religion, to gain insight into their responsibilities today. In addition to its leadership training programs, the museum sponsors onsite and traveling exhibitions, educational outreach for teachers and students, and Holocaust commemorations, including the annual observance of the Days of Remembrance in the U.S. Capitol. Its Jack, Joseph and Morton Mandel Center for Advanced Holocaust Studies fosters the continued growth and vitality of the field of Holocaust studies in an academically creditable environment. Its Simon-Skjodt Center for the Prevention of Genocide works to educate, engage, and inspire the public to learn more about past genocides—for example, Rwanda, Bosnia, and Darfur—and to consider what can be done

Annotated Bibliography | 179

to prevent genocidal atrocities in the future. Since its founding in 1993, the museum has welcomed more than forty million visitors, including ninety-nine heads of state and more than ten million school-age children. Its website is among the world's leading online resources on the Holocaust.

Vidal Sassoon International Center for the Study of Anti-Semitism (SICSA), Hebrew University, Jerusalem, Israel

The Vidal Sassoon International Center for the Study of Anti-Semitism (SICSA) at the Hebrew University of Jerusalem was established in 1982 as an interdisciplinary research center dedicated to an independent, non-political, and critical approach to understanding the phenomenon of anti-semitism. The center is primarily interested in providing a high-level platform within academia for understanding the historical and contemporary contexts of antisemitic prejudice, its occurrences, and its mechanisms, including comparative perspectives on other forms of discrimination and racism. Research at SICSA intentionally covers a broad spread of disciplines: history, political science, psychology, sociology, law, economics, literature, and the arts. SICSA's activities encompass research projects, doctoral and postdoctoral fellowships, a wide range of publications (books, monographs on current topics, a research journal, and annotated bibliographies), a computerized bibliographic project, conferences, symposia, monthly seminars, and lectures. Its Analysis of Current Trends in Antisemitism (ACTA) unit conducts research on worldwide trends with a focus on changes in local, national and regional areas and their impact on public opinion; the arts; the mass media; and ideological and political movements.

World Jewish Congress (WJC), New York, NY

The World Jewish Congress (WJC) is the international organization that represents Jewish communities and organizations in one hundred countries around the world. It advocates on their behalf to governments, parliaments, international organizations and other faiths. Since its founding in 1936, in Geneva, Switzerland, the WJC has been at the forefront of fighting for the rights of Jews and Jewish communities around the world. Its programs include advocating for justice for Holocaust victims and their heirs, including the payment of reparations for hardship suffered under the Nazis; protecting the memory of the Holocaust; obtaining restitution of, or compensation for, stolen Jewish property and negotiating a settlement with the Swiss Banks for assets held in so-called dormant accounts;

180 | Annotated Bibliography

campaigning for the right of Soviet Jews to immigrate to Israel, for those who wish to do so, or to stay and practice their religion freely; countering anti-semitism and the delegitimization of Israel; and continually supporting the state and people of Israel in their struggle to live in peace with their neigh-bors. It also maintains relations with the Holy See in its continuing dia-logue with the Roman Catholic Church. The WJC is also engaged in fostering interfaith relations with other Christian churches, representatives of Islamic communities, and other faiths.

Yad Vashem, the World Holocaust Remembrance Center, Jerusalem, Israel

Yad Vashem, the World Holocaust Remembrance Center, is a primary source for Holocaust education, documentation, and research. Yad Vashem is at the forefront of unceasing efforts to safeguard and impart the memory of the victims and the events of the Shoah period, to accurately document one of the darkest chapters in the history of humanity, and to effectively grapple with the ongoing challenges of keeping the memory of the Holocaust relevant today and for future generations. Yad Vashem's four pillars of remembrance—commemoration, documentation, research, and education—remain foundational to its mission.

Yale Program for the Study of Antisemitism (YPSA), New Haven, CT

The Yale Program for the Study of Antisemitism (YPSA) seeks to bring the resources of Yale and its faculty to bear on the pernicious problem of antisemitism. Housed at the Whitney Humanities Center, the program invites scholars from across the university—including sociology, political science, law, history, literature, art history, philosophy, religious studies, and psychology—to analyze antisemitism in an atmosphere of interdisci-plinary collaboration and scholarly inquiry. YPSA focuses on both the past and present forms of antisemitism. It promotes the study of the perception of Jews, both positive and negative, in various societies and historical moments and encourages comparisons with other forms of discrimination and racism. YPSA regularly sponsors talks and lectures by scholars, both from Yale and other institutions, including the Benjamin (Yale 1962) and Barbara Zucker Lecture Series. It also hosts an annual conference focused on a specific theme related to antisemitism.

Index

Page numbers in **bold** indicate the location of main entries.

Academic Engagement Network (AEN), 14

Adversus Judaeos, **1–2**

Agobard, 19

Ahmadinehad, Mahmoud, xxxii, 39, 50, 65

al-Banna, Hassan, xxxi, **2–4**, 115; Muslim Brotherhood, 3, 114

al-Husseini, Mohammad Amin, xxxi, **5–6**, 42

Alt-Right, **6–9**

Ambrose, St., xxv

Anglin, Andrew, 7, 65; Daily Stormer, 7

Anti-Defamation League (ADL), xxxiii, 10, 45, 51

Anti-immigration, 6

Anti-Zionism, 14, 37, 111, 146; Jewish Occupational Government (JOG), 142; Zionist Occupation Government (ZOG), 25, 97

Apion, xxii, 19

Appollonius Molon, xxxiii

Augustine, St., xxv

Baker, Alan, xix; "Draft International Convention on the Prevention and Punishment of the Crime of Anti-Semitism," xix

Bannon, Steve, 8

Barnes, Harry Elmer, **10–12**, 23, 64

BDS (Boycott, Divestment, Sanctions) Movement, **12–16**, 70

Beilis Affair, **16–18**; Beilis, Mendel, xxviii, xl

Bernard of Clairvaux, 19

Black Death, xxvi, xxxviii

Black September, xli

Blood Libel (blood accusation), xxviii, xxxviii, xl, 17, **18–21**, 31

Bonaparte, Napolean, xxvii; Assembly of Jewish Notables, xxvii; Sanhedrin, xxvii

Brimelow, Peter, 8

Butler, Richard Girnt, 25

Cameron, William, 25

Camps, Nazi: Auschwitz, 60; Belzec, 60; Bergen-Belsen, 60; Buchewald, 60; Chelmo, 60; Dachau, 60; Dora-Nordhausen, 60;

182 | Index

Camps, Nazi (*Continued*)
Flossenburg, 60; Gross-Rosen, 60; Maidanek, 60; Mathausen, 60; Natzweiler-Struthof, 60; Neuengamme, 60; Ravensbruck, 60; Sachsenhausen, 60; Sobibor, 60; Struthof, 60; Theresienstadt, 60; Treblinka, 60

Carto, Willis, 11, **22–24**, 64, 103; Institute for Historical Review, 22, 23, 49, 64, 66, 73, 146; Liberty Lobby, 11, 22, 146; Noontide Press, 11, 23

Cernovich, Mike, 8

Chabad Center, Poway, CA, xli

Chaeremon, xxiii

Christian Identity, 12, 22, **24–26**, 122, 138, 139

Chrysologus, Peter, 34

Chrysostom, St. John, xxv, 1, 34; "Eight Homilies against the Jews," 1

Codreanu, Corneliu, 8

Comparet, Bertrand, 25

Coughlin, Charles E., 22, **26–29**, 146; Christian Front, 27

Crusades, xxv, **29–32**

Damascus Affair, 20

Dar al-Harb, 97

Dar al-Islam, xxx, 97

Davidowicz, Lucy, 11

Deicide, xxiii, **33–35**, 100, 105

Democritus, 19

Dreyfus Affair, xxviii, **35–37**; Dreyfus, Alfred, xxviii, xl, 35; Drumont, Eduard, 36; Drumont, Eduard, *Jewish*

France, 36; Esterhazy, Ferdinand Walsin, 36; Henry, Hubert-Joseph, 36; Herzl, Theodor, 36; Herzl, Theodor, *Der Judenstaadt*, 37; Picquart, Georges, 36; Zola, Emile, xxix, 36

Duke, David, 8, **37–40**, 113, 122, 139; Euro-American United and Rights Organization (EURO), 38; Knights of the Ku Klux Klan (KKKK), 38; National Association for the Advancement of White People (NAAWP), 38; New Orleans Protocol, 39

Edward I, King of England, xxxviii; Edict of Expulsion, xxxviii

Enlightenment, European, xxvi, 60

Eugene III, Pope, 30

Eugenics, xxix, 125, 138; Grant, Madison, 138; Haeckel, Ernst, 125

Eusebius, 1

Evangelical Lutheran Church in America, 14

Evola, Julius, 8

Faisal, King of Saudi Arabia, xxx, 110

Farhud, xxxii, **41–43**; Ghazi I, King of Iraq, 42

Farouk, King of Egypt, 3

Farrakhan, Louis, **43–45**, 71; Fard, Wallace D., 44; Malcolm X, 44; Million Man March, 44; Mohammed, Warith Deen, 44; Muhammad, Elijah, 44

Index | 183

Fascism, **46–49**, 118, 145

Faurisson, Robert, 23, **49–50**

Ferdinand II, King of Aragon, xxvi, xxxix, 127; Edict of Expulsion, xxxix

Fields, James Alex, 7

Flaccus, xxiii

Fourth Lateran Council, 31

Frank Trial and Lynching, **51–52**; Conley, Jim, 51; Dorsey, Hugh, 51; Frank, Leo, 17, 51, 70; Mann, Alonzo, 51; Phagan, Mary, 51, 79; Slayton, John, 51

Gale, William Potter, 24

Gibson, Hutton, 12, 65

Glock, Charles Y., xviii

Goldstein, Baruch, **53–55**; Jewish Defense League, 53; Kahane, Meir, 53; Rabin, Yitzhak, 54

Gottfried, Paul E., 6–7

Griffin, Brad, 8

Grynszpan, Herschel, xl, 76

Halimi, Ilan, xxxiii

Hamas, 3; "Covenant of the Islamic Resistance Movement," 3

Heimbach, Matthew, 8

Heyer, Heather, 7

Hilberg, Raul, 119; *The Destruction of European Jews*, 119

Hitler, Adolf, xv, xxviii, xxxix, 5, 12, 22, 37, 41, 47, 59, 63, 73, 75, 91, 93, 100, 105, 109, 120, 121, 125, 133, 141, 147; *Mein Kampf*, 109

Hochhuth, Rolf, 119; *The Deputy*, 119

Hoggan, David L., 11; *The Forced War: When Peaceful Revision Failed*, 11

Holocaust/Shoah, xxix, 10, 11, 15, 37, 41, 45, **56–63**, 72, 82, 86, 87, 88, 90, 100, 137; *Arbeitslagers*, 60; Auschwitz Trial, 61; Bielski brothers, 62; Buchenwald Trial, 61; Dachau Trials, 61; Doctors' Trials, 61; *Dolchstoßlegende* (stab in the back), xxxiv, 56; *Einsatzgruppen*, 61; International Military Tribunal (IMT), 61; *Konzentrationslagers*, 60; *mischlinge*, xxix; *Porajmos*, 56; Sobibor Uprising, 62; *Vernichtujgslagers*, 60; Versailles Treaty, 59; Warsaw Ghetto Uprising, 62

Holocaust, Denial of, 37, **63–67**, 97, 103, 111, 122; App, Austin, 65; Black, Don, 65; Buchanan, Pat, 65; Butz, Arthur, 50, 65; Garaudy, Roger, 65; Hoffmann, Michael A., II, 66; Leuchter, Fred A., 66, 73; *negationnisme*, 64; Nizkor Project, 64; Rudolf, Gemar, 50, 66; Smith, Bradley A., 66; Smith, Bradley A., Committee for Open Debate on the Holocaust (CODOH), 66; Zündel, Ernst, 50, 66, 73

Hugh of Lincoln, xxxviii

Hussein, Saddam, 43

184 | Index

Icke, David, **68–69**
Ignatius, xxv
Inquisition, xxvi, xxxix
International Criminal Court, 15
International Holocaust
    Remembrance Alliance, xviii;
    Declaration of the Stockholm
    International Forum on the
    Holocaust, xviii–xix
Intersectionality, **69–72**; Black
    Lives Matter, 71; Collins,
    Patricia Hill, 70; Dershowitz,
    Alan, 71; Haidt, Jonathan,
    71; Krenshaw, Kimberly, 70;
    Mallory, Tamika, 71; Sarsour,
    Linda, 71; Women's March,
    71
Irenaeus, xxv
Irving, David, 23, 66, **72–74**
Isabella, Queen of Aragon, xxvi,
    xxxix, 127
Israel, State of, 11, 13, 15, 42, 45,
    87, 90, 97, 116, 146; 1948
    Arab-Israeli War, 3, 5, 13;
    Second Intifada, 13; Zionism,
    xxx, 4, 5, 6, 45

Jews, 4, 5, 7, 10, 11, 20, 25, 38,
    85, 97, 100, 111, 130, 142,
    146
Joffe, Josef, xviii
John Birch Society, 103
Johnson, Greg, 7
Josephus, xxii, 19

Khelmnytsky Uprising/Massacre,
    xxvi; Khmelmnytsky,
    Bohdan, xxvi, xxxix
Kielce, Poland, xli

Kishinev pogrom, xl
Kristallnacht, **75–77**; Beer Hall
    Putsch, 75–76; Funk,
    Walther, 77; Goebbels,
    Joseph, 76; Goering,
    Hermann, 76; Sasse, Martin,
    76–77
Kuhn, Fritz, 146; German-
    American Bund, 146
Ku Klux Klan (KKK), xxxiii, 22,
    37, 51, 65, **78–80**, 138; Civil
    Rights Act/Ku Klux Klan
    Act, 78; Dixon, Thomas, Jr.,
    78; Forrest, Nathan Bedford,
    78; Grant, Ulysses S., 78;
    Griffith, D. W., 78; Simmons,
    William Joseph, 78

Langmuir, Gavin, xvii
Lenin, Vladimir, 91
Leopold I, King of Austria, xxxix
Lewis, Bernard, xviii
Lipstadt, Deborah, 11, 66
Livingston, Sigmund, xviii
Luther, Martin, xxv, xxxix, 76,
    81–83, 93; *On the Jews and
    Their Lies*, xxxix; *On the
    Unknowable Name and the
    Generations of Christ*, xxxix
Lysimachus, xxiii

MacDonald, Kevin B., 8, 113
Manetho, xxii
Marcion, 1
Marcus, Jacob Rader, xviii
Marcus, Kenneth L, xix
Marr, Wilhelm, xxi, xxxix, **84–86**;
    Antisemiten-Liga, 85;
    Antisemitismus, 84; Haeckel,

Ernst, 85; *Judenhaas*, 84;
"A Mirror to the Jews," 84, 85;
Rosenberg, Alfred, 85;
Stoecker, Adolf, 85;
"Testament of an Antisemite,"
84, 86; "The Way to Victory
of Germanism over Judaism,"
xxxix, 84
Martin, James L., 11
Martyr, Justin, xxv, 1
Martyrdom, Sanctifying the Name
of God, 29, **86–90**; *Akedat
Yitzhak*, 87; Akiba, Rabbi,
88; Bar Kokhba, 88; *Hillul
Ha-Shem*, 87, 89; Kedoshim,
87, 88, 89
Melito, xxi
Menken, Henry Louis (H.L.), 9
Methodist Church, 14
Miller, Stephen, 8
Mosely, Sir Oswald, 146; British
Union of Fascists, 146
Muhammad, xxx, 5, 115
Mussolini, Benito, 5, 22, 46, 47, 91;
"The Doctrine of Fascism,"
47; Franco, Francisco, 48;
Peron, Juan, 48; Salazar,
Antonio de Oliviera, 48

Nasser, Gama Abdel, xxxi, 115, 146
National Socialism/Nazism, 47,
91–95, 105, 118, 145;
Alternative für Deutscheland,
93; Chamberlain, Houston
Stewart, 93, 133, 136;
Chamberlain, Houston
Stewart, *The Foundations of
the Nineteenth Century*,
133–134, 136; de Gobineau,

Arthur, 93, 133, 136; de
Gobineau, Arthur, *An Essay
on the Inequality of the
Human Races*, 133, 136; de
Lagarde, Paul, 93; *der
Führerprinzip*, 93; Diedrichs,
Eugen, 93; Fichte, Johann
Gottlieb, 93; Fidesz, 93;
Golden Dawn, 93; Günther,
Hans F. K., 93; Langbein,
Julius, 93; *Lebensraum*, 91;
Lueger, Karl, 93; National
Socialist German Workers
Party (NSDAP), 91;
Rosenberg, Alfred, 93, 137;
Rosenberg, Alfred, *The Myth
of the Twentieth Century*,
137; Stampel, Wilhelm, 93;
Volksgemeinschaft, 91; von
Schönerer, Georg Ritter, 93
Nationalism, **95–98**
Netanyahu, Jonatan ("Yoni"), xli
New Testament, xxiii
Nuremberg Racial Laws, xxix, xl,
61, 96, 119

Oberammergau Passion Play,
99–101
Origin, xxi

Palestine, 3, 15
Patterson, Charles, xviii
Pearl, Judea, xx
Peinovich, Mike "Enoch," 8
Pelley, William Dudley, 24
Perednik, Gustavo, xx
Phillip the Fair, King of France,
xxxviii; Edict of Expulsion,
xxxviii

186 | Index

Philo, xxiii

Phineas Priesthood, 25

Pierce, William Luther, 23, 37, **102–105**, 122, 139; Franklin, Joseph Paul, 104; *Hunter*, 102, 139; Lane, David, 104, 138; Lane, David, "White Genocide Conspiracy Theory," 138; Lane, David, "White Genocide Manifesto," 139; MacDonald, Andrew (pseud.), 102; McVeigh, Timothy, 103; Matthews, Robert Jay, 104; National Alliance, 23, 102, 122, 139; National Vanguard Books, 102; National Youth Alliance, 23, 103; Nichols, Terry, 103; Resistance Records, 102; Strom, Kenneth Alfred, 102; *The Turner Diaries*, 102, 139; Youth for Wallace, 103

Pilate, Pontius, xxiv

Pius XII, Pope, **105–108**, 119; Pope Benedict XV, 105; Pope Francis, 107; Pope Pius XI, 106; Pope Pius XI, *Humani generis unitas*, 106; Pope Pius XI, *Mit brenender Sorge*, 106; *Summi pontificatus*, 106; "The Vatican and the Holocaust," 107; Vatican Information Service, 106; Weimar Republic, 105; Zolli, Israel, 106

Posidonius, xxiii

Pranaitis, Justinas, 17; *Talmud Unmasked: The Secret Rabbinical Teachings Concerning Christians*, 17

Presbyterian Church, 14

Protestant Reformation, 60

Protocols of the Learned Elders of Zion, xxvii, xxx, xxxii, xl, 22, 25, 27, 64, 68, 92, 97, **108–111**, 131; Ford, Henry, xxviii, 22, 109; Ford, Henry, *The International Jew: The World's Foremost Problem*, xxviii, 22, 109; Goedsche, Hermann, 108; Goedsche, Hermann, *Der Schmuggler von Biarritz*, 108; Goedsche, Hermann (Sir John Retcliffe), 108; Graves, Philip, xxviii; Hamas Charter, 110; *Horseman without a Horse*, xxxii; Joly, Maurice, xxvii, 111; Joly, Maurice, *Dialogue in Hell between Machiavelli and Montesquieu*, 108; Nilus, Sergei, xxvii; Nilus, Sergei, *The Great within the Small: The Coming of the Anti-Christ and the Rule of Satan on Earth*, 109; Okrana, xxvii

Proud Boys, **111–113**; Chapman, Kyle, 112; Chapman, Kyle, Fraternal Order of the Alt-Knights (FOAK), 112; Invictus, Augustus Sol (Arthur Gillespie), 112; McInnes, Gavin, 111; McInnes, Gavin, *Vice Magazine*, 111; McInnes, Gavin, Vice Media, 111; Tarrio, Enrique, 111

Pseudo-Gregory, 1; "Testimonies against the Jews," 1

Index | **187**

Qutb, Sayyid, xxxi, **114–117**; al-Qaeda, 114, 116; Hamas, 116; Hezbollah, 114; *Our Struggle against the Jews*, 115

Racism, 6

Rand, Howard B., 24

Rassinier, Paul, 49, 64, **118–120**; *Debunking the Genocide Myth: A Study of Nazi Concentration Camps and the Alleged Extermination of European Jewry*, 120; *The Drama of European Jews*, 119; *The Lie of Ulysses: A Glance at the Literature of Concentration Camps*, 119; *Operation Vicar: The Role of Pius XII before History*, 119; *Those Responsible for the Second World War*, 120; *The True Eichmann Trial or the Incorrigible Victors*, 119; *Ulysses Betrayed by His Own*, 119

Richard the Lion-Hearted, 30

Robb, Thomas A., 23

Rockwell, George Lincoln, 23, 25, 37, 93, 102, **120–123**; American Nazi Party (ANP) 23, 37, 65, 93, 102, 121; Arrowsmith, Harold Noel, Jr., 121; Koehl, Matt, 93; Lane, David, 93; McCarthy, Joseph, 121; National Committee to Free America from Jewish Domination, 121; National Socialist Movement (NSM), 93;

Schoep, Jeff, 93; *This Time the World*, 123; *White Power*, 123; World Union of Free Enterprise National Socialists, 121

Roman Catholic Church, 14; *Nostre Aetate*, 34

Saladin, 30

Samuel, Herbert, 5

Sartre, Jean-Paul, xviii

Sawyer, Rueben H., 24

Scapegoatism, xxxiii

Smith, Gerald L. K., 24

Social Darwinism, xxix, **124–126**; Darwin, Charles, 124; Darwin, Charles, *The Descent of Man, and Selection in Relation to Sex*, 124; Darwin, Charles, *On the Origin of Species by Means of Natural Selection, or the Preservation of Favoured Races in the Struggle for Life*, 124; Galton, Francis, 125; Malthus, Thomas, 124; Malthus, Thomas, *An Essay on the Principle of Population*, 124; Spencer, Herbert, 124; Spencer, Herbert, *Principles of Biology*, 125

Southern Poverty Law Center (SPLC), 45, 78, 103, 112

Spanish Inquisition, **127–129**; de Torquemada, Tomas, 127; Netanuahu, Benzion, 129; Netanuahu, Benzion, *The Origin of the Inquisition in*

188 | Index

Spanish Inquisition (*Continued*)
   Fifteenth Century Spain, 129;
   *Tribunal del Santo Officio de
   la Inquisición*, 127
Spencer, Richard B., 7
Stalin, Joseph, xv, xli; Doctors'
   Plot, xli
Stark, Rodney, xviii
Streicher, Julius, 19, 136; *Der
   Stürmer*, 19, 136
Swift, Wesley, 24

Tacitus, xxiii
Taylor, Jared, 8
Tertullian, 1; Pseudo-Tertullian, 1
Tlass, Mustafa, xxviii, 20;
   The Matzah of Zion,
   xxviii, xxxii
Toledot Yeshu, 35
Tree of Life Synagogue,
   Pittsburgh, PA, xli

Unite the Right, xli, 7, 112, 122;
   Kessler, James, 139
United Church of Christ, 14
United Nations Relief and Works
   Agency (UNRWA), 14
Urban II, Pope, 30
Usury, **130–132**; Dickens,
   Charles, 131; Fagin, the Jew,
   131; Marlowe, Christopher,
   131; Marlowe, Christopher,
   The Jew of Malta, 131;
   Shakespeare, William, 131;
   Shakespeare, William, *The
   Merchant of Venice*, 131

Voltaire, xxvii
vom Rath, Ernst, xl, 75, 76

Wagner, Richard, **133–135**, 136;
   Adorno, Thedor, 135;
   Adorno, Thedor, *In Search of
   Wagner*, 135; German-Nordic
   Richard Wagner Society for
   Germanic Art and Culture,
   134; "Jewishness in Music,"
   133; Nietzsche, Fredrich,
   135; Nietzsche, Fredrich, *The
   Case of Wagner: A
   Musician's Problem*, 135
Walker, Alice, 69
Wallace, George, 23
White Supremacy, 6, 37, 103, 111,
   136–140; Bowers, Robert,
   139; Camus, Renaud, 139;
   Camus, Renaud, "Great
   Replacement Conspiracy
   Theory," 139; Carlson,
   Tucker, 139; Coulter, Ann,
   139; Savage, Michael, 139;
   White genocide, 7, 38; White
   nationalism, 6, 8, 22, 37, 111,
   145; White separatism, 6
White Terror, xl
William of Norwich, xxxviii, 18
Wistrich, Robert, xviii
World Church of the Creator,
   140–144; Church of the
   Creator, 140; Creativity
   Alliance (CA), 141;
   Creativity/Creativity
   Movement (CM), 140, 141;
   "Five Fundamental Beliefs,"
   142; Hale, Matthew, 142;
   Klassen, Ben, 140; Klassen,
   Ben, *Nature's Eternal
   Religion*, 141; RaHoWa
   (Racial Holy War), 141;

Index | **189**

"Sixteen Commandments,"
142; Smith, Benjamin
Nathaniel, 141; *White Man's
Bible*, 143

Xenophobia, xxxiv

Yiannopoulos, Milo, 7; "An
  Establishment Guide to the
  Alt-Right," 8
Yinger, John Milton, xviii
Yockey, Francis Parker, **145–147**;
  Bolton, Kerry, 147; *The
  Enemy of Europe: The
  Enemy of Our Enemies*, 147;
European Liberation Front
(ELF), 146; *Frontfighter*,
146; *Imperium: The
Philosophy of History*,
145–146; Oliver, Revilo P.,
147; "The Proclamation of
London," 145–146; Spengler,
Oswald, 145; Spengler,
Oswald, The Decline of the
West, 145; Varange, Ulick
(pseud.), 145

Zakim, Leonard, xviii

About the Author

STEVEN LEONARD JACOBS returned to the Department of Religious Studies as an associate professor and the Aaron Aronov Chair of Judaic Studies on January 1, 2001, and received tenure as of August 2004. He was promoted to full professor as of August 2017. He received his BA from Penn State University and his BHL, MAHL, DHL, DD, and rabbinic ordination from the Hebrew Union College–Jewish Institute of Religion. As a resident of Alabama for four decades, he taught at Spring Hill College in Mobile; the University of Alabama at Birmingham, Birmingham-Southern College, and Samford University in Birmingham; and the University of Alabama in Huntsville and Calhoun Community College in Huntsville. He also served congregations in Birmingham, Mobile, Huntsville, and Tuscaloosa, Alabama, and in Dallas, Texas.

Dr. Jacobs's primary research foci are in biblical studies, translation and interpretation, including the Dead Sea Scrolls; Jewish-Christian relations; and Holocaust and genocide studies. His books include *Shirot Bialik: A New and Annotated Translation of Chaim Nachman Bialik's Epic Poems* (1987); *Raphael Lemkin's Thoughts on Nazi Genocide: Not Guilty?* (1992); *Contemporary Christian and Contemporary Jewish Religious Responses to the Shoah* (2 volumes, 1993, editor); *Rethinking Jewish Faith: The Child of a Survivor Responds* (1994); *The Meaning of Persons and Things Jewish: Contemporary Explorations and Interpretations* (1996); *The Holocaust Now: Contemporary Christian and Jewish Thought* (1997, editor); *The Encyclopedia of Genocide* (2 volumes, 2000, associate editor); *Pioneers of Genocide Studies* (2002, coeditor); *The Biblical Masorah and the Temple Scroll: An Orthographical Inquiry* (2002); *Dismantling the Big Lie: The Protocols of the Elders of Zion* (2003, coauthor); *Post-Shoah Dialogues: Re-Thinking Our Texts Together* (2004, coauthor); *The Jewish Experience: An Introduction to Jewish History and Jewish Life* (2010); *Fifty Key Thinkers on Holocaust and*

192 | About the Author

Genocide (2012, coauthor); and *Lemkin on Genocide* (2013, editor). He has also authored more than fifty referred articles in a wide variety of professional publications as well as numerous book reviews.

Dr. Jacobs's professional and civic involvements have included the Alabama Holocaust Commission; the Board of Advisors for the Center for American & Jewish Studies, Baylor University, Waco, Texas; the international editor of the Papers of Raphael Lemkin; the International Advisory Board of the Centre for Comparative Genocide Studies, Macquarie University, New South Wales, Australia; the Editorial Board of "Studies in the Shoah," University Press of America, Lanham, Maryland; the Editorial Board of *Bridges: An Interdisciplinary Journal of Theology, Philosophy, History and Science*, Monkton, Maryland; an Educational Consultant to the Center on the Holocaust, Genocide, and Human Rights, Philadelphia, Pennsylvania; the Board of Advisors of the Aegis Trust for the Prevention of Genocide, England; and the Associate Editor of the *Journal for the Study of Antisemitism*. He is also coeditor of the online database "Modern Genocide: Understanding Causes and Consequences" (ABC-CLIO) and the four-volume encyclopedia *Modern Genocide: The Definitive Resource and Document Collection* (2014, ABC-CLIO). (*Modern Genocide* has received two national awards: 2015 Choice Outstanding Academic Title and 2015 Outstanding Reference Source, Reference and User Services Association (RUSA) of the American Library Association (ALA).)

Dr. Jacobs regularly teaches REL 101 (The Violent and the Sacred: Religion and the Problem of Human Suffering), REL 110 (Introduction to the Old Testament/Hebrew Bible), REL 223 (The Holocaust in Historical Perspective), REL 224 (Introduction to Judaism), REL 238 (Philosophies of Judaism), REL 332 (Figures in Contemporary Jewish Thought), REL 347 (Jewish-Christian Relations), REL 372a (Religions, Politics, and Cultures of the Middle East), REL 372b (Antisemitism and the Crises of Modernity), and REL 410 (Religion and Genocide).

Printed in the USA
CPSIA information can be obtained
at www.ICGtesting.com
LVHW020312260524
781313LV00001B/153